CUTTHROATS

CUTTHROATS

THE ADVENTURES OF A SHERMAN TANK DRIVER IN THE PACIFIC

Robert C. Dick

BALLANTINE BOOKS • NEW YORK

Cutthroats is a work of nonfiction. Some names and identifying details have been changed.

A Presidio Press Mass Market Original

Published in the United States by Presidio Press, an imprint of The Random House Publishing Group, a division of Random House, Inc., New York.

PRESIDIO PRESS and colophon are trademarks of Random House, Inc.

Insert photographs courtesy of Robert C. Dick

ISBN 0-89141-884-9

Printed in the United States of America

www.presidiopress.com

OPM   9   8   7   6   5   4   3   2   1

This book is dedicated to all who fought the good fight and won it.

It is also dedicated to those on the home front who supported us in every possible way . . . who worked, who waited, and prayed for our safe return. Our victory was theirs, too.

There is nothing quite so exhilarating as being shot at and missed.

—WINSTON CHURCHILL

I've been shot at and missed. And I've been shot at and hit. Of the two, I much prefer the former over the latter.

—ANON.

Acknowledgments

There are so many people who have helped me in the writing of this book that I wonder how in the world I'll be able to list them all. Their assistance, suggestions, and expertise, and in many cases simply their friendship, has made the difference. This book is much better than it might have been without them.

In no particular order, here are a few.

My former crew members, who include Henry Fisher, assistant driver/bow gunner (and one-time fearless jungle fighter); Roy Greenup, loader; Jim Anderson, gunner; and O. W. French, my tank commander of #60. Others not in tank #60 include Eldon "Couch" Davenport, another fearless jungle fighter, tank #58. Tank #55 Commander Edward Metz (who calls me his "crazy hero," I don't know why). Ed was the single most "calming effect" I ran across during those hectic days. Officers I must mention are Ross Garner, A. A. Todd, and Carl Schluter. Also high on my list is my former infantry platoon leader Pat Phillips. These men stand out in my memory not only for their leadership, but for their concern for their men.

Don Dencker, historian of the 96th Infantry Division (the "Deadeyes"), and author of the great book *Love Company*, a narrative account of his World War II experiences as an infantryman in L Company, 382nd regiment, helped me in more than one instance. We agree that our paths must have crossed many times during our tank/infantry assaults on Leyte and Okinawa. Our mutual admiration continues to this day.

Comrades who I served with but who have passed on are just too numerous to list here, but are with me still.

Luck was with me the day I was browsing the Internet and came across a mailing list of Sherman-tank aficionados. The list name is G104 and is managed by Hanno Spoelstra of the Netherlands. Hanno is the guiding light of our group, which has members worldwide. A *few* of them are: Ken Hall, of Hall Graphics in London, Ray Merriman, and Russ Morgan (who has promised me he'd let me drive his M5 if I ever get down to his neck of the woods). And especially Geoff Winnington-Ball, Captain, Canadian Armor UP who has helped more than he realizes, I'm sure. Geoff is one of those guys who is so filled with enthusiasm he sort of picks you up and carries you along. His push in the early stages of my writing, when I hit a snag once in a while, always got me rolling again. Thank you, Geoff.

I can't leave this list without telling you about Joe DeMarco, of Baltimore, Maryland. Joe has helped me in so many different ways I am tempted to list him as coauthor. I stand amazed thinking back on his research in the National Archives, which has turned up facts and figures about facets of my old outfit. He has been researching World War II manufacturers of Shermans, and has verified his huge listing with individual serial numbers. His expertise is often sought by members of our G104 group. Another of Joe's pursuits is locating existing Shermans, especially those in the United States. Whenever I came across some sort of puzzling Sherman technicality, or perhaps something I couldn't find words or phrases to describe, Joe always came through. In the process we became great friends, and I treasure our association more than words can describe. The term *right-hand man* is applied 100 percent to Joe. Thank you, buddy.

Ron Doering, my editor and good friend. He held my hand throughout the process of what he calls "making a good book better." His comments, suggestions, and requests were all right on. I can honestly say that every e-mail he sent to me, over the months we worked on the manuscript, was on the mark and in most cases made a significant difference. A simple "thank you" falls far short of saying what I want to, but . . . thank you, Ron. Truly, I couldn't have done it without you.

Fleetwood Robbins, Ron's sidekick, made the difference in almost every page of the manuscript. Not only because of his keen eye when it came to "helping" my terrible grammar, but because his suggestions were often responsible for finding just the right word or phrase.

My final, but certainly not least, acknowledgment is to my dear wife, Linda May. She was and is my jewel. Her initial encouragement to write this book started with a simple "Why don't you write some of these things down?" to the point where I felt that if I didn't write, she'd kill me. That's not really true . . . but close. In more ways than I can say, Linda inspired me to write. She was always ready to listen, read, and criticize where it was needed. My wife, best girl, best friend, she's been my reason for everything. Including this book.

Contents

Author's Note

The reader might wonder how I was able to recall, in such detail, events that took place almost sixty years ago. When those events concerned my very existence, the impression that registered in my memory was there for keeps. As long ago as it all was, I found it was easy to recall. Exact words are sometimes difficult to remember, but I must say that in almost every instance, I remember vividly what was said, who said it, and what was going on at the time. We were, don't forget, experiencing combat for the first time, and I challenge anyone to talk with a World War II combat vet and not come away with that same feeling, the marvel of detailed memory of events.

That is, if they do talk about it at all, and a lot of them won't. If you have relatives or friends who are vets, please encourage them to talk with you about what happened to them, and what occurred around them. We are living history, and time is almost at an end for those of us who are still around.

The transition from civilian life to full-time soldiering was not the abrupt and oftentimes unbelievable change that most inductees underwent. Because of my National Guard service, I had close to three years training with an infantry outfit that was run strictly by the book. By the time our unit was mobilized into federal service, we were already prepared for military life. This is not to say that we were better soldiers. We just had a toe in the water before they did, and it was not long before we were all in the same pond together, doing what we could to stay afloat.

Looking back, it is an absolute wonder to me that any of us in my tank survived the vicious fighting on Okinawa. The enemy we faced was prepared to fight to the end, and did so. The cost in human life, to both sides, was unbelievable. During the (approximately) eighty-three days of fighting I experienced, more than twelve thousand American fighting men were killed, which includes army, navy, Marines, and air force. Within that same period, over 110,000 Japanese soldiers, sailors, and airmen were killed.

This book tells only about my personal experiences and, I am certain, relates to events that were common to most of my fellow tankers. I remember a conversation between a couple of the guys about those wonderful Sherman tanks of ours: "One thing about it, these things have a lot of armor between us and 'them.'" His buddy's reply echoed all of our thoughts on the matter. "Yeah, there's lotsa armor all right, but they are such hellish big-ass targets!" And they were. I think that every weapon the Japanese had was, at one time or another, used against our tanks. In one instance a Japanese officer, using his sword, tried to hack off a machine gun barrel, but of course failed. We were constantly under fire by everything from satchel charges and mortars to 47mm antitank guns and heavy artillery. To say nothing of land mines. On several occasions, aerial bombs were buried with the detonators covered by mud and leaves.

I saw what real heroes are. There can never be enough said about the courage of the American soldier. And that's especially true of the infantryman. It was an honor to support those men of the 96th "Deadeye" Infantry Division in combat, and I salute them.

A word now about the Japanese soldiers we fought against on Okinawa. They were courageous fighters and they must have been aware that their situation was hopeless. But they made us pay for every inch of ground we took. Their weapons were, for the most part, inferior to ours (their 47mm antitank gun was an exception), and they did not have replacement troops to fill depleted ranks. They used every trick in the book and came up short in all of them but one, courage. To see a lone Japanese soldier carrying a mine and running toward a 30-ton Sherman tank removes any doubt one might have about their bravery.

I worked on this book for over a year, but that space of time was devoted mostly to typing and revising. The raw content has been floating around inside my old memory ever since the events you read about here first occurred. I have honestly tried to bring you into my world, and for the most part I think I've been able to do that. The things, dear reader, that are not here for you to experience are the smells, the smell of dead humans—bloated, maggot-filled corpses. The stench of sulfur from our guns, the sharp concussion when high explosives landed nearby. And, finally, the gut-wrenching apprehension, the anxiety that lies in the pit of your stomach so long that it becomes a normal feeling, one you carry with you as you would a hidden birthmark. No one sees it, but we all know it and no one talks about it. The wonder of it all is that we continued to function as we had been trained to do. We followed orders, and even though we sometimes wondered about their logic, we did the best we could. Before Leyte, none of us had heard a gun fired in anger, nor had we fired one. Okinawa was our proving ground. As that old saying goes, "I wouldn't want to have to do it all over again . . . but I'm glad now that I was there."

—Robert C. Dick
Southern Oregon

Prologue

This story is about me and how I got involved in the World
War II military mix that took me by the hand and pulled me
kicking and screaming from late 1938 through September
1945. I suppose that the single most important thing I learned
was just how totally, completely frightened a person can get
and still function. And not have a heart attack in the process!

Looking back to those years, I am amused at the brashness
of my youth. Barely seventeen years old, standing six-foot-
two and a skinny 155 pounds, with brown hair combed in no
particular direction or style, mussed up beyond help, coupled
with ordinary blue eyes, I must have looked like just about
every other tall, skinny teenage kid in Southern California.
It's a wonder the personnel officer would even consider sign-
ing me up.

But he did, and there I was, in my innocence, looking for
adventure, and, as you'll see, finding it by the bucketful . . .
in surplus lots . . . and more.

I enlisted in K Company, 160th Regiment, of the 40th
Infantry Division, California National Guard, on October 10,
1938. The minimum age for enlistees at that time was eighteen, but because of my height I probably looked a bit older
than I was and had no problems convincing anyone that, at
seventeen, I was fully qualified recruit material, a "mature
man" of eighteen. Ahem.

In my enthusiasm, I managed to talk my best friend, Joe
Mason, into enlisting with me. We were students at El Monte
High School at the time, and we'd been involved in all the
usual adventures of teenage guys of that period. We both
were on the high school wrestling team, and while I did so-

so, Joe managed to shine. He was around five-foot-ten, built like a fireplug, with brown hair, brown eyes, and a fairly heavy beard, for a high schooler. His mustache was a thing of envy for the rest of us. And he was a genuinely nice guy.

When we enlisted in the California National Guard, we managed to stay together in the same squad. Matter of fact, we stayed together until I left the outfit. But that didn't happen for a while down the road. We joined the infantry, mainly because we were told that we'd be taught to fire a rifle and hit what we aimed at. And, I thought the uniforms were great. I learned also that we would get paid for attending the weekly drills at the armory at Exposition Park, in southeast Los Angeles. To make matters even better, there was a summer tour at Camp Merriam near San Luis Obispo.

During one of our summer training sessions, 1940 I think it was, we were ordered to Washington State for two weeks. We were told that these maneuvers would test our units as well as those of the Regular Army troops stationed at Fort Lewis, Washington. We were to be the offensive forces, with the Regular Army defending. Referees were attached to both sides, and the whole exercise, we were told, was to ascertain our degree of combat readiness. Or lack thereof.

The exercise started at midnight, and we took off on foot from Centralia, Washington, headed for the army. As luck would have it, it rained. Not only that night, but every day and night of the entire exercise! I was a platoon sergeant by then, and one night the CO requested that I send a small reconnaissance patrol out to see just exactly where the "enemy" was in our area, judge its strength, and all those good things. I told him that I'd take the patrol myself and would limit its size to a four-man unit. I left Sergeant Mason in charge, collected three of my men, briefed them as to the mission, and we took off in the dead of night. And, yes, it was still raining. Hard.

We had gone through the woods for about half an hour when my scout signaled for us to stop and motioned me to come on up front. When I got there I saw the problem . . . a narrow stream, maybe fifteen feet wide, was in our path, and the water was flowing very fast. So much so, I was reluctant to try crossing it. We weren't sure of the area, and I had no idea how far we might have to go to find a bridge. If we did find one, the chances of it being unguarded were fairly remote.

So, I decided to give it a try. We had only our personal weapons, having left packs and even helmets at the rear. I dropped back and informed the patrol that I would try the crossing, and if all went well, we could get the rest of them across. One of the men told me he couldn't swim. I told him that the water was rushing too fast to even consider swimming. If I couldn't get across, we'd have to figure out something else.

With my patrol huddled near the bank, watching me, I held my rifle away from my body in case I was knocked down by the current and took a small, tentative step into the stream. As soon as I did, I wanted to turn around, walk past the patrol, and return to my platoon. And, never, ever talk about this situation again.

What I found when I made that first step was that this wasn't a stream. It was a small, narrow backcountry asphalt road! The water rushing down it, at a hundred miles an hour it seemed, was only two or three inches deep! I took another step and was certain that, from the patrol's vantage point, it probably looked like I was, at last, walking on water! I had spent months trying to convince them that I was entirely capable of that, and now they had proof! Somewhat sheepishly, I returned and told them what the dreaded "river" really was. We all got a laugh out of it, and I made sure that they all understood that I had been ready to face the unknown danger, alone, on this "dark and stormy night." Most important, I also swore them to secrecy.

We finished our patrol and I reported to the captain back at the bivouac area. We had discovered an artillery outfit up ahead, and I gave him an estimate of the situation. Later I realized I had neglected to mention our river crossing. Ah, well, some things are best forgotten.

It was an interesting two weeks and, according to the referees, we, the offensive forces, had won the war. Not bad for a bunch of National Guardsmen.

Our division was mobilized into federal service on March 3, 1941, and we were informed that the length of this "emergency period" would be for six months. However, my three-year enlistment was coming to an end in October, so I decided to leave the army then and join the Royal Canadian Air Force as the Canadians were at war, and at this point the United States was still uncommitted.

My dad was a private pilot, and I thought there was nothing in the world better than cruising around in the sky. So I contacted the RCAF recruiting office in Vancouver, B.C. In a short while they sent me an application form, but I saw that the maximum acceptable height was six-foot-one. I filled it out and returned it with the note that I was six-foot-two-inches tall. The application was returned with the height restrictions crossed out. I was requested to sign and return it and informed that a class would be starting soon. Before I could take any steps toward getting out of the U.S. Army and into the Canadian armed forces, an official order came down from the United States War Department. All enlistments were frozen "for the duration of the emergency plus six months." That order went into effect on October 1, just nine days before I was to be free! My days of flying for the Canadians were over before they began.

My extended stay in the army did not get off to a good start when about this time I made a really stupid mistake that resulted in me and Joe being demoted from sergeants to corporals in the blink of an eye.

Joe had just gotten engaged and wanted to go to Los Angeles to see his girl. We were told that weekend passes for that area were all out, but we could have a weekend pass for San Luis Obispo. San Luis is about two hundred miles from Los Angeles, where we really wanted to go. I talked Joe into getting the weekend pass, and we went straight to L.A.

Naturally, on our way back to camp late Sunday night we blew a tire on Joe's old car and could find nothing open. We finally got the thing repaired and were hours late getting back. You might say we were officially AWOL, absent without leave. We came dragging into camp at midmorning. The entire company was already out on the field, and the first ser-

geant told us where we could find them. We would also find
the captain there. The next day we were busted to corporals.
I asked for and was assigned to the weapons platoon in
charge of a light machine gun squad. Joe stayed in the rifle
platoon as a squad leader, and we both settled down to try
getting back what we should have never lost . . . our sergeants' stripes.

After that little episode, we stayed on the straight and narrow as far as passes went. Joe's car was pretty shabby, and
we didn't want to risk making that long trip in it again, so we
"bought" a ride in another guy's car by chipping in on the gas
bill. It so happened that the fellow we were to ride with the
next weekend turned out to be a sergeant I'd had a little scuf-
fle with several months before, and I was pretty sure we'd get
turned down as soon as he saw me. As it turned out, he was a
pretty nice guy, and by the time our round trip was completed
we were good friends. Sadly, he later joined the paratroopers
and was killed during a combat operation in Europe.

During the last part of November 1941, we were placed on
a twenty-minute alert. Passes were halted. We knew something was up, but didn't know what. If we wanted to go to the
PX (post exchange), we had to go in groups, ready to return
to the company, a few hundred yards away, at a moment's
notice. It was all very hush-hush, and everyone sort of
walked around "on eggshells" waiting for we knew not what.

Just as mysteriously, the alert was lifted and passes were
available once again. Joe and I headed south to El Monte for
what was to be the last of our weekend passes for a long,
long time. It was December 6, 1941.

PART ONE

War, and Things
Start to Warm Up

1

On December 7, 1941, I was home on a weekend leave. My grandfather knocked on the door of the bathroom where I was, in the midst of shaving, and announced, "You're in for it now, boy!"

I asked, "In for what?"

"The Japs bombed Pearl Harbor. . . . It's on the radio and I just now heard it."

I thought it was some obscure U.S. Navy base in the Pacific. Of course, not long after that, everyone in the free world knew where and what Pearl Harbor was. I collected Joe and we drove back to camp immediately. On the way north toward San Luis Obispo we saw convoy after convoy of army troops heading south. Fortunately, our outfit was still in camp, and we got back just in time. My first assignment was nothing like what I had thought war would be. Our company was loaded onto trucks and driven to the rail lines close to camp. We were placed inside a boxcar and away we went, not having a clue where. "Where," for my machine gun squad, turned out to be just a few miles north, at Camp Roberts, a large army basic training station. So large, in fact, it consisted of two separate camps. The main camp, and the second one, North Roberts.

The train stopped midway between the two camps, just short of a bridge, and my four-man squad was ordered off, along with our tent; the machine gun, and all its paraphernalia; four folding GI cots; a small gasoline-fueled cooking stove; a shovel; four barracks bags; and several other miscellaneous bits of gear and equipment that we soldiers always seemed to accumulate above and beyond our issued stuff.

Thinking back on it, we must have looked like a potential yard sale getting set up.

Lt. Pat Phillips walked me up forward to the railroad bridge that spanned a wide but shallow river running between the two camps. "Your squad is to set up the machine gun here at the south end of the bridge and allow no one to pass across it other than railroad workers or other soldiers. No civilians. You will have the gun manned during the hours of darkness. That is from sundown to dawn. It'll not be necessary to man it during daylight hours."

"Do you think the Japs will attack us here, Lieutenant?"

"Corporal, just how in the hell would I know that?"

"Well, I guess somebody figures they might, otherwise we wouldn't be set up here, would we? If someone tries to cross at night, do we shoot 'em, or what?"

He just looked at me, turned, and started back to where the train was stopped. It was a steam locomotive, and I loved the sounds that came from it, the creaks, grunts, and groans, the hissing of steam. How I wished it would stick around for a few days so we all could just sit and listen to it. Trying to look sharp, I hurried after him and asked about food, mail, and supplies.

"Don't worry about anything like that. I'll have a weapons carrier up here tomorrow with everything you guys will need. Any other questions?"

I wrote down the telephone number of his CP and tried to think of questions that I knew would come up as soon as he left. Phillips and I had known each other for several years and got along very well. We first met when he was a sergeant. I liked him and I respected him. He had a great sense of humor, too.

We returned back to where the train was waiting, and I saw that a bunch of the guys had hopped off and gotten the tent up and staked down. Another twenty minutes and the four of us were standing alongside the tracks, watching the train disappear northward. I wanted to say, "Choo, choo," but didn't.

I got my gunner and we went for a walk up to the edge of the bridge, looking for a spot to place the gun. We found the perfect one just at the edge of the bridge, overlooking the entire "target area." It was a wonderful place for our gun. The fact that it had no cover or concealment didn't bother us for the simple reason we didn't think about it . . . dumb, dumb.

PFC Hubert White, my gunner, was a tall, lanky Kentuckian with a rare sense of humor and a ready smile. He had blond hair that seemed to be always mussed up, blue eyes, and a nice drawl that, I guess, was what folks from his state sounded like. He was the first person I had ever met from Kentucky, so I didn't know for sure. But it was nice to listen to.

It was early December, and the cold rains began. We rigged up cover at the gun position, using shelter halves from our individual packs, and while it wasn't like home, it kept us fairly dry. Not completely, but somewhat. The rail line was on an embankment about ten or twelve feet above the surrounding ground. Our big tent was down at that lower level, below, out of the wind as much as possible. But, we found out later, it was low enough to flood the dirt/mud floor with three or four inches of water if the rain lasted very long.

True to his word, Phillips returned the next day in a weapons carrier and left us with some rations and, best of all, mail. He told me he didn't know how long this routine would go on, but he'd see that we got rotated "once in awhile" back to the platoon CP for showers, new supplies, things like that.

One day, after we'd been there about a week, a Camp Roberts weapon carrier drove into our area. The passenger turned out to be a mess sergeant, an old-timer, a regular army guy, and he had gotten reports that we were guarding the bridge. He asked me, "What are you guys doing for chow?"

"Not much, Sergeant. They give us some rations, and we have a small field stove, but none of us is much of a cook."

"Well, how would you like me and my cook here to come by in the mornings and cook breakfast for you guys?" We were all inside the tent, sitting on army cots when he said that, and I think we'd have lifted him to our shoulders and paraded him around if we'd had the room. To this day I'm not sure what prompted his good-natured offer. Perhaps he just wanted to get off the post for a bit, or maybe our situation brought about some sympathy. Whatever it was, a wonderful thing happened. Especially in light of the terrible cooking each of us had managed to turn out.

The next morning he showed up with one of his cooks, as promised. This was after his own cooks and bakers back at camp had completed the morning's breakfast detail. We got fried eggs, bacon, and coffee. On the second or third day Hubert said he felt like eating a dozen eggs. I said I bet I could, too. And, we did. Ate a dozen each . . . with bacon and thick slices of buttered bread, and a cup of hot GI coffee. It was wonderful!

Our routine for guarding the bridge was two on the gun from sundown until midnight, then the second two men relieved us to guard until dawn. The gun, tripod, and ammo would then be taken down and placed inside our tent until sundown, at which time the whole schedule was repeated. This suited us very well. We all slept throughout the day. After a great breakfast, that is.

One morning, just after our mess sergeant friend had left, I heard a jeep drive into our area. We had laced the front of the tent fly so it was open at the lower end, about a foot above the water-and-mud floor.

I figured it was Lieutenant Phillips, as he was about due for his regular visit. We heard splashes as he approached, and then he tried to unlace the tent fly. That's when I yelled out, "Get down on your hands and knees and crawl in like we do."

During the pause in the activity outside, we heard some muttered curses. I knew Pat was a good sport, so I didn't worry about it. We waited, and pretty soon an officer's black-and-gold-braid overseas cap appeared. Then his shoulders. Resting on each shoulder tab was a silver eagle! It was a full colonel, a guy just one step away from being a general . . . on his hands and knees . . . in the mud, and looking for all the world like a wounded bear. He filled the only door opening, otherwise I swear I'd have taken off. I yelled, "Ah . . . ten . . . shun!" And as he got up on his feet, we were all standing, rigid as statues, eyes front . . . or in my case, quivering.

He looked around, and I became aware of just how crappy

our little hovel must have looked to him. We were all in GI shorts and undershirts. He yelled, "Who in the hell is in charge of this . . . this dump?"

"I, ah, I am, sir," I said. I was near fainting.

"And just who the hell are you?"

I gave him the standard GI answer. "Dick, Robert C., Corporal, sir."

"Well, corporal, where in the hell are your guards? You're supposed to be guarding the railroad bridge, aren't you?"

"Ah . . . yes sir, but we guard it only during the hours of darkness, sir, that is."

"I see. Well, that's all changed now. You *will* post guards on it twenty-four hours a day, seven days a week."

"Sir, begging the colonel's pardon, but my orders are to guard it during the hours of darkness only . . . sir."

"Uh-huh. Well, Corporal, you now have new orders, or didn't you understand what I just told you?"

The four of us were still standing at attention, the colonel never having given us an "At ease" order.

"Yes, sir, I understand what you said, but I can only take orders from my commanding officer."

"And, who is your commanding officer, Corporal?" responded the colonel most sarcastically.

"Well, sir . . . he's Lieutenant Phillips . . . um . . . Pat Phillips . . . Second Lieutenant Phillips, that is. Sir."

"Okay, and where is this commanding officer? I want very much to talk to him. Meantime, you might as well prepare to resume guard duty twenty-four hours a day. You'll hear from me very soon . . . Corporal."

I gave him Pat's phone number, which he proceeded to copy down into a small pocket notebook. He then got down on his hands and knees and gave us a view of his majestic butt as he squished through the mud on the way out. As soon as we heard his jeep engine start, we all relaxed, sat down on our cots, and everyone looked at me. I had just refused a full colonel's orders. Oh, my God!

I knew then just how an accused person must feel when the foreman says, "Guilty!"

I dressed as fast as I could and was up on the highway in nothing flat. I hailed an army jeep and got a ride to the main entrance of Camp Roberts. I walked inside and saw that the provost marshal had an office right there. I went in and explained that I was in charge of the railroad bridge guard detail and I had to phone my CO right away. The sergeant on duty showed me a phone I could use, and I dialed Pat's number. It rang a couple of times and I heard him say, "Lieutenant Phillips speaking."

I said, "Pat, we're in a world of shit. . . . I mean that really, really deep stuff."

A pause, and then, "Is that you, Corporal Dick?"

I said, "You know it's me. . . . This is no time to be funny. I just had a visit from a full-bird colonel, and he's as mad . . . you'll see . . . I mean he's reeeeally pissed off. He'll be contacting you any minute now."

Phillips asked me what I had done this time, and I gave him a full accounting of the situation, including the "get down on your hands and knees" thing. There was another pause, and I heard him making some noises that I couldn't identify. First I thought he might be coughing, but he was either laughing or crying.

After he came back on the line, he told me to go back to the tent, keep our regular routine, and not to worry about anything. We said our good-byes, and I added a "Good luck" in there, too.

I thought I was okay after that, but it was just wishful thinking. When I started to walk out of the main gate, the guard there demanded to see my pass. I told him I didn't have a pass . . . that I'd just come in to use the phone and borrow a cup of sugar, but he wasn't buying that. After a spell of some very nasty army words, glaring, foot stomping, and the usual threats, I simply walked out, crossed the highway, and bummed a ride back to the bridge.

We never saw the colonel again, but within the next day or so we observed some soldiers from the north camp setting up a guard post at their end of the bridge. I walked over and talked with them, but all they knew was they had received orders to guard the bridge. Twenty-four hours a day!

2

We were moved from the Camp Roberts bridge a few weeks later and dropped off at yet another railroad installation. This one was right on the central California coast, guarding Sudden Tunnel. We were taken to it via the boxcar method and, as usual, dropped off with our old tent, machine gun, and my same little group: four of us, counting myself. This time, however, we had company . . . a full complement of rail workers, and a Chinese cook named Hoo.

We pitched our tent on the east side of the rails, with an embankment rising above us for a few hundred feet. A few feet away ran the rails, and across the rails was another set of them. Sitting on this second set was a cook's car, a dining car, and two coaches that housed the workers. I'd guess there were around twenty-five or thirty. Their daily routine was simple. They'd be fed breakfast in the morning, get on their little handcars, and head out to do repair work somewhere. They would take a packed lunch the cook gave them, to be eaten at midday on the job. Late afternoon saw them return for an early dinner in the dining car.

We had our daily rations supplied by our own cook back at platoon CP, and they hadn't improved at all. One day I walked over and had a chat with Hoo (no, I didn't go into an Abbott and Costello routine, although sometimes I felt like the whole thing was not real). The upshot was that Hoo would feed us breakfast and dinner in trade for our rations.

And, we would have to do the dishes.

I talked it over with my men, and they were all in favor of it. If we had been happy with our situation back at Roberts, we were delirious with this one! Breakfast was unimaginable. Hotcakes, eggs fried or scrambled, bacon and sausage, toast and biscuits, and so it went. Dinner was even better. Hoo was a wonderful cook, and every meal seemed just different enough from the last one that it was always a new, great eating experience. Those rail workers really tied into the food, too, and seemed to consume twice as much per man as any of us. They paid Hoo one dollar per day, per man, and everyone was happy, whereas Hoo soon saw less and less value in what we were offering in exchange. We lasted only a few days in the kitchen before Hoo ran us out with a very large butcher knife. We were not allowed back into his "kingdom.". . . Not that any of us wanted to wash pots and pans. In the meantime I picked up a reputation for taking good care of my men, foodwise, that is, even though I seemed to attract full colonels.

Sudden Tunnel got its name, I think, because it was located near a fairly sharp curve in the tracks. A train headed north would round the curve and there, about a hundred feet or so ahead, was the tunnel. Incidentally, on the other side of the rails from us was a cliff that dropped straight down to the Pacific Ocean, maybe a hundred feet at least.

Our routine here was identical to the one we had at the Camp Roberts bridge. We guarded the tunnel during the hours of darkness. I felt fairly secure from colonels here because the only way they could get to us was either by parachute or rail.

One late afternoon, just before sundown, I heard someone moaning. It was PFC George Hill, and he was complaining of a pain in his abdomen. He told me that he thought it might just be gas, or something he ate. I told the next detail to go ahead and get onto the gun. As time passed, Hill was hurting more and more. I checked him by probing his stomach and abdomen and finally came to the conclusion that he might have appendicitis. I walked up toward the tunnel and yelled for White to come on back to the tent and the other man to stay on the gun. When he got back, I told him to take three torpedoes and go back down the tracks, around the curve for a couple of hundred feet or so, and install them on the rails about six or eight feet apart. These things were railroad issue, and I had been informed that three of them going off was the signal for a train to immediately stop. Meanwhile, I got some ice from Hoo and packed it onto Hill's abdomen. He was running a pretty fair fever, which scared the hell out of me.

White returned and said that all we had to do now was wait. No kidding! After what seemed to me several hours, we heard a train coming. Because of the wind that blew off the ocean and the curve that shielded us from approaching trains, the noise of a train was seldom heard until it was almost on us. At the same time that we heard this train's engine, we also heard those torpedoes go off . . . *bang, bang, bang!* It came lurching around the curve, sparks flying from the steel wheels, passed us, and finally came to a halt just before it got to the tunnel entrance. I looked at it and saw that it was a passenger train. We had not seen anything go by except freight trains since we'd gotten here, so this was a big surprise. A second look told me that we had a troop train on our hands, which I figured was a good thing as surely they'd have a medic on board. I told White to get hold of a noncom or an officer and have Hill loaded aboard. By then I was genuinely afraid that Hill's condition had deteriorated to something extremely serious from the "something I ate" category.

About this time a figure loomed out of the darkness and there, standing in front of me, was a full colonel! Another one! The woods must be full of these guys, I thought. No, I couldn't believe this. I could only stare, and then snapped to attention, saluted, and waited for what I just knew would be a commendation for a medal for saving Hill's life.

"Are you the asshole who stopped this train . . . ?"

"Well, sir, yes, I guess I am . . . the one. That stopped the train, I mean."

Leaning closer to get a good look at me, he snarled, and I truly do mean snarled, "Corporal, are you out of your friggin' mind? Do you want to spend the rest of this century in jail? Don't you know that this is a troop train?"

"Ah, sir, I mean . . ." I was wondering if there was a special training center for full colonels that would teach them how to come close to exploding, without actually doing so.

Before I could complete my sentence, he continued, "Soldier, it's against regulations. . . . You cannot just stop a troop train."

He made that statement to me while his troop train stood quietly, stopped, about twenty feet behind him. I didn't quite know how to call his attention to this basic fact, and while I pondered that, he reiterated, "You cannot stop a troop train, do you understand?"

I looked him in the eyes and raised both arms, pointing one at the engine up front and the other toward the tail end of the train, as if to say to him, "Hey, this bastard's stopped, Colonel. Take a look!"

There was dead silence while each of us considered the situation, and I took advantage of the silence by saying, "Colonel, I really didn't know that your train was a troop train. But I would have had to stop it, despite regulations, because one of my men has a burst appendix [I didn't know that for sure], and he is in need of medical treatment if his life is to be saved." He stood there in the darkness, running over what I'd just told him, I think. Then, with a snarl (they must practice that at their colonels' seminar, too), he said, "Just be goddamn careful in the future, Corporal. Stopping troop trains cannot be done." I wanted to, once more, point to the train, but I honestly didn't think I could hold up under another full colonel attack. So I just muttered a quiet "Yes sir" and saluted his retreating back. I may not have given him a regulation salute, but who's to know in the darkness? White had returned by then and said that a medical officer told him that there was no doubt about it. . . . Hill had appendicitis, and it was lucky as hell that we got him on the train when we did. I told White that it was lucky as hell we could get the thing stopped . . . that you couldn't stop a troop train. We stood there in the darkness, looking at the train pulling out, and White said, "Thank the Good Lord for torpedoes." I watched the train as it slowly gathered speed and said, more to myself than to White, "Damn the torpedoes . . . full speed ahead." It wasn't very original, but somehow it fit the situation.

From the coastal positions we were then sent to Los

Angeles Harbor, guarding drawbridges and other similar port installations. We had been there a week or so when one day our orders changed. My machine gun was to be positioned at the island side of the Terminal Island drawbridge, and we were to stop and search all vehicles coming off the island. Most of the installations were shipbuilding and repair. There was also a commercial fisherman's marina, and that day the Japanese-American fishermen would be returning for the first time since Pearl Harbor. We were there to arrest all male Japanese over the age of thirteen and place them in waiting army trucks.

Come quitting time for the island shipyard workers, and what a situation! All of them were tired and eager to get home, and any delay had to be frustrating. Yet they gave us no problems when they learned we were rounding up Japanese fishermen from the incoming fleet. There was, after all, a war going on, and all Japanese were suspect even though there had been no evidence that they were anything but loyal American citizens. By the end of our shift we had picked up twenty or thirty Japanese . . . maybe more. I do recall one white couple that had driven onto the island and were bringing back with them several Japanese friends. They too were taken under custody. The couple was furious with us, but there was nothing we could do about it, and they knew it, too.

One morning I was awakened by Lieutenant Phillips.

"Wake up, Sergeant. Get your lazy ass out of the sack."

I opened my eyes and told him that he must have the wrong guy, that I was a lowly corporal. Well, he told me that I was once more a sergeant and that "we" had work to do.

It turned out that he had been assigned the task of forming a cadre whose mission was to teach basic training to draftees. "Come on, Lieutenant, I've had basic training up to my eyebrows. I absolutely refuse to go through that shit again. . . . "

Our basic training unit was at Camp Hahn, across the highway from March Field, in Riverside, California. Everything was there except the men. The good old pyramidal tents, mess halls, officers' tents, the whole shebang. Within a day or two the draftees, or, as we were told to say, "inductees," arrived. Bewildered, half scared to death, all of them dressed in ill-fitting fatigues. They looked like a bunch of Indians. As it turned out, that's what they were . . . Navajo Indians. There were a few Apaches, but 99 percent were Navajos.

We started them out with the basics. How to stand at attention, parade rest, at ease, things like that. I had a difficult time making them understand that officers rated a salute and were to be addressed as "sir." It was almost impossible to get them not to say "sir" to noncommissioned officers. As a group, they were as nice a bunch of guys as you'd want. As soon as they found out that we were all on the same side, it became a lot easier all around. We taught them close order drill . . . lots of discipline, scouting and patrolling (I felt sort of strange teaching Indians about scouting, but they took it all okay). There was only a scattering of non-Indians in the group, and we all got along just fine.

One guy stood out from all the rest. He was white, about six-foot-four-inches, with blond hair, blue eyes, and a ready smile.

As I went down the line the first day, it was a bit of a shock to see this fellow standing in line with all the much smaller soldiers. I looked him up and down and saw he was wearing civilian loafers. I started in on him about wearing only GI issue clothing and shoes. It turned out that the army had no shoes his size . . . really big ones. They were on order, so we had to make do as best as we could. I found out later that he was Ben Gage, Bob Hope's announcer from his radio show, and once he had basic training under his belt, he was slated to go to Special Services and take part in USO shows.

One evening after chow, I was visiting some of the Indians in one of their tents, and while we were talking, for whatever reason, I slipped my right little finger through the barrel ring on a bayonet guard. The bayonet was strapped to the side of a pack that was hanging at the end of the cot I was sitting on. While we talked, I sort of fooled around with the thing. After a while, a runner came to the tent and told me that Lieutenant Phillips wanted to see me in the orderly room right away. Well, I couldn't get my blasted finger out of the bayonet ring, try as I might. And the longer it was stuck, the more it swelled. In a little while the runner came back and said the lieutenant was getting pissed off. I'd better get it in gear. Finally, I went to the orderly tent, where Pat was waiting. I kept my right arm and hand slightly behind me. I didn't dare salute him when I entered.

"Where the hell have you been? Didn't you get the message? I wanted you up here then, not a week later . . . and, what the hell have you got behind you?"

"Ahh . . . sir . . . ahh, well, I was talking to some of the guys and . . ."

"Sergeant Dick, what do you have behind your back?"

"Nothing, really, Lieutenant. . . . It's just a bayonet" (I lowered my voice and sort of turned my head to one side as I mumbled the word "bayonet").

"Just a *what*?"

"A bayonet, sir. . . . You know, those long knifelike things that go on the end of . . ."

"Damn you, Dick, what in bloody hell are you doing with a bayonet on your finger . . . and, incidentally, I do know what one is . . . are you planning on attacking me or what?"

"Sir, the thing is stuck . . . on my finger . . . I mean I can't get it off . . . sir."

"Well, you are sure gonna have to be extra careful when you go to the latrine, Sergeant. Heh, heh. Just how the hell did you manage that? No, skip it. . . . Go get some shaving soap and get the thing off. Then come back here. I want to go over tomorrow's sked with you. Now, get out . . . out, out, OUT!"

After running several classes through basic training, we, the cadre, received orders to rejoin our outfit, which entailed a nice, long train ride. We were to proceed to Fort Lewis, Washington, to train for duty in Alaska . . . or so said the rumors.

Our coal-burning, steam-powered locomotive pulled us northward through some of the most beautiful country I'd ever seen. We ran alongside rivers for miles, and from what we could see, there were no roads in sight. We were seeing things that average vacationers would never get close to unless they were backpackers.

One of the important lessons we learned right off the bat

was to be handy with the windows. A coal-burning engine can produce the absolutely blackest, stinkiest, most choking smoke ever put out by any machine on the face of the planet. And when the engine entered a tunnel, and there were more than a few on our route, all that belching yucky stuff would stream through any open window and fill the entire car in a split second. Much to the utter disgust of all of us. It not only smelled foul, but it left us with soot on our faces, on our clothes, and on everything in the car, including our rifles and packs. And, the soot was not just black; it was greasy. Without the luxury of showers and with limited washing facilities, we began to look anything but what we thought we were—a first-class fighting outfit. Instead, we ended up looking for all the world like a traveling minstrel show! By the time we got to Fort Lewis we were ready to throw in the towel, despite the great scenery we'd seen along the way.

3

Having had my sergeant's stripes returned, I really fell back into it. The new TO (table of organization) assigned the platoon sergeant's rank as staff sergeant. Hot dog! This was a real case of coming out smelling like a rose.

Training at Fort Lewis consisted of the usual infantry routines. Lots of walking into the beautiful areas around the camp and, of course, doing our full share of details around the barracks. As a staff and platoon sergeant, I rated a private room. It was on the left as you entered the two-story wooden barracks. One Sunday morning I slept in and was awakened by someone knocking on the door. I told him to come in and saw Hubert White standing there . . . in civilian clothes! We were forbidden to wear anything except uniforms, and here he was in civvies. He came in grinning, with some of the other guys tagging along.

"Hubert, what the hell's going on? You can get yourself in a world of trouble wearing that."

"Sergeant, I've decided to go over the hill, and I came to tell you good-bye." He kept grinning at me like it was some kind of joke. Yeah, that must be it . . . he wouldn't, or would he?

"Okay, White, what's going on? I know you too well, and I know you aren't that dumb . . . so, what's the deal?"

I no sooner finished saying that when White stepped into the room, thankfully still in his GI uniform, and everyone broke into some wild-ass laughing. I couldn't believe my eyes. There were two of them! Two Whites! White, the one in civvies, stuck out his hand and we shook. He said, "Sergeant Dick, I'm Herbert. Hubert and I are identical twins." To which I said, "No shit."

Turns out that his brother and he had flipped a coin, and Hubert had won, or lost, depending on your point of view. They were the only means of support for their mother, and they lived on a farm in Kentucky. Anyway, Herbert, who had gotten the military deferment on the coin flip, had somehow gotten a ride cross-country to see Hubert, and what a pair they made. I got Hubert a weekend pass, and later the first sergeant kept giving him passes until his twin finally left for home.

On another Sunday morning when I was sleeping in, again I was awakened by knocking. The three or four soldiers were all excited and told me that I *had* to come upstairs and see Al Cartello. I got a pair of pants on, and our little group went up to the second floor. Down the aisle we went and stopped at Cartello's bunk. He was on his face, snoring away as only he could. He was bare to the waist, and there, for all the world to see, was his brand-new, only one in the world like it, tattoo.

It was a thing of beauty. It covered his back, starting at the nape of his neck, going down to his waist, and running from one side to the other. It was a full-rigged, old clipper ship. A three-master, under full sail. On one side was an American flag, and the other side had palm trees. Across the bottom

was a ribbon/scroll that read, "Sailing Home." It was magnificent and, I knew from personal experience, also painful.
So painful that he wouldn't be able to carry a pack on his
back, and that meant getting company punishment from the
first sergeant. Parts of the tattoo were not filled in, and that
meant more work on it had yet to be done . . . which might
mean more missed duty hours and more details for Al. I'd
love to see it again.

One Saturday morning, as inspection of our quarters and
personal gear was coming to a close, Lieutenant Phillips
drew me aside and asked if I was going on weekend pass. I
told him that Joe and I had been planning on it . . . what's up?
Pat's wife Georgia, a most wonderful and beautiful red-
haired saint of a woman, had come to Washington to stay
with him for a short while, and they had a small apartment in
nearby Olympia. He asked me if Joe and I could drop by the
apartment when we got into town, he had something he
wanted me to take care of. And of course I said yes.

The apartment was on the second floor, and while it was
small, it looked great to a couple of guys who had spent the
last year living in tents or barracks. Pat said that we would
have to keep this under our hats, and naturally Joe and I took
the oath not to say a word to anyone. With that, the lieutenant
pulled his footlocker out of the closet. The three of us stood
there, admiring it, and I said, "Lieutenant, I know that I speak
for Sergeant Mason here, when I tell you that we'll never say
a word about your footlocker, or your closet, or anything like
that, sir." I sort of rolled my eyes at Joe and edged toward the
door.

"Wait a minute, you dummy. . . . Never mind the footlocker or the closet. I want you to paint something on the lid
of the dad-ratted thing. Okay?"

"Well, sure Pat . . . what did you have in mind?" I could
see that his name, rank, and serial number had already been
stenciled on the lid . . . what more could he possibly want?

"Palm trees, some clouds, maybe a hula girl, stuff like
that."

"Lieutenant, we're supposed to be headed to Alaska and
you want me to . . . oh!" The light dawned. I looked over at

Joe and he looked back at me, and then the nut began strum-
ming an imaginary ukulele. Both of us were grinning. Who
wants snow and ice when they can have the tropics! Phillips
had gotten the inside word from someone, and we didn't care
who. I had painted my footlocker back at San Luis Obispo,
and Pat had remembered that, while it wasn't professional-
looking, it wasn't too bad.

No one said anything further, but we all understood what
the deal was.

"Pat, when you get ready to ship this thing, you're gonna
have to say that you painted it. Otherwise they'll know that
we were in on the deal." It was no sweat, he assured me.

He said he'd already thought about that. He and Georgia
were all set to go to some officer's function, and before leaving he pointed out a gallon jug of cherry brandy, about half
full. He said it had been a present from his dad, and Pat
didn't really care for it. So, it was ours. We were also told
that if we got hungry, the refrigerator was well stocked. He
had bought a couple of small artists' brushes and a few small
cans of enamel paint.

They left, and I began to lay out the lid for our master-
piece. Joe poured me a glass of cherry brandy, one for him,
too. After some time, Joe decided to scramble some eggs and
make toast. Damn, we were rolling now. The painting,
cherry brandy, and food kept getting better as time passed.
After a while I ran out of cigarettes, and while Joe snoozed
on the couch, I put on a jacket and went downstairs to the
drugstore I'd noticed on the corner. By the time I got the cigarettes and was back upstairs, Joe had woken up and was sitting there, staring at me.

"What's wrong? Is my fly open or what?"

"No, but you're impersonating an officer."

I had picked up Pat's half-coat and naturally, him being a
lieutenant, he had bars on everything, including his half-
coat. I was wondering why all the GIs had saluted me, and
figured that my reputation had preceded me. Heh, heh.

By the time Pat and Georgia returned, the lid had been
painted, I was fast asleep on the couch, and Joe was on the
floor nearby with a pillow and a blanket. What a great time

we'd had. And next morning, looking at the footlocker lid, I found that while it wouldn't win a ribbon, it didn't look too shabby. All things taken into consideration, of course. Things like cherry brandy come to mind.

Back at Fort Lewis, whenever the guys started talking about Alaska, Joe and I would look at each other, smile, and not say a word.

4

Troop trains were now a thing of the past, and we sailed out of California going west. While most of the troops still thought we were Alaska-bound, I would catch Joe's eye once in awhile when we were topside, and we'd both break into big grins. And, yep, after about a hundred years of the ship zigzagging across the Pacific, we arrived at the Big Island of Hawaii. And, what a beautiful sight it was. Didn't look a thing like Alaska, either.

Our first assignment was at a place called South Point, down at the end of the island where I don't think it ever rained but the wind certainly blew, and with a vengeance. We were stationed there for a week or so and then moved back closer to Hilo, the major city on the island, where we guarded a fuel dump just outside Olla in a tropical fern forest.

After we settled in, our company was split up around the east and south portions of the island, manning observation posts, or, as we called them, OPs. The OPs were small positions, maybe four men, and the main duty for them was to spot and report any enemy ships or suspicious activity. At each OP was an alidade board. This was a large circular board, maybe a yard or so across, marked off in degrees and looking exactly like a compass card. Pivoted at the center was a strip of metal that had at one end a pointer, and at the other end a peephole, kind of like a gun sight in its most basic form. When an unidentified ship came in view, we would swing the pointer around until it was dead on to the ship. The OP would then phone the CP (command post) and report the OP number and what they had observed, plus the angle of the pointer. When another OP phoned in, its angle of observation was also noted on a master map at the CP. Where the two lines of sight crossed would be the precise location of the ship.

Because no one knew for sure if the Japanese would invade Hawaii, the army held evening and morning alerts to keep everyone on their toes. Every man, regardless of assignment, had to be up and ready for a period of a half hour before sundown, or sunup, until a half hour afterward. Gas masks and personal weapons were to be present. No exceptions were allowed.

One of my first assignments in Hawaii was to install and maintain a series of OPs in and around the city of Hilo. My CP was a two-story civilian house that sat on a point of land overlooking Hilo Harbor; a truly beautiful setting. The driveway was circular and passed under a roof overhang at the front entrance.

My platoon leader was 2d Lt. Floyd Hammond, a former sergeant himself, who had gone to OCS and was now an officer and a gentleman, at least according to Congress. He was one helluva nice guy. He'd been an enlisted man and knew all the ins, outs, and problems that faced us common folk. One evening Floyd and I were out imbibing, as the saying goes, and we had had more than our share. Good drinking whiskey was extremely hard to come by at the time. There was some stuff brewed in Hawaii called Five Islands. There was Five Islands gin, whiskey, rum, you name it, but except for the coloring, it all tasted exactly the same. Really bad.

On this night Floyd and I came back to the CP very late, and as we passed the sentry on guard at the door, the lieutenant told him to not wake either of us for the morning alert. Sometime next morning I was being wakened by the lieutenant shaking my shoulder.

"Wake up, Sergeant. . . . Come on, wake up."

"What's happening. Lieutenant?"

"The colonel's here, and we missed the alert. He's mad as hell!"

"How do you know he's here?" I asked.

"Because the son of a bitch just woke me!" I noticed that his voice was shaking slightly. Which didn't do much for my confidence. Sleeping during the alert, we had been told, was akin to sleeping on guard. A capital offense during wartime.

I looked out the front window and saw the colonel pacing back and forth on the front porch, his jeep parked nearby. By the time we got into uniform and outside, he had roared away, wheels spitting gravel as he spun out of the driveway, and turned left for battalion headquarters. Well, shit, another full colonel attack. Later that day I got into my jeep and drove over to battalion headquarters. I asked to speak to the colonel and was granted a few minutes. I came in, saluted, and thanked him for seeing me. I said, "Sir, I was supposed to wake Lieutenant Hammond for alert this morning, and I just slept through it. It was my fault, plain and simple."

He looked at me for a bit and then said, "That's interesting because a little while ago, the lieutenant was here and told me that it was his fault. That he was supposed to wake you. You guys had better get your stories straight next time. Now get the hell out of here." For whatever reason, nothing ever came of this, but needless to say, the lieutenant and I, from then on, were always on time for the alert. No exceptions, as the saying goes. Not all colonels are bad guys!

A month or so later my platoon and I were transferred to the Laupahoehoe area, up the coast a number of miles from Hilo. This also was an OP operation, with the posts strung out for several miles up and down the coast from the main CP. While on leave I dropped in on a small bar a few miles outside of our OP operations area. The place was owned and run by a Japanese American, a very nice guy. One day I was mentioning how rotten the Five Islands liquor was and how I'd love to get my hands on a bottle of Canadian Club. He told me that if he ever came across any, he'd save it for me.

A week or so later I got a phone call from him. He said he

had just received a bottle of Canadian Club and it was mine if I'd come and get it that evening. He said otherwise he'd put it on the bar shelf the next day. I told him I would see him in a little while. It was about 7:00 p.m. and had begun to rain. I got hold of my driver and told him we were leaving in about fifteen minutes and to be ready. I then phoned company headquarters and spoke with my first sergeant, John Clement. I told him I was going to pull a surprise inspection of OP #2. It sat on top of a small hill and its only access was by a dirt road, which, because of the almost constant rain, was usually mud. Sergeant Clement told me to be very careful driving in the poor road conditions in the dark. That done, we got into the jeep and headed for my Canadian Club in the next town, out of my jurisdiction.

A few miles down the road we came to a long, narrow bridge. I was sitting in the passenger seat with my legs pulled up and my knees resting on the metal dashboard. As we entered the bridge, I could just make out an object in the middle of the narrow road, as the rain was very heavy and made vision difficult. We were traveling probably close to forty miles per hour, and I suddenly realized that there was a cow in the road, on our side. I didn't want to yell at the driver because I thought he surely must have seen it. He didn't, and we plowed into the poor thing, head-on.

I took the full shock on both my knees, and I knew right then that I'd never walk again.

We crawled out and inspected the damage. The cow was dead. The heavy channel-type bumper on the jeep had been bent in the middle and shoved against the radiator, which was now leaking. I staggered around, in agony, and between some choice words asked the driver, "Why the hell didn't you stop?" He was newly assigned to me, and this was the first time I'd had him drive me at night. Turned out he couldn't see worth a hoot at night. Damned way to find out!

We got the jeep turned around and managed to drive it back to our CP. I told my driver to keep his mouth shut and to get a water hose and clean the blood and fur off the front of the vehicle. After that was done, we bent the fan blades back so they stopped grinding away at what was left of the radiator. I went into my headquarters' room and again phoned the first sergeant. I told him I'd been delayed in starting up to OP #2, but was leaving now. Again he cautioned me about the road hazards. We left and, fortunately, no one had seen the condition of the jeep.

About halfway up the road to the OP, I had the driver stop the jeep, and together we managed to get it over the side of the road and into a ditch. We walked on up to the OP and I phoned the first sergeant again. I told him that he had been absolutely right, and that we had skidded off the road about halfway up and the jeep was in a ditch.

Years later, after the war, John and I were having dinner in a small restaurant near his home. Of course we began talking about the "good old days." John remembered the time my jeep slid off the road on the way to OP #2. He said, "Don't tell me . . . there was something fishy about that one, wasn't there?" So I confessed the whole thing. He asked, "Was that bottle of Canadian Club worth all that hassle?"

"John," I said, "I never got the stuff. By the time I finally got back to my CP, I was so tired and disgusted I just said to hell with it!"

"So I guess you learned a bit of a lesson, didn't you?"

I said, "You're damn right . . . from then on I always checked with my drivers to be sure that their night vision was okay."

John just looked at me a moment, shook his head, and ordered another round. I can't remember for sure, but I'd like to think we were drinking Canadian Club at the time.

5

As a platoon sergeant I had forty-eight men under my command, and we had all trained together for so long I felt that we were up to any situation we might encounter. All except one. My left ankle began bothering me during a march.

Our routine called for a ten-minute break for every one hour of walking. At the end of the ten minutes' rest, I could hardly put any weight on my ankle because of the pain. It felt like a very bad sprain. After I resumed walking for a few minutes, the pain would subside a little. I went on sick call and was sent to the army hospital just outside Olaa, Hawaii. X rays didn't detect anything wrong, so I was assigned a whirlpool treatment. The whirlpool tank was a stainless steel affair about three feet across and about the same depth. I was sharing it with another soldier, Jack Harley. He had sprained his right ankle, and so there we sat, an hour each treatment, three days a week, he with his right leg in the whirling warm water and me with my left one in it, both of us griping about the service in general and our fearless leaders in particular. I learned that Jack was a driver of an M3 light tank, which I had first seen during maneuvers in Washington State. For whatever reason the tanks had intrigued the hell out of me, and I couldn't get enough of Jack's colorful descriptions of life as a tank driver.

A few days after meeting Jack, I learned that I was going to be transferred out of the infantry to a noncombat unit; quartermaster, administration, MPs, wherever there was no marching involved. All of my service life had been predicated on one day seeing combat, and this news really unsettled me. Naturally, I talked about this latest situation with Jack. I figured that if I could ride in a tank, my ankle would be of no consequence. I asked him if there were any openings in his outfit, the only tank unit on the island at the time. The next day he told me that he'd talked to his CO, and I had an appointment with Capt. Ross Garner that afternoon.

I kept the appointment and found, to my disappointment, that there were no openings in my grade (staff sergeant), although the captain was eager to have me. I learned that he was an infantry buff and thought that anyone who served in that branch was a real soldier. He said he'd advance me as rapidly as possible, but that I'd have to take a bust to private in order to get into his unit, having no openings in any other grade.

I thought long and hard and decided to take a chance. I typed up a request for a transfer to C Company, 763d Tank Battalion, as a private. My reason was "for the good of the service," stating that I desired to go to OCS (officer candidate school) in the Armored Forces and wanted to get some background experience in that branch before requesting OCS. My transfer request was granted, and within a matter of days I found myself a buck private in a real live tank company.

The company was an activated National Guard unit from the South. That was okay, except I had difficulty understanding their dialect. I had always enjoyed the rich accents of those from the Deep South, but try as I might, I missed a lot of what was being said. The fact that I was a Yankee didn't set too well with them, either. I mentioned that I was born in Fort Worth, Texas, and that helped a little . . . but not much. I casually mentioned that I had lived in Southern California before getting into the service. . . . Hey, that's in the South, right? That one almost got me killed! Two other strikes against me were that I had been an infantryman and a non-commissioned officer. They disliked both. Other than all of the above, I was as welcome as the flowers in May. Those guys were "clannish" to the point where I began to feel like a member of the Hatfields dropped into the midst of a family of McCoys!

PART TWO

I'm a Tank
Driver . . .
More or Less

6

I had been in the company for a while and had managed to survive all the pitfalls newbies usually dig for themselves. And, because I liked to draw, the word got around that I was something of an artist (I wish), and soon I was painting pinup girls on some of the tank turrets. Every tank had a name painted on it, according to what the crew thought they liked. One day, orders came down from battalion headquarters that put the brakes on things. We were told that all tank names had to start with the same letter as the company. This meant that all the tank names in our outfit had to start with a C. Radio procedure, we were told. Also, another low blow . . . nothing else was to be painted on the turrets. Just the big white star and the number. That was it. All my great-looking gals were now covered. What a pity because some of them weren't all that bad.

The radio procedure did sound like a good idea, however. It was explained that using this "new system" would prevent any possibility that a tank from another unit might come along with a duplicate name. And then, of course, pandemonium would reign even more than it usually did.

Before leaving the tank name discussion, I must say that D Company came up with a wonderful series of names for the five tanks in one of its platoons. You can imagine our appreciation of their cleverness when one day this particular platoon paraded on by, telling the world about "Dinah"; that is, DINAH . . . DINAH MITE . . . DINAH COULD . . . DINAH WOULD . . . and DINAH DID.

Try as we might, none of us could come up with anything half as good for C Company despite a whole lot of deep and serious thought. Our crew's tank finally ended up with the very plain-Jane name of CUTTHROATS. Hey, what can you expect from four guys all wanting to name a tank after *their* girlfriends (wife, dog, or whatever)? At any rate, we were stuck with the new radio call signs that would, in the end, simplify things. From now on, on the radio, our battalion's code name was "Hitchhike," our company was "Charlie," and individual tanks would use their turret number. For example, a typical tank-to-tank radio transmission would go like this: "Hitchhike Charlie Five-Five to Hitchhike Charlie Five-One."

I soon found that there were a few non-Southerners in the company, and after a couple of weeks of training I, thankfully, ended up as driver for tank #60, commanded by Sgt. Ovid W. French. "OW" (pronounced oh-dub-ya) had been a lobster fisherman in civilian life and hailed from Rumbly, Maryland. He had a slight Down East accent but was perfectly understandable. He was a quiet guy, on the husky side, and what we nowadays would call "cool." Standing about five-foot-ten with an open face, blue eyes, and dirty blondish hair, he was as polite as could be.

Our loader was Jim Anderson, who came direct from Kansas. His accent sounded, to my ears, sort of like a "good old boy" from the Midwest which, of course, he was. Jim was five-foot-ten or so, and he, too, had blue eyes, blond hair, and was on the husky side. He was very strong, and he looked it. He had a temper, and together we used to plot against the you-know-whos for all the good it did.

Our assistant driver was Roy Greenup, from Visalia, California. He had not a trace of an accent and sounded like an ordinary human being. I say he had no accent, and that's true, but he did have a slow way of speaking, almost a drawl. Dark hair, brown eyes, and dark eyebrows, Roy seemed to always have a ready grin to share. We four were kind of an "us against them" crew, and we were all happy with that.

Now, a word or two here about our light tank. The M3 Stuart weighed thirteen tons and was powered by an air-cooled, radial engine, a Guiberson diesel. The main gun was a 37mm cannon, and the Stuart was also equipped with .30-

caliber machine guns. There was one in each sponson, and the driver fired them by squeezing a pair of levers located on the steering laterals. They were aimed by simply steering the tank toward the target and squeezing the levers. To say that the designer of this particular part of the weapons system was an optimist is, at once, obvious. The tank commander was also the gunner. He moved the cannon up or down by using a shoulder hook or U-shaped metal half circle covered with foam rubber. It was designed so that the commander/gunner could insert his shoulder into it and, by raising and lowering his body, cause the gun to elevate or depress. Traversing the gun was done by hand cranking the turret until the gun sight was on target.

The commander had one other duty that stands out in my memory. When standing in the turret, he gave the driver commands by using his foot on the back of the driver's head and shoulders! There was no intercom, and the noise was too loud to hope to be able to shout commands. Kicks and pushes on the poor driver had to do the job. A light tapping on the driver's helmet meant "Go ahead." A steady push between the shoulder blades meant "Stop." A rapid tapping on the back of the driver's helmet meant "Back up." A push on the right shoulder meant "Turn right," and a push on the left shoulder meant "Turn left." One time when OW wanted me to stop really quick, he almost pushed me out through the hatch opening!

Starting the little dear was always a lesson in dramatics. Because of the configuration of the radial engine, some of the cylinders were on the bottom, so there was the possibility, nay, the probability, that while the engine was shut down, oil might have seeped past the cylinder rings and settled in the lower combustion chambers. Oil doesn't like to be compressed, and given this fact, we had to drain the lower cylinders so when the engine was fired up, we wouldn't blow the bottom end of the thing to pieces. Good reasons all, but to drain the oil we had to hand crank the engine. Hand cranking a diesel is one of those things you can forget. Won't work. Unless, of course, you do something about the compression.

The first step in this somewhat magical procedure was to pull what we called the "decompression rod" from the engine. Okay, rod out, no compression, let's crank. So, out came a strange looking "crank" and the driver and assistant driver were in for a bit of exercise.

The crank was a short length of steel tubing with a claw affair at one end. At the aft end of the transmission case, where the driveshaft came out, was a kind of gear. The engine was turned over several times by engaging the claw/crank to the gear. Lazy drivers sometimes took a chance and started the engine without doing all that cranking. Present company excluded . . . of course. Ahem.

It should be understood that this hand-cranking operation was not necessary each and every time the engine was started; only if it had sat, say, all day or overnight. If it had been running an hour or so before, no sweat.

Once the oil was drained out of the lower cylinders, via the exhaust pipes, it was time to get down to business. First, we pushed the decompression rod all the way back in, thus ensuring that the open valves were now closed and the engine was in a "normal ready to start" status. On the inside of the turret, on the rear wall, was a device that looked like the breech end of an old-fashioned break-open shotgun. The engine's starter shells were packed in what looked exactly like a coffee can. They appeared to be 12-gauge size, but none of us knew for sure. When things were ready, transmission in neutral, magneto selectors on "both," the starter switches were thrown. There was a loud bang, and if all went according to the group prayer meeting we'd held beforehand, the engine would start with a loud roar and a cloud of black smoke. Told you it was dramatic.

Sometimes while we were driving along, the engine would begin to lose power. Almost certainly the decompression rod had vibrated out slightly, and the engine was losing compression. Rapid action would then be taken. Normal procedure was to pass the crank up to the turret. The crank, that piece of steel tubing with the claw on the end, then became a hammer. The commander would bang furiously on the decompression rod, and soon the engine would be back to its usual growling, snarling self.

Our little tank had rubber blocks on the tracks that would, hopefully, prevent us from tearing up any paved streets we might be lucky enough to find. The tanks' five-speed transmission was manually shifted, and it had to be double-clutched when shifting up or down the gears. The driver sat on a seat that had its cushion almost flat on the floor, his legs extended straight out between the steering laterals. There was a clutch pedal on the left and an accelerator pedal on the right. No brakes. In order to stop, gears had to be shifted down, double-clutching each time until the tank had been slowed to almost a walk. At that point, both steering laterals could be pulled at the same time and hopefully the vehicle would then come to a halt. Hopefully.

There are two volcanoes on the Big Island. Mauna Loa (Long Mountain) has the active volcano, Kilauea. The inactive one is Mauna Kea, which, if memory serves me, means White Mountain. The "white" part of the name comes from the fact that there is snow on top of the mountain just about year round. Matter of fact, there is a Hilo Ski Club, or at least there used to be. Imagine that; a ski club in the Hawaiian Islands!

One day we loaded up and drove our tanks up the Mauna Kea road, as far as it went. We were to stay overnight, and our crew decided to lay out the big tarp, which was large enough to cover a tank. There was some discussion as to how and which way to install it. Finally it was decided to lay it out flat on the ground, fold it in half, and crawl under it for the night. Needless to say, I got in first and ended up where the fold was. Almost immediately it began to rain. Cold, almost icy rain. As the rain ran down the slope of the mountain, it entered our canvas covering and ran down to where you-know-who was. I stood it for a while and then deserted the crew for the tank. Got inside that cold chunk of iron and sat in the commander's seat, listening to Tokyo Rose play good American jazz, and tried to sleep. I was not a happy camper that night, but the music was good.

Next morning I was talking to Howdy Haight, one of the

maintenance crew. Howdy drove midget race cars before the war and was from San Diego. The maintenance vehicle was a half-track, and because mine was the last tank in the column, somehow or other Howdy and I decided to race down the mountain. I lagged behind as the company drove off, and when I decided that they'd gotten far enough ahead, I put my foot in it. Howdy stuck right on my tail, and we thundered down the mountain, having the time of our young lives. The road had a series of dips and rises, and at the top of one of the small hills, I decided to shift down because it looked pretty steep ahead. I reached back for the shift lever and found that it was in neutral! The tank was gaining speed, and I had no brakes and no gears to slow us down. In desperation I floored the throttle and, with the engine wide open and the clutch pedal out, pushed the pedal in and somehow got the thing into third gear. We were almost on top of a sharp turn to the left, and I just took my foot off the clutch pedal. No easing it out . . . just let it go. The tank literally stood on its nose, the engine screamed, and we slid around the curve. I shifted down to second gear and finally got us stopped.

Howdy came up behind us and we both went around to the rear to look the engine over. When I opened the engine compartment doors, there was oil leaking from every nut and bolt on the old dear. Howdy looked at it for a minute and said, "Well, it looks like you've got a bad engine here . . . got to get it replaced as soon as we get back. Assuming we can get it back." We did, and yes, we got a new engine, and no, Howdy and I did not, repeat, did not do any more racing. At least in the mountains.

One of the joys that came with the driver's job was exploiting the speed and agility of the M3 light tank. There were eighteen tanks in C Company, and our tank, old #60, was the last one in the column. During a road march a favorite practice of mine was to slowly drop back until we were a fair distance behind the rest of the column and then go full-bore catching up. One time in Hawaii we were rolling along a paved road, and it was raining. The company had gotten quite a distance ahead of us, and OW gave me the signal to catch up. I got us up to around forty miles per hour, came sailing around a curve . . . and there sat the entire company at the side of the road! Apparently, they had stopped for a break. I started downshifting, and by the time I got us stopped, we were sitting directly alongside Captain Garner's parked lead tank. I had passed seventeen tanks before we stopped! He just looked at me, smiled, and motioned OW to have me back up to our proper place in the convoy . . . at the tail end of the line. By the time we finally got back to where we were supposed to be, the signal was given to start engines and move out. I had managed to cheat us out of our ten-minute stretch. But, ah, it was worth it, every minute of it.

We were living in tents with wooden floors and wood frames, each housing six men. One of the men in our tent was Pvt. Don Weller. Weller was a quiet individual and kept to himself. He had one very unusual thing that he'd do. After evening chow, when guys were sitting around playing cards, writing home, or just plain bullshitting, Weller would take out his wallet and count his money. Then, he'd count it again. And again. All the time laughing quietly to himself, and once in awhile, he'd bark. Not real loud. Or continuously. But, bark he would. He would do this most every evening, and we soon ignored it. He wasn't hurting anyone, and Lord knows there were enough flaky guys around without pointing a finger at Weller.

One morning after breakfast and our usual physical exercise session, several names were called out. Mine was among them. The first sergeant said he didn't know what it was about, just that we should be at the company headquarters tent at such and such a time, in a class A uniform. Class A meant our chinos with ties.

At the appointed time we gathered in front of the headquarters tent, and after a wait (there's always a wait), we were loaded into the back of a weapons carrier. There were seven of us, including Weller. No one had a clue as to what was going on. But there was nothing new in that . . . the army always worked in mysterious ways, didn't it, and who were we to ask questions?

We were transported to a building just outside Hilo, the main town on the island. We unloaded and were told to go inside, have a seat, and wait for our names to be called. We did that, and the first name was Weller's. He disappeared through a door and didn't come back out. About twenty minutes later, one of the other fellows' names was called. He came back out a few minutes later, with a strange look on his face, and left the building. After a bit, my name was called, and in I went. I was told to be seated. A long table with several officers seated behind it was across from me. Private Weller was seated in another chair, alongside me, about ten feet away. He had his regular smile and looked perfectly normal . . . as "normal" as any of us, that is.

I went through the usual dance with the officers, stating my name, rank, and serial number. I was asked if I was acquainted with Private Weller and I said yes, I was. The officer then asked me if I had ever observed Weller doing anything, "well, unusual"? I could see where we were headed and decided not to say anything unless it was in answer to a direct question. So I asked, "Do anything unusual, sir?"

"Yes, make any strange noises, actions, things of that nature."

"Ah . . . yes sir." I could see Weller out of the corner of my eye and he was still smiling. I was very embarrassed.

"Okay, what did you see or hear?"

"I'm not real sure what you mean, sir."

He was getting impatient. "Did Weller make any strange noises?"

"Ummm, well, he'd bark once in awhile. . . ."

"You mean, bark like a dog?"

I found that I really had to laugh. Out loud. And, maybe a touch hysterically. But I kept quiet. And, I mean, just barely.

"Yes, sir, like a dog." I prayed, silently, that I wouldn't be asked the breed.

"Anything else?"

"You mean any other animal, sir?"

Angrily, "No, did he do anything else out of the norm?"

"Well, he'd count his money . . . a lot. And, he'd laugh while he was doing it."

"And, bark?"

"Yes, sir, barking is one of his favorites." I had figured out by then that Weller was looking for a Section 8, a medical discharge by reason of mental deficiency. Nutty, in other words.

Weller left the company shortly after that hearing, and I can only guess that he got what he had wanted all along . . . that good old ticket to the USA. And in my imagination, I could see him sitting at home, counting his money, laughing every once in awhile, and barking.

Kona, at the north end of the island, had a wonderful climate, but the week we were there, it got very cold at night. One evening I was corporal of the guard, and one of my duties was to make the rounds of the posts and see how things were going. Our showers were inside a building that also housed some very large hot water heaters, so the room was always nice and warm. As I walked by, I decided to step inside, smoke a cigarette, and get warm at the same time. The floor was concrete, and as I stood there warming up, I noticed a small field mouse at the other side of the room. He'd move a little bit, stop, and move some more. I kept watching him, and he continued to move . . . in my direction. When he was about five or six feet away from me, he put on a sudden burst of speed and crawled right up my pants leg! I made a panicky grab and got hold of the rascal. I was holding a handful of pants leg cloth, with mister mouse trapped inside. The tanker's standard fatigue uniform was coveralls, and that's what I was wearing. I also had a pistol belt around my waist. Holding the mouse with my right hand, I unclipped the pistol belt and unbuttoned my coveralls with my left hand. After I was unbuttoned, I had to get my arm out of the left sleeve . . . no easy task. Once I had half my outfit off came the crucial move . . . changing hands. I managed that, as only a person holding a mouse at bay could. I now had the mouse trapped in my left hand, and proceeded to get out of my right sleeve. Once free, I dropped the whole shebang, stepped out of it, and took mister mouse outside (still enveloped in my coveralls). I set him free, and as I went back inside to get dressed, I thanked my lucky stars that no one, at any stage of this thing, had happened to walk in on me. The word would have spread about the intrepid corporal of the guard, armed with a .45-caliber pistol, who had encountered a fierce field mouse and, using modern technology, had defeated the poor creature. Or words to that effect.

That same night I got myself involved in something of a more serious nature, although at the time I passed it off as nothing. As I was approaching one of the guard posts, I saw someone coming up our long dirt driveway. He was weaving, and once he fell. As he came closer, I could see that it was Pvt. Fred Kamp, one of the men in our company who had a reputation of being a very heavy drinker. We talked for a bit and I found that he had been into town. He had gotten loaded and overstayed his leave and was now trying to get back to his bunk with minimum trouble. Rather than put in a report, I helped him locate his tent, saw him inside, said goodnight, and forgot about the incident. It was to pop up again a few days later.

As had happened with Weller's hearing, several of us were loaded into the back end of a weapons carrier and taken into Hilo for a hearing regarding Kamp's drinking. The word had been out on him for a long time, and either the first sergeant or one of the officers, or both, had decided to get rid of him once and for all. Kamp must have heard about it because he discussed it on the way into town. There were four of us, not counting Kamp, and we decided that "no brass was going to railroad old Kamp into a lot of trouble." We didn't agree to lie, outright, but we were going to avoid telling the truth if at all possible.

When it came my turn, I was asked if I had seen Kamp the night he came back from pass. "Yes, I'd seen him."

"Was he drunk?" I didn't know, I was no authority on drunkenness. Yes, sir, I smelled liquor on his breath, but that didn't mean he was drunk, did it, sir? And so on.

Finally, we were all literally tossed out and the hearing ended. As we got back into the weapons carrier, Kamp spoke up and said, "Hey, guys, in celebration of my victory, what say we all go out tonight and tie one on?" He got no takers, only disgusted, dead silence. I wondered at the time, what was it going to take to drive home to this guy what kind of problem he had? As it turned out, the solution was coming. Once in awhile I think that maybe if we'd all told the truth, Kamp would have ended up much better than he eventually did.

Sometime in September 1943, I was flown home on an emergency leave. My grandfather was critically ill, and the Red Cross had made a request that I be allowed to get back before it was too late. He had been stricken by a cerebral hemorrhage and there was no chance of recovery. My grandparents had raised me and were the only real mother and father I knew.

I got a ride in a converted B-24 bomber and the flight from Hickam Field, Honolulu, to Oakland, California, took twelve hours. From Oakland I had terrible luck getting a ride south to El Monte and finally ended up on a Greyhound bus. I arrived the day after the funeral. I tried to get an extension on my leave in order to assist my grandmother with some business, but it was refused. I was ordered to report to Angel Island, in San Francisco Bay, and wait for transportation by sea back to my outfit.

One day while at Angel Island, I noticed a couple of GIs looking at me, and pretty soon they walked over. One of them asked if I had gone to El Monte High School, and I said yes . . . how did you know? Turns out he had been a few grades behind me, but recognized me. He, like myself, lived in El Monte. His name was Pete Goni, and his buddy was Eldon Davenport. Davenport wanted to be called Al, but I decided that with his name being Davenport, "Couch" was much better. Neither of us was to know it at the time, but our friendship was to be a lasting one.

I found that Couch was from Santa Ana, in Southern California, and both he and Goni were armored force troops headed to a replacement center on Oahu. Goni was a likable guy and had the slightest trace of an accent, which I think was pure Spanish. He had little use for Mexicans, I remember. He was stocky and dark-haired, with brown eyes, and as nice a guy as you'd find. Couch was about five-foot-ten with brown wavy hair, and he sported a mustache. I asked him how he had gotten away with that in basic training, and he claimed he'd told them he had a harelip and it was doctor's orders! He was always looking at the bright side, and the three of us had a good time with our gab fests. I kidded Couch about being from "San An-tone," and he was quick to correct me . . . "Santa Ana" was his response.

We all got assigned to the former cruise ship, the *Luraline*. On the way to Hawaii, I regaled them with stories of my outfit, those Southern guys, and the few Yankees in it. When we hit Oahu, we parted ways. They were off to the replacement center, and I went back to the Big Island of Hawaii. A couple of weeks later Goni and Couch showed up. They were our latest replacements, and after all the foreboding tales I had laid on them, I could only guess at their feelings as they climbed off the truck.

7

Sometime later in 1943 our battalion was upgraded from a light tank outfit to medium tanks. We turned in our little M3s, and we were shipped over to the Hawaiian island of Oahu where we picked up brand-spanking-new Sherman M4 composites at Pearl Harbor. They were fresh from the factory, and regardless of it being the first time any of us had even seen one of these big guys, we drove them the twenty miles to Schofield Barracks.

The thirty-ton Sherman tank was an altogether different beast. It had a 75mm cannon in the turret along with a coaxial-mounted .30-caliber machine gun. The ammo for the 75mm (which we loaded a few days later) consisted of around 90 to 100 rounds of various types. There was WP (white phosphorus), AP (armor-piercing rounds with provision for delay ignition—great for taking out pillboxes, dugouts, etc.). We also had canister ammo; a flat-nosed projectile looking for all the world like a large can of beans. It was nothing more or less than a big "shotgun" round, throwing shrapnel after traveling a very short distance from the muzzle. Our most-used round was HE (high explosive). There were two more .30-caliber machine guns. One was in the assistant driver's area and poked through the front armor. It was on a swivel and could be used in a "spraylike" manner. The third .30-caliber machine gun was stored inside the turret and served as a spare gun. It could also be set up outside as an antiaircraft gun. Originally the tank was equipped with a .50-caliber machine gun mounted on the outside of the turret and intended for the same purpose, but the captain decided to trade it for a .30-caliber to keep the number of different types of ammunition to a minimum.

The turret crew consisted of the commander, the gunner, and the loader, and the turret had state-of-the-art radio equipment and something else that I appreciated—an intercom. No kicks to the head . . . all right! Now if you want me to turn, just say so. Downstairs was reserved for the driver and the aforementioned assistant driver/bow gunner. The power plant in this model Sherman was a Continental, air-cooled nine-cylinder, 385-horsepower radial aircraft engine. Like the diesel radial, it had to be cranked over before starting if it had been sitting for any length of time. The cranking was done manually via a long handle inserted in the rear. Some drivers used to "cheat" and turn the engine over by using the starter, but not switch on the ignition. It was against the rules, so of course we never did anything like that in our tank . . . Sure.

This tank used aviation gasoline for fuel, and after the comparative safety of the diesel that we had enjoyed with the M3, we were a bit apprehensive about fire. Word got around pretty fast about the hazards of smoking and gasoline, so a number of the fellows who smoked changed over to chewing tobacco. At that time I smoked cigarettes and figured that smoking wasn't good for you anyway, now it was a double threat! So I got myself some Red Mule and bit off a big chunk of it the next time we went for a ride. I'd like to go on record, right now, that there is no place, no way, that a guy can spit, safely, in a Sherman tank. Also for the record, let me say that holding a mouthful of spit and tobacco juice for a long time does not bode well. After a couple of drives, most all of us went back to smoking. To hell with that chewing stuff. And if we do get hit, it won't matter a heck of a lot if we're smoking or chewing at the time.

Compared to the light tank, the Sherman was gutless, no power at all. The steering was heavy, the driver sat, almost stood, upright when the hatch was open and the seat raised. The steering laterals were between the driver's legs and, to me, felt awkward. It had no brakes, and, like the M3, had to be double-clutched when shifting gears. Top speed on a paved surface was around thirty miles per hour ... if you were lucky. Fuel consumption was approximately three gallons per mile ... not miles per gallon.

When we first got our hot, sweaty hands on our new #60, it was sort of like Christmas. The thing was filled with equipment and, wonder of wonders, it was all new. All except for one large bundle of *Life* magazines found in one of the storage compartments under the turret floor plate. They weren't new, but what a great gift! Attached was a note from one of the ladies who had helped build our tank. Because I had "discovered" them, I took it on myself to drop them a note of appreciation. Their message had been that they were all praying for our safety and hoped we'd have a lot of success with our tank. On behalf of the crew, I wrote and thanked them, and echoed their hopes, too. What a nice thing they did.

I discovered one other thing under the turret floor ... the battery. The thing was bigger than most small car engines and, I soon found out, packed a whole lot of power. To this day I can't remember why I had a large crescent wrench in my hand, but I did and, yeah, I somehow managed to get one end of it across the positive terminal and the other end touching a nearby piece of metal. The wrench immediately welded itself to the tank's structure and we had to get Smitty from the maintenance section to rescue us.

This is a good time to mention a bit more about that magical turret floor. It was diamond plate and pretty heavy-duty stuff. A section of it was cut into a pie-shaped configuration, hinged, with a one-inch hole drilled into it. By inserting a finger in the hole, the hinged, pie-shaped "door" could be raised or opened. Below the turret were compartments, and by slowly traversing a full 360 degrees, all of them could be accessed. In one of the compartments we found headphones and some newfangled microphones.

We soon discovered that the new earphones were impossible to use. They looked for all the world like the ear ends of medical stethoscopes! When we put them on and then placed our helmets over them, the pressure from these "plug-ins" was very painful, and they were impossible to wear for more than a few seconds at a time. Every time my helmet brushed against something, I received a jab directly in the ears. Yow!

The microphones were intended to replace our old hand-held mikes, and I suppose in any other job they would have worked out just fine. But, not in a tank. The mike was put on by slipping the loops over your ears (where the stethoscope plugs were) and adjusting it so that it rested on your upper lip. We all looked like Adolf Hitler! They proved to be very distracting and uncomfortable. Some of the men also claimed that the audio quality from them was poor.

We had left our old helmets with our light tanks, which were now in a storage yard near Pearl Harbor. The tanks had been shipped there from the Big Island right after our unit had left it. After trying on our new equipment, we, as a group, made the trip back to Pearl, found our old tanks, and rescued our helmets, headphones, and microphones, leaving the new ones behind.

All of our new .30-caliber machine guns were wrapped in some sort of brown paper that was water-resistant and did a good job of protecting them from rust and corrosion. The large FM radio unit was already installed and occupied a big chunk of space across the back wall of the turret.

In the turret we found a small gasoline-powered, air-cooled generator that could furnish enough power to keep us in business, powering up the radio, intercom, and primary electrical system. We used the pistol port on the left side of the turret to toss out empty 75mm shell casings. Those things would otherwise get underfoot and be a very real hazard for the loader . . . especially during a firefight when the loader became just about the most important guy in the tank.

Alongside the pistol port was the breech of the fixed "gun" we used for firing smoke shells. It broke open like an old shotgun, a shell was inserted, and the trigger was pulled. Simple and effective.

Seating in the turret was barely adequate. The gunner's seat had a low back to it, so that he could get over it from behind in order to sit. However, I heard that some gunners had the back removed, not only for easier entry, but also to make it a lot easier to get out of in an emergency. The commander's seat was almost directly behind the gunner. That was just about the only location left for him, but it was also a good spot. If the gunner saw something he wanted the commander to view, he would lean to the left and the commander would simply bend forward and the gunner's periscope/sight was right there. The commander's seat was only about nineteen inches in diameter and could be folded up vertically. If the commander had a very big butt, he was in trouble.

The loader had a small adjustable seat similar to the commander's, and it could be raised and lowered. Unlike every other seat in the tank, there was no seat belt provided.

The driver and assistant driver/bow gunner had the downstairs all to themselves. They were separated from each other by the huge transmission case between them. The assistant driver sat on the right side of the tank. In front of him was his periscope and a tad above his waist level was the breech end of a .30-caliber machine gun. The bow gun. To the rear of his seat, on the floor, was the escape hatch, one of the most important features of the whole shebang. It could be unlatched and dropped by the assistant driver, and it had two lifting handles for bringing the hatch back up where it could be dogged in place. Dropping and then retrieving the escape hatch was a physically demanding job because its location was to the rear of and below the assistant driver's seat. The operation required a lot of twisting, bending, and straining to get the heavy hatch back up into position.

The driver's seat was, well, good and bad. Like the commander's seat, the cushion was nice and thick and the backrest was adequate. But the thickness of the seat was the result of springs, not padding, and for me the thickness was literally a pain in the ass. When the seat was lowered as far as it would go, my helmet just touched the underside of the padded hatch. I wondered what might happen if we got a hit while my head was in contact with the hatch . . . a broken neck, a concussion, what?

The seat wouldn't go down any farther, and of course I couldn't remove the padding on the hatch (it was only about three-quarters of an inch thick, anyway), but I finally developed a scheme that I used all through combat. It worked, but it was painful.

I would drop the seat all the way down, put the seat belt on very loosely, and slide forward on the seat as far as I could without falling off. As I slid forward, the space between the top of my helmet and the underside of the hatch increased. When I had slid forward on the seat as far as I could, I'd cinch up the seat belt as tight as I could, thus insuring that I would stay in place. It worked well enough. We went over some rough terrain and I never bumped my head on the hatch. But I have to say that at the end of the day, after hours up on the line, my ass was on fire. When I unbelted and got out, it felt like a hot wire had been laid across the cheeks of my butt. Talk about giving your all for the cause . . . !

And then there were the periscopes. Get outside the tank, hold a spare periscope in your hand, and look through it, and it works great. Vision is clear, and everything can be seen by simply turning in whatever direction you want to look. Now get back inside and install the periscope in its slot in the middle of the hatch, and the situation changes drastically. The periscope was mounted in a swiveling, circular assembly that we tightened or loosened so it could be held in a fixed position or swivel freely.

Okay, I start the tank, engage the gears, and begin to drive forward. As the terrain goes up and down, and the tank begins its usual bob and weave, I must keep the periscope level—with a free hand I don't have!—so I can see where the hell we're going. My other hand must contend with two steering laterals and, to make it even more fun, I might shift gears once in awhile. In the midst of all of that, think how wonderful it is when the commander comes on the intercom and says, "Watch out for mines." Those babies have a detonator about the size of a little finger and are buried in dirt and grass, leaving just that small tip sticking out. Fun City!

Before we leave the interior of our little home, let me add that the entire inside of the hull was painted white enamel, as was the engine compartment. Very nice touch, and hell on wheels to keep clean enough to pass our Saturday morning inspections.

8

After getting our new mediums, most of the time was spent familiarizing ourselves with them. Each crew member now had brand-new surroundings to explore, and while it doesn't seem like it would take very long to get used to the new machines, some of the stuff was so different from our old tanks that we did need the time. We had also picked up an addition to our little family . . . a loader. We now had OW as our commander, Jim Anderson was the gunner, Roy Greenup our loader, Henry Fisher the assistant driver, and me, herding the whole conglomeration around.

Between the loader and the gunner, the 75mm got a lot of attention. When loading a shell into the 75, the loader learned to turn his right hand slightly so that as the horizontal breechblock slid closed, it hit the heel of his hand and pushed it away. On firing, the gun automatically ejected the empty casing, and that was what allowed for rapid fire. If the loader could have a new round ready when that empty came flying out, the new one could be inserted, the breech closed, and we were ready for action again in a second. When we were providing indirect fire on Leyte, we figured we were keeping a round in the air all the time; while one was impacting the target area, another was in midflight, and the third was being fired.

I should mention that the gunner was jammed into his area tighter than anyone else, or so it appeared to me. When he was seated, he had the turret wall to his right. Sticking out just forward and to his right was a black "L"-shaped handle. By leaning it to the right, the turret traversed to the right. Leaning the handle to the left caused the turret to move to the left. On the handle was a trigger. That was the thing that fired the cannon, and it seemed to me that it was most perfectly placed . . . swing the turret, and pull the trigger, all with the same hand.

To the left was a small wheel, which was used to elevate and depress the gun. Alongside the wheel was a large, round, button-type switch. Pushing on it caused the coaxially mounted .30-caliber machine gun to fire. Our gunner sighted in the .30-caliber so it impacted about a hundred yards ahead. Now, all he had to do to knock out an emplacement at one hundred yards or closer was to fire the .30-caliber machine gun until the tracers were hitting the target, then squeeze the firing switch on the 75mm cannon. If the target was farther away than one hundred yards, he just raised the barrel a wee bit and fired the big gun. The cannon's trajectory was so flat at these ranges that Kentucky windage was hardly ever necessary.

The office, that is, the driver's area, was large enough to be fairly comfortable . . . except for my ongoing battle of butt versus seat. The instrument panel was to the left and set at an angle for easy viewing. During combat I used to place my Thompson submachine gun behind the dash. It lay there at hand, easy to get a hold of in a hurry.

To the right and slightly behind was the shift lever. Five speeds, if you'll allow the word "speed" to be used here. The engineering of the transmission as far as speeds go was, in my opinion, bad. Really bad. For example, to put the transmission in first gear, a button, or clicker, had to be pushed down and the shift lever moved to the left and forward. You were now in first gear. Straight back would get you into reverse.

So, what's the problem? Well, first gear's top speed was just too slow for starting off and going to a higher speed. The ratio was so low that after you picked up "speed" and peaked the engine, the tank was barely moving. To go faster, a higher gear had to be selected . . . second gear. But by the time the shift lever was moved from the first gear slot, back and over to the right, and up into the second-gear position, the tank would have come to a stop. There was not enough speed in first gear to keep the thing rolling until second gear could be engaged. What to do? Easy, from a dead stop we'd start in second gear. But now we had another problem. Second gear was too high a ratio to start from, so in order to get the tank rolling, we had to slip the clutch until the tank's speed built up to where second gear could pull the weight. Second gear should have had a gear ratio low enough to pull the tank at starting. First gear could be left alone and used in those situations where the terrain or conditions would require that ratio.

Our arrival at Schofield Barracks was not an occasion for us to rejoice. Our quarters were, basically, piles of lumber, nails, all sorts of material, and the tools you'd expect to get hold of if you wanted to build a shelter. And that's what we did. We built our own barracks, and they came out fairly well. Actually, we didn't build from the ground up. What we had to do was repair and rebuild several existing units until they were livable. And, as I say, they came out fairly decent. For a bunch of tankers, that is.

9

We hadn't been at Schofield very long when orders came down that we were to attend Jungle Combat Training School at the far end of the island. The rainy end. Unfortunately, this school had absolutely nothing to do with tanks, and at this point I really was sorry I hadn't ended up in Alaska as the Good Lord intended in the first place. Or flying with the Canadians. While in the infantry I had run classes on basic training, scouting and patrolling, cover and concealment, and so on until I was sick of it. I could see the value in all that when I was in the infantry. But I was a tanker now, and this bullshit was not for me. Jungle fighting? No way. No sir.

We arrived there in the rain, of course, and right off I noticed that the instructors weren't into smiling much. Or, at all. Well, I didn't much feel like smiling, either, so I guess we were starting off on the same level playing field. The course lasted two weeks and involved just about everything you've heard or thought about training for fighting in the jungles.

We fired all weapons "combat style." That is, the .30-caliber light machine gun was fired from the hip at pop-up targets. And even though there were no mortars in our company, we were given a 60mm mortar tube, which we fired without the base plate or using sights. In short, this was a *real* "combat course."

One of the classes taught us how to properly cross a stream while carrying our personal weapons. Even the guys who didn't know how to swim had to do this. We learned to take off our pants, tie the legs in a knot at the cuffs, dip the whole thing in the water to make the porous cloth nonporous, swing the saturated pants over our heads, and "scoop" up some air in them. Holding them together at the waist and lying across them, they made a fairly good life preserver. Good enough so that it allowed me to dog-paddle across a deep stream. We also learned how to float a jeep. Placed onto the shore, a jeep rolled onto a large canvas tarp, the sides of the canvas were pulled up and lashed in place, and, after being manhandled into the water, the thing floated like a boat! About four or five guys then held onto the sides and, by kicking with their feet, powered it to the far shore.

The most memorable part of the training was the segment on demolitions. When we arrived at the open-air "classroom," we found seats made from palm tree trunks laid out in rows, and standing on a low platform or stage was one of the instructors. We knew he was an instructor because he wasn't smiling. Looking back on the class, I can understand why he didn't find anything humorous about us, the new day, or the future. He, after all, had to teach a bunch of greenhorns how to handle the weapons, the jungle, and the enemy. I would have volunteered for the French Foreign Legion or the Japanese kamikaze air corps before I'd consider taking his job.

After introducing himself, he held up what looked like a large chunk of putty. He had been kneading it as he talked, and he then began to tell us about it.

"The material I have here is a high explosive. It's called Composition C, and I have enough in my hand right now to do more damage than any of you can imagine. It's wonderful stuff to work with, and absolutely safe." He then inserted what looked like a short piece of brass tubing, maybe an inch long. He said, "Composition C can be burned, dropped, and shot at and will not explode. It will," he continued, "explode if a cap and fuse is inserted, like the one I just placed in it. When the burning fuse reaches the cap or, as we call it, the detonator, then we'll have an explosion."

As he was talking, he left the platform and walked a short distance toward us and ended up standing in the "aisle" next to me.

"I'm putting what we call a fuse lighter on the end of the

fuse. When I pull the ring here on the end of the lighter, you'll see smoke come out of the end of the fuse." He then pulled the fuse lighter and, by golly, smoke began to come out just as he said it would. He stood there looking us over and then asked, "Are there any questions?"

I held up my hand and he nodded at me. I said, "Sergeant, what do you plan to do with that thing? . . . I mean right now?"

He actually smiled, and I had the feeling that that was his quota for the day. He walked a short distance to the rear and tossed his smoking package over the side of a cliff. Almost at once, or so it seemed, we heard and felt the thing go off. And it was one hellish bang, let me tell you.

We spent the rest of the day learning about the various ways Composition C can be used. Along the way we had a chance to observe and use quarter-pound blocks of TNT. Those blocks tied together could make an almost limitless-sized charge.

One of the things that fascinated me was called a "shape charge." Using some of the Composition C, our instructor shaped it into what looked like a cone about eight or so inches at the base and tapering to a point ten or twelve inches away. Of course, these charges could be hand molded into virtually any size or shape. After the cone was ready, the inside was scooped out, and we now had a hollow cone.

"Okay, men, if you'll just assemble over here, I'll show you what a shape charge can do." He walked down a steep slope while we remained at the top. He placed his demo shape charge on a piece of sheet metal that looked to be about a quarter to a half inch thick. After inserting the detonator, fuse, and fuse lighter, he pulled the string and walked back up to where we were. There was a loud boom, and the sheet of metal was knocked off the rock it had been resting on. From where we were, we could easily see the hole that had been blown through that piece of steel!

Explosives that are simply laid on a surface tend to expand in all directions unless confined and "guided." Oftentimes a simple layer of mud will suffice and cause the explosion to direct its power downward, away from the shielding layer.

That, we were told, was exactly what happened when we made a cone out of Composition C. The material itself formed a covering layer, and the explosive force was sent downward toward the open end of the cone. I couldn't help wonder about the enemy and if they were using this sort of thing.

Graduation at the demolitions class was memorable for me. Each of us was given a glob of that good old, safe Composition C. We were told to form a "grenade" out of it, similar to what our instructor had started things off with in that first class. We molded it into a ball, inserted a cap, then the fuse and, at the end, a fuse lighter. We formed a line and each of us, in turn, would step up alongside the instructor. He would then have us cut a small slit in the fuse a short distance from where it entered the cap. Now, we had to pull the fuse lighter, watch the smoke coming out of the tail end of the fuse, but, most important, watch very, very closely that little slit. As the burning material inside the fuse passed by the slit, a spurt of smoke would come out. That was the signal to get rid of the thing. And I mean right then. Well, when it was my turn, and my "grenade" was completed to my instructor's satisfaction, I pulled the fuse lighter and waited. And waited. Oh boy, I figured I hadn't cut that slit deep enough and the warning smoke I was waiting for would not do its job. It wouldn't spurt. But, I bet I would. Well, it did, and I threw the damned thing, with much enthusiasm.

Gee, what a great demonstration, what a great instructor, what a great class. Let me get the hell outta here!

At one of our classes an instructor told us about all the "delicious and nutritious" things we could find to eat in the jungle. They included but were not limited to such goodies as all sorts of bugs, roots, weeds, snakes, and stuff like that. I mentally eliminated snakes because I would never ever be hungry enough to try and catch one. I just didn't want to get that close. No bugs, either. I was left with roots and weeds, but heck, I'd already gone that direction when I was a kid. We used to pick and chew on most everything that grew except poison ivy. That's a one-timer.

The last day of our two-week session was graduation time. We were paired off in what were called Tiger Teams. Jim Anderson and I were a pair, but considering it now, I hardly think that the tag "tiger" could be fairly applied. "Kitty cats" maybe. Anyway, the idea was for the teams to follow a narrow trail through the jungle. Along the way we would encounter some sort of obstacle or challenge that would make us utilize some of the instruction we had received in the course.

Along the way, our instructors were hidden, grading us. Some were posted in trees, where they could control and release a sandbag suspended at the end of a rope. These guys had done this many times and knew just when to release the sandbag so it would strike an unsuspecting "tiger." We had been warned that "things might happen" and told that we should be constantly on guard as we wended our way warily along the trail.

All sorts of cunning devices had been pre-positioned for our benefit. How nice!

We crossed a stream by walking on a single, thick rope while holding on to two ropes about armpit high. The "bridge" was ten feet above the water, and if we did fall in, about all that would happen would be that we'd get wet. We hoped this was not too tough, except that they kept detonating explosives in the water, which was highly disconcerting, especially with that footrope swaying side to side and the hand ropes as slippery as hell from all the water being flung to and fro.

The one little trap that got me was the sandbag-drop along the trail. I was in the lead, and as we approached a large tree I heard a faint squeak. What I didn't know was that the noise was coming from a rope going through a pulley, with the feared sandbag at the rope's business end.

I hunched my head a bit and *wham,* the sandbag hit me from behind right between the neck and shoulders. I not only went down, I also slid off the trail down into a ravine. I was tired, it was raining, and I was mad as hell.

I could hear at least one of the instructors laughing, and then he yelled, "You're dead, mister." I hollered back several colorful army phrases that I'd picked up during the course of my hitch, and while I had no idea what they meant, I felt good saying them.

It seemed a fitting way to end the Jungle Combat Training course; as it had begun, with a lot of cussin'. I mean, colorful army phrases.

10

We'd been back at Schofield a week or so when the order came down to clean up our tanks and give the exteriors "shine" by using diesel oil. Rumor had it that we were to be reviewed by some big shot, and the battalion had to be up to snuff.

Came the big day, and the entire battalion drove over to a major road on Schofield and lined up perfectly. It was a wonderful sight. Eighty-two tanks lined up precisely at the curb. We removed all the firing pins from our weapons and left all of our grenades behind. We lined up in front of our tanks and were told to come to attention when the reviewer passed in front of us, and if he stopped to talk with us, we were to stay at attention and answer using "sir" even if he was in civilian clothes!

Naturally we waited a long time. That didn't surprise any of us; after all, that's the name of the game . . . right? Sometime later we were called to attention as the motorcade approached, going about forty miles an hour. The cars weren't military vehicles. All of them were limousines. Cadillacs. Staring straight ahead, I caught a glimpse of one car that, except for the driver, was empty. Almost empty. In the backseat was a wheelchair. Our big-shot reviewer was the president, Franklin Roosevelt. He not only didn't stop to talk with anyone, he didn't even slow down. He may have waved, but he was going so fast it was hard to tell. I know that none of us waved back.

Now all we had to do was drive our tanks back to company area and try to scrub off all the diesel we had so lovingly applied to the paint. The tanks did look great all shined up like brand-new cars. But with the oil coating, by the time we got back to our area we had dust stuck on every square inch. Not quite so pretty now.

A schedule was passed down, and we drove our tanks over to battalion maintenance to have the outsides steam cleaned, and by this time it was around midnight. Surprise, surprise. I only regretted that election time wasn't near and I could vote. I had a pretty fair idea of how I would . . . if I could . . . which I couldn't.

Rumors abounded that we were getting ready for combat, and all sorts of targets and places were mentioned. Ammo for the machine guns was taken out, inspected, cleaned, and placed back into the tank. With the 75mm shells loaded into the storage racks, there was no question of what was in the works.

An interesting piece of equipment was installed on the rear of our tank. It was sort of a flat, oblong, smokestack affair. It was an air intake for the tank, and allowed us to enter water deeper than the tank had been designed to go through. The stack was in two parts, with the top part falling away when a cable was pulled. That was done after we were ashore.

We had only to be told when and where. Cutthroat's crew all chipped in, and a couple of the guys went on leave to a small town nearby. They came back loaded with civilian canned goods. We had good soup, all kinds of beans, fruit, things like that. No GI food. We even had some saltine crackers. These packages we wrapped in OD-colored tape and smeared with waterproofing gunk on the outside. The crowning item was Coca-Cola syrup! Our plan was to mix it with the five gallons of water we had in a container in the turret. And, the last little treasure was a bottle of champagne! None of us were heavy drinkers, and we all agreed that we'd better stay sober if we wanted to stay alive. So the champagne was carefully packaged and stored with all the other goodies under the turret floor. We were going to war in style and, hopefully, would celebrate victory the way it should be celebrated!

Apparently we weren't scheduled to leave right away . . . weekend passes were still being issued. A friend of mine, PFC Roy Agnew, proposed that we get a weekend pass and go over to the Big Island. That sounded good to me. Honolulu was solid service personnel, and everybody was a tourist. We got our weekend passes and headed to Fort Ruger, near downtown Honolulu, to arrange for transportation. We were told that there was nothing available that day, but we would be booked on the interisland steamer for the next day. We were also informed that our pass time would not begin until we arrived at the Big Island, which suited us just fine. I had already assumed that we'd end up spending our pass time sitting at Fort Ruger.

Next morning we boarded the boat and it was a rough, wild ride. Even the crewmen were seasick. I felt woozy and had a lousy headache. I might have felt better if I'd heaved everything over the rail, but for some reason I couldn't.

After a somewhat miserable trip we arrived, our passes stamped as to time and date, and we were free for three wonderful days. Sleep as late as we wanted, no details, nothing we didn't want to do. Sort of like paradise. Like what we'd always imagined Hawaii to be. For three days we became civilians, did all the scenic spots, saw the lava boiling while we ate lunch at the Volcano House on the lip of Kilauea volcano. On our last day, when we reported at the docks to the little office where we would be given our transportation orders, we found a long line of GIs waiting. We went to the end of the line and pretty soon a guy came out of the office building and announced that that was all for today. No problem. Our passes were extended by a day, and all we had to do was to show up the next day. But we quickly figured that if we showed up a wee bit late each morning, our passes would be extended again and we would have another day in paradise!

After three or four days of this, reality dawned; we were

almost out of money. We'd be kicked out of our room. We'd have no money to buy food. We had to get out of here and no kidding! So the next morning we got up bright and early and went down to the dock, and there the line was, as long as ever. We found out that the place was full of guys in our same circumstances, and as a result they all were getting there early. Earlier than we had figured on.

The next day, early as it was, we still didn't get any transportation. As luck would have it, we were in downtown Hilo later in the day when I spotted an officer I knew. I was able to borrow enough money to keep us out of the ever-present rain and buy a few meals.

The next morning we still couldn't get close to the office building. We had been there a little while when a sergeant stepped out of the place and announced, "All personnel from the 96th Division and attached units, get aboard the trucks you see over there." We were taken to the airport, loaded onto a C-47, and flown to Oahu. Our unit was ready to move and we were not going to be left behind, if they had anything to do with it. Which was just fine with me. Combat, here we come!

PART THREE

Shipping Out

11

But we had forgotten the old engraved-in-stone army practice of playing the "waiting game." It seemed that we had done everything necessary to be ready, but still there was always that "one more thing." Inspections were rampant. Some were scheduled and others were of the surprise variety. One morning I was sitting in #60's driver's seat, brushing off all the dirt and dust I could reach with the dry paintbrush I kept for that purpose. In the midst of my brushing and thinking of things other than brushing, I heard a *pop,* and the next thing I knew there was a smoking hand grenade in my lap! I had no idea what was happening, but I did have one great idea: Get the hell out in a big-ass hurry. And I did.

When I landed, in a heap, not at all as gracefully as I would have done had this been a movie, I heard a lot of laughter, looked up, and saw a half dozen guys standing in a half circle, all of them looking at me. It was one of those jokes that's funny as hell as long as you're not the guy who is "it."

Funny, guys. Our jokers had unscrewed the bottom plug and emptied all the powder out of the grenade. Being "one of the guys," I couldn't make too big a deal over it. You had to be a "good sport" and not lose your cool.

Still, even as I write this, after all these years, I can still remember how I felt when that smoking chunk of iron dropped through my hatch and landed in my lap.

Because I took it so well, I was told that they were going to do something spectacular at the PX beer shack, that night . . . so be there.

At the appointed hour, I arrived to find a very long lineup for beer. Each man was allowed to get two beers at a time. If you wanted more, you had to go to the tail end of the line and work your way back to the counter. I had been in line for a while when a guy from my outfit came in, holding a grenade behind his back. There was an MP present whose job it was to keep order. Well, here our hero came, and as he approached the MP, he held out the grenade and said, "I don't know what to do with this thing." As the MP looked at it, our hero dropped the ring to the ground. Now all that kept it from "exploding" was the handle, which was still being held. The MP, with a look of sheer terror on his face, danced around in a little circle and yelled, "This is a job for Ordnance . . . they should fix it for you."

I think he was honestly trying to talk our boy into leaving the area to go hunting for an Ordnance company. Meantime, the center of the line, which was closest to the action, sort of bent away, and it now looked like a snake. The guys wanted to get out of there but didn't want to lose their place in line.

About that time, our grenadier dropped the grenade to the ground. The handle flew off, the thing went *pop*, white smoke began coming out of it, and the MP screamed hysterically. Someone else let out a yell, and total panic ensued. While everybody took off for Dodge, the few of us in the know walked to the counter and waited until the GI who was on that detail came back. We bought our two beers each and walked back to the barracks, happy and laughing. It sure is funny when it happens to somebody else.

About this time another "incident" happened that, more or less, seems to shed some light on our mood and psychological mind-set. We were all edgy, and perhaps we were getting too close to being fine-tuned. I don't know. But, I do know that what happened was far from normal. It began and ended on a fine evening at the barracks.

As it was getting close to lights out, I stepped out on the steps to have a cigarette and enjoy the moment. Inside, everyone seemed to be either writing a letter home or sitting around yakking. As I stood there, I saw one of our sergeants walking by. He was coming from the PX and had had his share of beer. That was quite obvious in his walk.

He saw me and stopped, looked hard at me for a minute,

and before I could do or say anything he had pulled a knife out of his pocket. It was a switchblade, and with a little *snick* it opened. He held it to his side and began walking toward me, keeping eye contact all the time. I wasn't afraid of this guy, but I didn't like knives at all. I reached behind me, opened the screen door, and backed into the barracks. I had backed up about ten or so feet when the door opened and in he came, still staring at me. The two of us kept this little position as we made our way down the aisle between the rows of bunks. I desperately hoped someone would jump him, but with that knife added to the mix, no one did, and I couldn't blame them.

By this time all conversation had ceased, and everyone was just watching. It was well known that this particular guy and I didn't much care for one another, so while this threat wasn't expected, it wasn't too surprising, either.

I had come off guard duty a bit earlier and my .45 pistol still had a loaded clip in it. When we got to my bunk, I reached down, slid the pistol out of the holster, and drew back the slide on the gun and let it go. It now had a live round in the chamber and was ready. So was I. He stopped, folded the blade of his knife, gave me another few seconds of staring, then turned and left.

Talk resumed and life went on. The men had arguments once in awhile, but this was the most serious thing that happened to me. Looking back more than fifty years since it happened, I find it hard to believe we all were that stupid. The man with the knife, I am certain, didn't want to kill me. I'm sure that he just wanted to frighten me in front of everyone . . . and he certainly succeeded. If he hadn't stopped when he did, I would have shot him. A .45 at close range in the middle of the body would almost certainly have resulted in death.

We were young tigers then, young and a bit foolish. If he were to walk up to me now, I'd shake his hand and buy him a beer and I like to think he'd do the same.

12

We were limited to one barracks bag per man, plus whatever we could stow away in and on our tanks. Footlockers and spare barracks bags were stored and would be available later . . . uh-huh. Last-minute spare parts, extra socks, underclothes, paperback books, all those kinds of things somehow found a place inside the tank. We looked sort of like a tracked, armored Goodwill store. And our tank was typical of the rest. A traveling gypsy caravan would best describe the entire company.

We were given last-minute shots by the medics, and some of the stuff they put into us didn't even have a name. I asked the medic giving me my shots what they were for. He told me "yellow fever, plague, and one I'm not sure what it is." Great!

As we passed through the line, I was hit on each shoulder. Two shots on the right and one on the left. I kept my eyes to the front, and after I felt the stings, I started forward. The medic said, "Wait a minute, soldier." I looked back and saw that one of the needles on the right had pulled loose from the syringe and was still stuck in my arm. About that time I heard something that sounded like a sack of potatoes being dropped. It was the guy in line behind me. I swear that they gave him his shots as he lay there, before he came around!

In the early morning hours of September 13, we drove our tanks the twenty miles or so from Schofield barracks to Honolulu Harbor. Once there, we refueled and loaded onto LCMs (landing craft, mechanized), one tank per individual boat. I had mixed emotions about what all of this meant. The firepower of our eighteen tanks represented an almost unbelievable amount of destruction for the enemy. We were actually a series of movable artillery pieces, with accompanying machine guns.

Our LCMs headed for a big ship that we found was an LSD (landing ship, dock). As our LCMs approached the big ship, I could make out the number 5 painted on it. LSD 5 had a rakish line to it and didn't look like a dock at all. Where did they come up with that designation, I wondered. I soon found out. As we got closer, our LCM maneuvered around to the rear, or stern as they like to call it. I could then see what all this was about. The entire rear portion of the ship had been opened up, like two huge barn doors. The inside had water in it, enough so that our LCM motored happily in, to the far back end. There we floated, waiting for the other seventeen boats to join us. As it turned out, all eighteen tanks were brought in, three LCMs abreast, six rows. The noise was deafening, with each boat's twin diesel engines going, times eighteen. Imagine thirty-six diesels roaring away, churning the water, and waiting for the final step in this procedure. The stern doors were slowly closed, and the well deck was pumped dry. The LSD now had all eighteen LCMs, each with a thirty-ton tank aboard, sitting on the dry deck! Our tank became our home, and we set up folding cots in the forward part of the LCM, just ahead of our tank. We also spread our tarp over the 75mm gun barrel and brought the sides down so that it formed a sort of tent affair. I think that the navy personnel must have thought of us as a bunch of gypsies. I know we felt much like that.

The next morning found us under way, and to a man we thought that at long last we were heading into combat. Not so. We were moving out into an area between Oahu and the island of Molokai, there to allow the cox'ns to practice taking their LCMs out (with us along for the ride), circling, and then reentering the LSD. This was to be the only practice these guys would get, and I hoped that our pilot was going to be on the ball.

All the LCMs' engines were fired up, and a few of us went up the steel ladder built into the side of the well deck. We walked to the stern to watch the first few rows take off. Our plan was to then hurry back to the ladder, scurry down it to our LCM, and go for a ride. As we approached the stern, we could see and hear some navy guy yelling at the cox'n in the boat in the first row. The fellow in the first LCM yelled that they were taking water. The other guy, the one on deck, yelled back, "Use your pumps and get the hell out of the ship. You're holding up the fuckin' parade, sailor." The sailor hollered a few obscenities back and emphasized that he was taking water faster than the pumps could pump it out. The man on the deck, we learned later, was the chief bosun's mate, the most powerful noncommissioned officer on the ship. He shouted that he didn't give a good God damn about the sailor's opinion of the pumps, just "get that piece of shit out of the way . . . there are seventeen LCMs waiting." He further said that once the last LCM was clear of the ship, the leaking one could come back inside. When the well deck was full of water it was only about three or four feet deep, so it was apparent that they wouldn't sink any further than that.

To make a long story short, the cox'n did move out and began to circle a short distance away, waiting for all the other boats to get out of the ship. As he circled, even to my untrained eye I could see that he was very low in the water and near sinking. Well, sink he did, complete with an almost new Sherman medium tank that had all the personal gear of the crew aboard plus all the ammo, the radio, spare parts, guns, the works. We returned to our tank just in time to join the group that was already out, circling. The navy and army people aboard the LCM that had sunk were picked up by one of the other boats, so at least we still had our crew intact. All of the other seventeen boats and tanks came back aboard, the well deck was pumped dry, and the LSD went back to her assigned position just offshore of Pearl Harbor.

The tank crew was ferried ashore and picked up another tank, resupplied it, and returned on a replacement LCM, all in the surprisingly short time of a few days. Now we were ready. Eighteen dry, in-good-condition LCMs loaded with eighteen perfectly good tanks, and all of us chomping at the bit. At least, that's what we told each other.

13

Life aboard LSD 5 was an interesting adventure. The mix of navy life and army activity seemed at first to be a water and oil thing. Two completely different military lifestyles would make it impossible to come to a point where either group would or could completely accept the other.

We were awakened in the morning by a shrill whistle over the PA speakers and a voice that said something like, "Now hear this . . . sweepers man your brooms . . . sweep down all decks and ladders . . . fore and aft." I couldn't for the world understand why, if this was a daily routine, they had to announce it each and every morning. Did someone think that the "sweepers" would forget and have to be reminded each day? I asked one of the sailors about this, and he just looked at me as if I'd asked a question that should never be asked. His answer was equally dumbfounding. "I don't know why they announce it. . . . They just do, always have on every ship I been aboard. . . . What's the big deal, don't hurt nobody to announce it, does it?"

The tankers assembled each morning on the foredeck for their regular physical exercises. We were already in good shape, but the easy life we were leading on the ship tended to make us lazy. So, exercise was not only in order, but for the most part, welcomed. We'd been at sea a few days when one morning, after our exercise session, a large board was brought out, complete with an attached map. It was mid-September, and we were told about our destination, our future battleground. It was the island of Yap. Yap? What the hell is that? We all wondered where it was, how many of the enemy were on it, what it was going to be like. None of us had been in combat, and we really weren't sure of what kind of questions to ask. What kind of info did we need to know? Not to worry, we were briefed soon, and very thoroughly, too.

Several things stand out in my mind. One was the strategy planned for the battle. We were to attack the island on one side, and a Marine division was going to hit it on the opposite side . . . at the same time! At the same time? The army was going to move onto the island, head across it, firing away, and directly opposite would be the Marines doing the same thing. I could only wonder who the hell had dreamed up this one. The plan was that once the Marines and the army met in the center of the island, they would turn and sweep, abreast, toward the far end, taking out all enemy and installations they came across.

While we were trying to recover from our shock, we were given another fact to think about. Money on Yap consisted of stone wheels that had a hole bored in the middle. Most of the wheels, we were told, were volcanic rock, and the wealthier folks had wheels that were four and five feet in diameter and as much as ten inches thick. No one knew for sure, but it appeared that some of these money wheels could be rolled from one house to another depending on the luck of the previous and/or new owner.

The final piece of information got the most attention; the ladies on Yap were bare-breasted! None of them wore any sort of covering above the waist. Where once we were reluctant to give the upcoming battle many good points, it appeared that, finally, something interesting was going to come out of the whole nasty mess.

The company was broken down into individual platoons, and a lot of intense study went into the basic plans and the platoon's mission. We learned that naval aircraft had already started occasional bombing of the island, and that three days prior to our landing it would come under intense naval shellfire as well as aircraft bombing.

As we continued to sail westward, we crossed the International Date Line. As it happened, we crossed it at night and during a fairly fierce storm. The LSD was a flat-bottomed craft, and despite all that weight in the well deck, we still rolled quite a bit. I was sergeant of the guard that night, and as I made my way up to the post farthest from our well deck, I found the sentry hanging onto a piece of the ship's structure . . . a vertical post of some sort.

Our guards' primary duty was to enforce the blackout rule. No smoking was allowed on deck at night. This despite that every once in awhile the ship would cruise through a large mass of ocean creatures that gave off a phosphorescent glow as we pushed them aside with the hull. The entire area would light up and could be seen for miles on a clear tropical night . . . and yet, we weren't allowed to smoke on deck. I told the guard to forget about making any rounds, to just sit tight and hang on until I could get a replacement for him.

It was, as I recall, a Thursday night. Next morning I heard that in crossing the date line we had "jumped" forward a day at midnight. . . . It was now Saturday! I tried in vain to get our guard credit for pulling a full extra day's duty, but no one would listen to me. So what else is new?

A few days later we were informed that Yap was being by-passed, for whatever reason. Maybe the thought of all those bare-breasted ladies had influenced the brass into thinking that the army had no place among such things. "Things" being the . . . well, the natives. At any rate, there we were, sailing along, loaded for bare . . . er, bear, and nowhere to go. Well, we know better, don't we. It was a cinch that the army was not going to have us prepare for battle, go through all we had, and then allow us to meander about the Pacific, cruise ship–style. No siree, Bob.

I mentioned that there existed a "situation" between the old-timers and us no-good Yankees. As time passed, tensions eased somewhat, but the feelings were still there, just below the surface. And every once in awhile, they would make themselves known. Again. Such was the case when we crossed the equator. As we understood it, the ship would be brought to a stop, and King Neptune would come aboard to initiate into his kingdom all who had not made the crossing before. Which meant every soul in C Company, 763d Tank

Battalion. The navy was going to conduct its own ceremony, complete with Neptune's court. It was at the court where various forms of punishment were handed out. For example, the ships' cooks were charged and found guilty of trying to poison the crew. They were then forced to consume some ungodly mixture of who knows what much to the delight of everyone who wasn't a cook. And, so it went.

The army was allowed to have its very own King Neptune, hold its own court, and issue whatever punishments the court felt were appropriate. The problem, from us Yankees' point of view, was that the entire court, Neptune and all, was made up of, you guessed it, those good old boys. Oh, oh.

We were allowed to watch the navy's ceremony, and it really was a fun thing, a lot of good-natured shenanigans went on, and no hard feelings.

And then it was the army's turn. That was when we Yankees faded from sight and established ourselves toward the rear of the ship, in a tight little defensive position. The loudspeakers soon called for all army personnel to assemble forward to participate in Good King Neptune's Court. Yeah, right.

Soon we heard all the laughter and yelling and knew that the action was going full blast. I was sure that it was just good old guy fun, unlike what we'd be in for.

And, it wasn't too long before things quieted down up in old Neptune's court, and we knew that new victims would soon be searched out. Meaning, us. And sure enough, here came Captain Garner . . . and what a sight he was. As he approached us, we could see something odd in his hair. When he finally arrived, we saw to our utter astonishment that his hair was hidden under a mass of what appeared to be thick, black axle grease mixed with sawdust. Or something very similar. He was dressed in shorts. Period. And I can only imagine what the sergeant (who was the army's King Neptune) had put him through.

He stood in front of us and, I'll say this for him, he maintained his bearing and dignity as an officer should, and I had to admire him for it. It was plain to see that he was distressed over our little "mutiny" and wanted us to reconsider our actions and go along with him. To the slaughter, I might add. There was nothing, of course, in army regulations that would require our participation in this thing, and so we all stood fast. If it hadn't been for the "us against them" thing, we'd all have been right in the middle of things, having our share of fun. But, as we knew, it would be closer to one of those college hazing things we'd heard about, but not nearly as nice.

We were told that if we didn't attend, then we'd not be eligible for a certificate showing that we were genuine "shellbacks" and had crossed the equator, blah, blah. We already had our Order of the Golden Dragon for having crossed the date line, so why be greedy? And so, we missed the Shellback thing by that much and remained what is known among hairy-chested navy men as "pollywogs." And, in the process, we kept our health and didn't have to inflict injury on any of the "old-timers," which we surely would have before the thing concluded.

I don't remember how long we'd been at sea, it was before we got to the equator, but one early evening we pulled into the harbor at Eniwetok Island. It was late September. As it got darker, we soon found out why we were there; to load ammunition for the guns aboard our LSD 5 plus other navy ships.

By this time it was dark, and I told Anderson that I had found a great spot to sleep in. It was out of the way, up fairly high, and we might catch a breeze once in awhile. It was in one of the starboard 40mm antiaircraft gun tubs. We took our musette bags along to use as pillows, climbed the iron rungs to the walled tub, and settled in. We could hear a lot of activity on deck, but figured it had nothing to do with us. Soon the loudspeakers came on with an announcement, "Now hear this, all hands lay forw'd and join the ammunition loading party. Army personnel are included."

Jim said, "We'd better get going." I told him to just stand fast . . . they'd never look up in a gun tub. About that time we heard someone climbing the ladder and soon saw a sailor poke his head over the edge. "All right you guys, lay forward on the double . . . you heard the announcement." I told him to forget it, that we weren't going on any navy loading party. He replied that if we didn't get our asses in gear, he'd see that the chief bosun's mate would deal with us personally. I told him that neither the chief bosun or his friggin' mate had anything to do with us . . . so shove off. Or words to that effect.

He left, and Jim said, "Well, we're in big trouble now."

"What are they gonna do to us, Jim . . . send us into combat?"

"I don't know, but that guy is nobody to fool around with."

Soon we heard somebody coming up the ladder again. His head came into view and, by golly, it was the chief bosun, in person. I said, "Hi, Chief Bosun . . . where's your mate?" Well, we found that he wasn't in a very good humor, and it was at that point that I decided that having no sense of humor was probably a prerequisite for his job.

He began shouting at us and was using some really bad language. I was horrified. We just lay there, listening, and finally I thought to hell with this shit. I stood up, looked at him, and used a few choice army words of my own, which mostly boiled down to the simple fact that we were army troops and we weren't going to load any of his chickenshit navy ammo, and for him to take off. He stood there a second or two, didn't say a word, and left. Jim started laughing quietly. "Bob, when you stood up in the dark, you looked nine feet tall."

"Yeah, and I felt ten feet tall. Screw him and the horse he rode in on. . . . He don't mean shit to me. Let's get some sleep."

Between the heat and waiting for a group of sailors to come and drag us away, it was a long time before I finally fell asleep. By the time I did, the loading party was over. I didn't think the chief could identify us because it was dark up there in the tub. But, Jim and I did vacate it early, just in case he came back. Which he didn't.

It wasn't so much that we were afraid of this guy. We just didn't want to take a chance, seeing as how his sense of humor tank was empty and we really didn't have a leg to stand on. I told Jim later that it must have been the heat that made me do it. Gotta blame it on something. Little did I know that the heat we were experiencing there in the Eniwetok area was like a breath of spring compared to what was ahead as we continued west and south.

14

Three degrees south of the equator bakes Manus in the Admiralty Islands group. It was a British possession, and the U.S. had a navy base there. Our convoy pulled into the harbor on October 3, and if we thought it was hot before, this place would make the outskirts of hell feel comfortable. It was so hot, it was difficult to get a lungful of oxygen. Touching anything metal topside resulted in a sure blister, guaranteed. Sitting in the open sun was impossible. A consensus had the temperature at around 120 degrees, plus or minus a few more.

Rumor had it that some big powwow was going on, and we would find out about it in due course. Which meant that, as usual, we would end up getting just enough info to allow us to make educated guesses at the real situation. Meanwhile, we were allowed to go ashore and buy two cans of beer at the navy facility there. It was Carling's Red Cap Ale, and was so cold it had small slivers of ice in it. As the brew slid down your throat, the little ice crystals would melt. Heaven!

I went back for another round and managed to get two more of the lovely cans before they closed the PX for the day. Hot as it was, and it was as hot as I'd ever felt it, I would have volunteered to stay on the island (almost) just to get some of those cans of Red Cap each day. With slivers of ice inside.

The second day we were there, I met an old-timer from the

navy. He showed me around the part of the island they were restricted to, and it looked like something you'd see in the movies. It really was a beautiful place. Coconut palm trees, inlets where there was hardly a ripple, seagulls coasting by silently, and on the horizon, beautiful white clouds in a blue sky no artist could ever duplicate. If it just weren't so blamed hot. While we were standing near a small bay, I saw a native outrigger canoe approaching us. The sailor grinned and said, "This guy likes to trade for stuff. It's against regulations to give them knives, but just about anything else is okay."

The native beached his small boat and walked toward us. If I'd been alone, I think I might have left, in a hurry. His appearance was intimidating. He wasn't very tall, and his skin was sort of blue-gray black. His features were very coarse, his nose broad and fairly flat. His hair was like an afro, and he had a loincloth for clothing.

Hanging on his chest was a dry gourd suspended by a vine that went around his neck. The gourd had the top part cut open, and I could see that it was about half full of a white powder. Sticking into the powder was a thin bamboo sliver that looked for all the world like a skinny chopstick. He was grinning, and his teeth were a deep, deep red-black. Mostly black. I asked my friend what the deal was, and he told me that the stuff was betel nut. He said it had a mild kick and was habit-forming. He also said that all the islanders used it, women as well as the men.

The native and my guide began talking in what I later learned was pidgin English. It was almost . . . *almost* understandable to my untrained ears. It went something like, "You long time no here by and by for trade." "Long time much big work work and no trade 'em." Or words to that effect. The upshot was that the native had something he wanted to trade. My guide told him that I would trade if it was a good item and the price was right. Not in those exact words, naturally, but they sounded close to it.

It turned out that he had a small stone statue, about ten inches high. It was crudely done, but it had a certain charm about it, and I knew that I really wanted it. It reminded me of those large stone statues on Easter Island. I didn't have anything on me that interested him. He did eye my K-bar knife, but he didn't mention it and neither did I. In the long run, with my navy guy doing the talking, I came away with my "Oscar." Cost: $2.50. I felt like I had gotten a good bargain and was told that it "wasn't a bad price."

Aboard our ship I had met a sailor who hailed from San Jose, California, and while I'd never been to that city and he had never been to Southern California we still felt a certain kinship. I showed him Oscar and asked how he sent stuff home. He said that there was a detail set up to handle mail, going both directions. Mail from home, and outgoing mail, too. He said that he'd be glad to mail Oscar home to my mom for me . . . no charge. Skipping ahead, I must say that Oscar never arrived. But I have no doubt that somewhere he is proudly displayed on someone's mantel . . . perhaps in San Jose? After a few days our convoy weighed anchors and we pulled out, headed north toward the equator, and parts unknown. Unknown to us, I mean.

15

It wasn't long before we were informed that we were now members of Gen. Douglas MacArthur's Southwest Pacific forces. When we had left Pearl Harbor, we were in the Central Pacific area of operations, under the command of Adm. Chester Nimitz. MacArthur was in command of the South Pacific area of operations and had, to my way of thinking, decided to use our ready-made battle group to make his initial assault on the Philippines, thus keeping his promise of one day "returning."

Actually, I found that he was using his own troops from his Southwest Pacific groups at the same time. The combined package of both area commands made good sense, and my initial reaction was not only incorrect, but mean-spirited as well, I suppose. MacArthur was referred to as "Dugout Doug" among us, and that was not a complimentary term, either. His leaving the Philippines while the battle was ongoing left all of us with a bad taste regarding him, and now he was going to use us to fight "his" battles.

We found that we would be hitting Leyte, one of the largest of the Philippine Islands, situated almost in the center of the chain. Aerial bombing had already begun, and soon the navy would bring its big guns to bear on the beaches. Our study of Leyte began in earnest, and we found that the plan for it was not quite as simple as the Yap operation had been. It was mid-October, and the rainy season wouldn't start for a month or so. That's what they said. It turned out that our weather weenies didn't really know wet from dry, because we got hit with weather that was hard to believe. After we started to kind of get used to it, it would change. And, always for the worse.

Leaving Manus Island, we began taking one tablet of Atabrine each day after lunch. Word was that this small yellow pill was for malaria. No, it didn't keep us from getting infected with the disease, it just kept us from feeling the effects. The first sergeant adopted what I felt was a "small-town approach" to the taking of this medication. We were required to form a line in the well deck after noon chow, and when a man moved up to the head of it, our medic would have him "open wide" and he'd pop a pill into his mouth, hand him a cup of water, and make sure he had really, really swallowed the thing. Our first sergeant was standing by, and after getting the thumbs up from our medic, he would put a check mark alongside the man's name. I don't know what they figured on doing once we got into combat, but I'd be willing to bet they wouldn't visit each of us with pills and a checklist.

One day, after Anderson and I had finished lunch, we started back toward the ladder going down to the well deck and our pill line. Looking down, I could see that most of the company was there, waiting their turn. I told Jim that I was reading a good paperback book and was going to the stern to read for a while. I'd wait until the line got a bit shorter. I went on back, found a shady, comfortable spot, and began reading. And, of course, I forgot all about the damned pill. They were smaller than an aspirin and very easy to swallow. In other words, it was no big deal, and not worth trying to skip. I just forgot.

I had been there for what I thought was only ten or fifteen minutes when a shadow fell across my book. I looked up and there was my old "friend," the first sergeant. I knew at once that I'd missed the lineup, and that was what he was here for. I got to my feet and walked by him as he started berating me. Said if I thought I could sneak out of this thing, how could I be trusted for anything else. Alluding, I thought, that in combat I wouldn't perform. And, so he raved and ranted for about twenty or thirty feet. I looked down at the tanks below in the well deck, and it seemed that the entire company was looking up at us, listening. They could hear because the top kick was yelling. I stopped, and he did, too, just out of reach. I turned toward him and told him I wasn't some kind of dog that had to be herded, that I was capable of finding the medic on my own. That pissed him off, and he said, "You know, those stripes ain't welded on." I had three stripes by then, and since I wasn't one of "his boys," he resented it something fierce and made no bones about it.

I said in a very loud voice, "Sergeant, you can have these stripes, point first, if that's bothering you so damned much." He said, "That's not up to me, that's up to the captain." So, I said, "Request permission to speak to the captain." Of course, he granted my request, and away I went, looking for Captain Garner. Meanwhile, I skipped the pill, just to rankle him when he next looked at his list. I found the captain in his cabin, and after knocking, he invited me in. I told him that I wanted to take a bust to private. When he asked me why, I told him that the first sergeant and I just didn't get along, and I didn't want him to feel he could hold any sort of threat over me. That if the stripes were gone, he'd have to figure something else out, and I didn't think he had brains enough to do that.

And then I began on the company . . . how bad some of the people in it were. For example, I said, "What about Sergeant MacBean? He can screw things up pretty bad, and I don't think you can afford that when we're in combat." The captain laughed and told me he was going to keep MacBean out of trouble and out of the way, if he could. I said that "a chain is no stronger than its weakest link," and that not only MacBean worried me, but several others as well.

Captain Garner was a lawyer in civil life, and looking back on our little session that day, I can only wonder why he listened to a smart-ass twenty-four-year-old tell him what was wrong with his outfit. I can only think that he was a most tolerant man, and I wish now, as I write this more than a half century later, that I could apologize for the petty problem I brought to him.

After a while I calmed down a bit, and he asked me to reconsider the offer of my stripes . . . to wait until the campaign was over, and if I still felt this way, he'd accept them. And so we came to terms. I'd go along and stop my bitchin' and do my job, and we'd wait and see what happened.

During our winding, zigzag passage across the Pacific, we had a lot of time on our hands. Henry and I had an ongoing chess game, that he always won. I accused him of using a crooked chessboard and crooked chessmen, but, being an Easterner with his nose in the air, he denied all charges. Actually, the board was the smallest I'd ever seen. It was about palm size and the chessmen were equally tiny. I distinctly remember one day when I finally won a game. That is, we both could look ahead a couple or so moves and see the inevitable outcome. And, what do you know . . . Henry "accidentally" knocked over the board as our ship took one of its slow rolls.

Couch and I were engaged in reading paperbacks and passing them back and forth, and comparing not only plots but individual characters as well. One book found its target with us. I can't be certain, but I think the title was *By Valor and Arms*. I remember it was about a scout back in the Daniel Boone period, and the guy was a fantastic shot with his muzzle-loader. We spent a lot of time talking about the hero and his tactics in the woods, stalking the bad guys, pesky redskins and all, never dreaming that one day soon we'd be doing some stalking of our own.

Jim Anderson and I were constantly trying to improve on the fine art of conversation. We talked about everything, especially our outfit and the upcoming battle. No matter how much we talked about them, we always found something new to add to the fire. In a way, those guys provided enough fuel for our discussion so that it really did help pass those long hours and days at sea.

In between reading, chess games, and yakking, we still put in a lot of time on our tank and its equipment. Especially the guns. The closer we got to our destination, the bigger our convoy grew. I had never seen so many ships within our immediate circle of vision. And, the closer we got to our target date, October 20, 1944, the better I felt about our crew and our tank. We didn't have John Wayne along with us, but with the five of us together, plus good old "Cutthroats" #60, seemed to be enough for us to hold our own. We'd soon see.

16

We learned that the 96th Infantry Division, of which we were now a part, would be on the right flank of the assault wave and that the 383d Regiment would be on its right flank. We would land on what the planning boys called Orange Beach with the 383d, and our tank battalion along with our company, C, would be on their right.

We were all gathered at the rails, watching the navy blasting shore installations, when the announcement came over the ship's loudspeakers: "Now hear this, now hear this. Tankers man your tanks. Tankers man your tanks." That announcement gave me the most gut-wrenching feeling I had ever had, including my first roller-coaster ride. It was, I recall, somewhere between fear and sheer excitement. And it seemed to me that I had waited for this moment all my life. Not knowing any different, I had been looking forward to the day I could get into combat . . . and here the moment had arrived. We went down the ladders and into the well deck and fired up our Shermans. What a noise, as eighteen 385-horsepower engines blasted the morning air. And amid all the tank engines was soon heard the big, twin GM diesels of each of the eighteen LCMs. Thirty-six boat engines and eighteen tank engines . . . a total of fifty-four of the things going all at once! If the sound hadn't been overpowering, then the exhaust gases would surely finish us off, and I began to look forward to fighting the enemy . . . anything to get out of all the noise, smell, and confinement of the well deck. However, there was nothing we could do about our current situation except endure it.

The well deck was flooded and the big stern doors opened. Getting aboard the individual LCMs was a little challenging, because once down the ladder, men whose boat was the center one in the row would have to go from one boat to another to get onto theirs. If your tank was on either side, then it was a simple step over the ladder.

The landing signal was given at 0845, October 20, and amid heavy gunfire from navy vessels, we circled in our LCMs, waiting for the proper time to move ashore. The sky was clear and the sun felt hot as it rose over San Jose Bay. Bombardment by aircraft had been hitting Japanese airfields for several days we were told, and on the nineteenth, the day before we were to land, the navy's big guns from battleships had fired into shore installations. Of concern had been the Japanese aircraft, but aside from one or two circling the fleet, we weren't bothered by them at all.

Our tank had been given the assignment of landing on the beach, going straight inland a short distance, crossing a small paved road, turning right, and running parallel to it. We were to follow alongside the road for about a half mile from where we had landed. We would then come to a bridge that crossed a small river, the Labiranan. We were to stand by there to stop and destroy any Japanese armored counterattack coming down the road. Failure to stop them would allow their control of the bridge. If the enemy could do that, it could then cross over the river and get behind our infantry units that were driving straight inland.

The 96th, regiments in line, was to land between Dulog and San Roque. Our tank had the responsibility for securing the Highway 1 bridge. The 7th Infantry Division was to move north of us through Dagami and capture the airfield at Dulog. Although they were on our right flank, we had no visual contact with them that first day.

Prior to the actual landing, the cox'n of our LCM and I had had serious discussions regarding his getting us safely ashore. It was his first time making an assault landing, as it was ours, and we were both in total agreement that he was going to do his best to see us make it to land in one piece . . . so that we could then go on and do our job. As our line of LCMs approached the landing zone, our boat suddenly came to a grinding halt, and immediately the cox'n dropped the front ramp for us to drive off. I yelled at him to have the other sailor on board use a long pole they had, the one with a hook on the end, to check the depth.

The ramp door was hanging straight down, and it didn't look to me as though we were anywhere near the bottom. I thought that we had gone aground on a knob or sandbar. The sailor stuck the pole overboard as far down as he could, and no bottom! I stared at our cox'n, and he nodded, backed us off a bit, brought the ramp back up, and we resumed our journey toward the beach. To this day I'm certain that if he hadn't done that, we'd have ended up underwater. Our Sherman wouldn't have floated worth a damn, either.

As we approached the beach, it was apparent to me that our cox'n had gotten us too far to the left of our intended position. Our boat scraped the beach, the ramp dropped down, and just like that we were on enemy terrain in the middle of a battle. Actually, we encountered little or no resistance, and it was difficult for me to realize that we were there, unhurt, and ready to go. Now, all I had to do was get us over to the right side of Orange Beach, where we had been designated to land.

As I drove #60 ashore, I observed MPs already there, directing beach traffic. Hard to believe, but there they were, and it seemed that all of them were waving their arms, gesturing at us, blowing whistles (even though we couldn't hear them), and pointing straight inland. Well, I could hardly blame them. Here in the midst of an orderly landing, with troops and vehicles moving straight inland, here came a "rogue" tank, all by itself, running parallel to the beach. We were buttoned up, and even though those MPs were standing out there with nothing but armbands and white helmets, we didn't know that the landing was going virtually unopposed. So we were hatches down, locked, and staying that way.

As I looked through the periscope, it seemed like a bad dream. I mean here were infantrymen, amphibious tanks, jeeps, everything you'd expect on an assault landing . . . all passing from right to left in front of us. And we were charging straight ahead, which is to say crosswise to where everyone else was going.

I got us to where I figured we'd been expected to land, gave it a hard left lateral, and turned inland, seeing for the first time, really, what the Philippines in general and Leyte in particular looked like. There were coconut palm trees everywhere, most of them shredded from the navy's gunfire, and some of them flat on the ground. I drove us straight ahead for a short way and soon saw Highway 1, the narrow asphalt road we had been told about. I looked both ways. Nothing in sight. We crossed over to the other side, and I turned old #60 to the right and began driving parallel to the road.

Almost at once I saw the biggest shell hole I'd ever laid eyes on. Well, up to then it was the only shell hole I'd ever seen, and it was a beauty! It was either from a battleship's big gun or a big bomb from a plane. I'm sure it was from one of those 16-inchers the navy had, and I know for a fact that at least two and maybe more Shermans could easily fit into it. I eased us over to the right, not wanting to get too close to the

edge . . . it looked like mostly sandy soil, and we easily
could find ourselves sliding down into that big hole.

As I got the tank over more to the right, I noticed a palm
tree trunk lying there with the butt end toward us. Still apprehensive about getting too close to the edge of the shell hole,
I tried to just ease by the tree trunk. Not to be. The right track
rode up on it, then slid down on the other side. We were now
driving along, straddling a palm tree trunk. As if that wasn't
bad enough, we suddenly came to a halt, both tracks off the
ground and turning. We were bellied up on the damn thing.
The intercom immediately came alive, but I wasn't in the
mood nor did I have time to chat about our situation. I kept
the transmission in gear, and slowly the tank eased over toward one side which, thank the good Lord, allowed a track to
gain some foothold and pull us forward. Yeah, we got off the
tree, and in the process I learned a basic fact: Do not straddle
anything high enough to lift the tracks off the friggin'
ground. Well, at least I missed the shell hole.

We drove on for a short distance and soon came to the
bridge. We could see the road on the other side of the river,
and it continued on along the coast then turned left, out of
our sight. Elements of the 3d Battalion of the 382d Infantry
Regiment of the 96th Division secured the bridge and established a position there as we stood by, with no targets in
sight. They also had the assignment of strengthening and securing our bridgehead position at the Labiranan River. Even
though they had not covered much ground since landing,
every man I saw was drenched in sweat. Near-exhaustion
was evident, and I couldn't help but wonder about our water
supply, if it was going to be adequate and could it keep up
with these men. Our own water was in the five-gallon can
plus our own canteens. We could see that water was going to
be a major daily need, and that we would need much more
than we usually used.

And so we sat, everyone tense, waiting for an armored
counterattack. And still we sat. And still no attack. Soon
some Filipino residents came along and began to chat with
us. By this time we had our hatches open, and what do you
know, these guys spoke English! All of them were males,

and every one of them was smiling and laughing. Talk about a bunch of happy people; these were as happy as any you'd see anywhere.

While we sat on-station, we heard a call over the radio that made me want to grab a microphone and call Captain Garner with an "I told you so" message. We heard Sergeant MacBean, and here is what he said, word for word: "Sergeant MacBean callin'. Sergeant MacBean callin' . . . [silence, then] . . . Sergeant MacBean callin'." And on and on.

Finally, Captain Garner replied: "Hitchhike Charlie four-two to unit calling. Say again. Over."

"Ah . . . Cap'n, I jest wanted to tell you that I'm here where you said for me to be, sir."

"Hitchhike Charlie four-two copies. Remain there until further orders. Out."

"Ah . . . yessir, we'll stay right here, Cap'n." I couldn't help but remember the little conversation Captain Garner and I had had aboard ship about this sort of thing, and MacBean in particular. It sounded as though the captain had assigned MacBean a safe area to park in and wait. I was all for that because I was convinced that if anybody could screw things up, it'd be him. Or one of his buddies. Several hours passed and still no action in our area. We could hear rifle and machine gun fire off to the west, some distance away, but it was sporadic and sounded more like a mopping-up exercise than a regular firefight.

By late afternoon we received a call to move back to the beach area where we had come ashore . . . that we'd RON (remain overnight) there. Driving back was one helluva lot easier and a lot less nerve-racking than our trip inland earlier in the day. I avoided all of the tree trunks, shell holes, and other obstacles. We arrived at our bivouac area without any surprises and got the tank situated so we had a clear field of fire and so we could, if necessary, move out in a hurry. And we prepared to eat our first meal ashore.

It was K rations, and I was looking forward to them, never having had the opportunity to try them before. The K ration box was a light brown cardboard carton with a waxlike coating to keep it waterproof. About five inches wide, ten inches long, and three inches high, each carton contained one complete meal for one person. For example, the breakfast box might have a small round can, similar to those that tuna is packed in today, that would contain eggs and bacon bits. Another might have a round, flat "cake" of some unidentifiable stuff, packaged in clear plastic and labeled "breakfast food." You could place it in your canteen cup, add water, and wait until it had begun to get soft enough to break up with your spoon. The cake would be a breakfast cereal with dry milk mixed into it. Once it had soaked up to the point where it was mushy, you added sugar to taste. And, yes, sugar was included in the packet. We also got crackers of some sort (they were hard as rocks), that were supposed to be loaded with vitamins, a small box of three cigarettes, and some toilet paper.

Other K rations included carrot-pork loaf, scrambled eggs, cheese, and bacon bits, and some other foods that I either can't remember or am trying to forget. C rations were in a standard-size can, and the only one of those that I liked was the meat & beans. That one tasted a lot like a regular can of pork & beans from back home. There was a corned beef hash that tasted and smelled like a popular brand of dog food. I don't know if it was good or bad . . . I never was hungry enough to try it after that first, cautious sniff and taste. At any rate, we all "feasted" that first night on K rations, and considering all things, our meal was a pleasant one.

In all of our training, we had never been informed or taught what to do at night. As a former infantryman, it was no big deal; just get out the entrenching tool and dig out a hole big enough to snuggle down in. Something that would offer protection in case of a firefight. But it was a cinch that we weren't about to dig a hole large enough to hide a Sherman tank. So, what do we do now?

17

As it got close to sundown, the crew had a group discussion. The subject: "What the hell are we gonna do at night?" This was a very serious matter because we had heard that a counterattack was still very much a possibility. None of us wanted to be caught in the open in the middle of a firefight. If we only knew where to hide, I mean establish ourselves.

The Sherman was certainly big enough to hide behind, but when you weren't sure which direction an attack was coming from, you couldn't be too sure which side was the side to rally to. OW said to hell with it and went back inside the tank for the night. He installed the big spotlight on the turret, saw that the coaxial .30-caliber machine gun was loaded, and dropped the escape hatch for us in case we wanted or had to get inside later tonight and join him.

Anderson and I decided to dig a hole in front of the tank, just under the nose. That way we wouldn't be too far from the escape hatch. Roy Greenup and Henry took the back area and dug just under the deck overhang.

In digging a hole to protect ourselves, we figured that it should be as deep as possible. And with that thought in mind, Jim and I started to dig. The fact that we were in the beach area helped a lot. It wasn't long before we reached . . . the water table, about three feet down. The hole was long enough for us to sit with our backs at each end of it facing each other, and wide enough so we had shoulder room and were not restricted in any movements we might have to make during our "Custer's last stand." We each brought our Thompson submachine gun, along with a few grenades, and I remember sticking my K-bar into the soft, sandy side of our hole, ready for the last-ditch hand-to-hand fight. We were indeed ready. For almost anything. Sort of. We hoped.

Darkness seemed to come on all of a sudden. It was light one minute and, bang, it was dark.

Jim and I sat at each end of our hole and looked at each other. We soon found that we'd dug the blasted thing too deep. In order to see anything, we had to stretch our necks and raise our respective butts off the sand. As we sat, whispering back and forth, wondering if it was safe to light a cigarette and too chicken to do so, we heard THEM coming!

It sounded like a platoon at least. As they drew nearer, I could hear what I thought was laughter! No . . . maybe they were drunk. We'd heard that the Japs would get drunk and charge anything worth charging and the devil take the hindmost. I just hoped that OW was still awake and ready. That 75mm would be a fearsome weapon at close range.

In a few minutes they arrived, at least a dozen, maybe more, some laughing, some singing. What the hell is going on? Craning my head up, I saw that "they" were in fact Filipinos. I also saw that they had a lot of wood with them, and before long they had one helluva big bonfire going not twenty feet away! As they stood around it laughing, it soon became apparent that they were discussing the day's events. I could see them making zooming motions with their hands, apparently talking about the dive-bombing our planes had done, about the gunfire from the navy, the whole enchilada. After a few hours of this, they began to wander away. A couple of them turned and waved at us before leaving, and I wondered if they saw us watching them. Neither Jim nor I waved, mostly because we didn't want to draw any more attention to ourselves than necessary.

Sometime in the middle of the night I saw movement to our right front. "Pssst . . . Jim," I whispered. "There's somebody over to your side and in front, moving around. Can you see him?" Yeah, Jim saw him, too, and the guy was moving real slow, sort of creeping up on us. I told Jim that I was going to use my tommy gun on him, and he said no, the muzzle flash would give our position away. Good thinking.

I fumbled around at the bottom of our hole and found a

grenade. I had never thrown a live grenade at a real live person before, so I sort of hesitated. I had my finger hooked in the safety ring, just about ready to pull it and toss the thing, when we saw what was happening. It was one of our GIs from a nearby unit, heeding nature's call. Next morning, Jim wandered over and asked who was out there last night. One of the guys said it was him and why did we need to know. Jim told him that he had been about three seconds away from losing his ass. The guy turned white as a sheet and mumbled something. I had a feeling that he'd take care of business, after this, while it was still daylight.

18

While we had pulled back to the beach, the 2d Battalion of the 383d Infantry Regiment on our left flank had moved straight inland. Word came back that they had encountered a swamp and, after crossing it, dug in for the night. They had moved about a mile and a half from their landing point and had not met with organized resistance of any size.

The 1st Battalion, on the right flank of the 2d Battalion, had also moved straight inland past the edge of the swampy ground, crossed the Labiranan River, and set up a roadblock at Highway 1 where it crossed the river. They consolidated their positions around 7:00 p.m. on that first day. We learned this from some of the men of the 3d Battalion, the outfit we were assigned to. Apparently, the 3d Battalion had remained on the south side of the river while the 2d had stayed on the north side. Both units were ready for a counterattack. We also learned that the 381st Infantry Regiment had remained as the "floating reserve" throughout the day.

The first thing we became aware of the next morning was the heat and humidity. Our clothes were wet from a combination of sweat and rain. Our shoes/boots and socks were saturated. Moving even a little bit was tiring, and we were urged to take our salt tablets and drink plenty of water. Oh yes, also don't forget that one tablet of Atabrine per day, even if no one is around to check on you. And speaking of heat, staying in the interior of our tank for any length of time was almost overwhelming. But I had managed to do one smart thing while we were still aboard the ship.

The cox'n of our LCM had been showing me around his engine room to look over the twin GMC diesels. The "room" was actually a fairly good-sized space belowdecks at the aft end of the vessel and, as I recall, didn't have full headroom, but was spacious around the twins to allow for maintenance work. While down in the cubbyhole, I noticed two rubber-bladed fans, about eight inches in diameter, and managed to trade a spare K-bar I had for one of them. I installed it so that it blew air over me while I was in the driver's position, hatch down and buttoned up. It didn't cool things down very much, but it did move the air around a bit, and that helped, I liked to think.

I honestly believe that we all would have been affected even more by the heat and humidity if the presence of armed enemy soldiers around us hadn't been so prevalent. That sort of grabbed our attention and held it. The heat became secondary . . . just barely.

We moved out about an hour after daylight and drove in column up a narrow road, northward. I say "road" only because there wasn't anything growing on it. The trees and other growth at each side defined where the so-called road was supposed to be. Actually, it was a ribbon of mud, and our tanks weren't helping the integrity of it at all. All of the so-called roads and trails we came across weren't simply mud. It was as though a giant mixer had ground up the earth/water and spit out a two-to-four-foot-deep mess. Walking in or on it was almost an impossibility for the infantry, and going straight through jungle growth was a terrible ordeal. I could see that moving much-needed supplies up this road was going to be close to impossible.

Movement was slow because our company was separated while we progressed forward. As we moved up, attempting to stay in close contact with the infantry, it was soon apparent to all that any attempt to move off the road would just about guarantee to getting us stuck.

Every tank had a cable preconnected to the left front shackle. From there it ran rearward up the front of the tank, bypassing the driver's hatch toward the outside, and continued to the back, where it was bolted down at a connecting point on the rear deck. If you got stuck, the commander (after a brief but to-the-point conversation with the driver) would crawl out of the turret and unbolt the rear cable eye. He would then bring that end forward, dismount, and bolt it to the rear shackle of the towing tank.

Not only was it oftentimes a "knee-deep in mud situation," it also meant the commander was out in the open, on foot, and vulnerable to enemy fire, a situation not at all familiar or comfortable to a tanker.

19

During the second day on Leyte, we found that the word "dangerous" was not just a description but, indeed, an actuality.

Our platoon was moving up a road when we came to a bridge. It was built to carry local traffic and apparently had either collapsed because of the heavy traffic ahead of us or been destroyed by the enemy. Whatever the case, it was unusable, and we had to move forward. We didn't know where the engineers were, so it was decided to drive down the near embankment, cross the fairly shallow stream, and drive up the far side.

The first tank started down the slope and crossed the stream just fine. But as it started to climb the steep slope ahead, its tracks began to slip and eat away at the mud. They were stuck. The rest of the platoon dismounted and began cutting palm tree trunks into lengths that would allow us to manhandle them and slide them under the tracks at the front of the tank. It was working and the tank moved up a bit, but then we ran out of logs and stopped. As some of the other guys were moving more logs into place, the bow gunner of the stuck tank decided that he needed or wanted something inside, by his seat. His hatch was open, and about five or six of us were standing in front of the tank, ready to resume putting logs in front of the tracks.

As the bow gunner crawled up the front of the tank, leaned over, and reached inside, a machine gun cut loose and sprayed the area in front of us. Probably a dozen rounds were fired, I'm not sure. I didn't remember moving, but I soon became aware that I was lying facedown in a small ditch alongside the trail. It was raining at the time, as it usually was, and as I hugged the mud, I saw blood floating by my face. I'd never been shot before, so wasn't sure how it was supposed to feel. Anyway, I checked myself by running my hands over my arms and then my legs. No blood.

I was looking at a pair of GI shoes directly in front of my face, and I said, "There's blood in the water . . . has anyone been hit?" The man in front of me hollered, "It's me . . . I've been hit . . . !" It was the youngest guy in our outfit, Timmy Bahrees. Someone yelled for us to stay down because we weren't sure where the enemy was, and none of us had brought our personal weapons along on this work detail. My tommy gun was still in the tank, as was everyone else's. Here we were, pinned down by enemy fire, and no one had a gun! How in the hell are we ever gonna win this war if we (myself included) are all this dumb?

Finally, one of the commanders managed to get into a tank and radioed for help. After a short interval, the medics arrived and Timmy was loaded onto a litter and taken out of the area. His wound was in the meaty part of the thigh and not life threatening, fortunately. The story of what really happened soon came out. When the bow gunner reached inside the tank, he got hold of the .30-caliber machine gun grip and swung the gun aside. Of course, as he moved the gun, he also had his hand on the trigger. Why more of us were not hit is one of those mysteries. We had been clustered right in front of the gun when it went off. Our first casualty was caused by accident, and one of the sad parts of it was, the guy who pulled the trigger was Timmy's best friend. Just goes to show.

That night our platoon was settled in not too far from where we had started all of this. That is, just a very little ways from the beach. We were not doing a thing to help the infantry, and between the rain, the mud, and the mosquitoes at night, we were only thankful that we didn't have the enemy breathing down our necks. At least, we didn't think any of them were close by, but later that night proved us wrong.

I had been fighting a bad cold since we had landed, and instead of getting better, it kept getting worse. About the only thing our medic could do for me was give me aspirin. He didn't say anything about getting plenty of rest and calling him in the morning. Sometime after dark, Fisher and I were sharing guard duty. We were together in a big hole we had dug, and had stretched the tank's tarp over us in a futile effort to stay dry. There was water in the bottom of our hole, and more coming in, but we were still drier than if we were standing out in it. Small comfort.

Henry and I were lying at the front of our dugout when I saw something moving. I whispered to Henry, "I think I see a Jap." He picked up his Thompson and aimed it at the figure. I stopped him (remembering Jim's advice) and told him the muzzle flash would give our position away. Toss a grenade instead. While Henry searched for a grenade, I saw the figure had stopped for a moment, right in front of us, about ten feet away.

It was really pouring now, and things were getting tense. Henry had his finger in the ring on the grenade's pin and was preparing to toss it when I suddenly had an overpowering desire to sneeze. Not exactly a desire, but a need. I mean it was a sneeze to go into the record books. As the noise of it exploded, the sound could be easily heard over the deluge. "Ahhhh . . . CHOOOO!"

Everything stopped except the rain. The Jap froze in his tracks, Henry paused with his grenade, and I, well, I was grateful that I hadn't blown my nose off in the sneezing process. In a split second the enemy was gone! I mean, he took off like a jackrabbit into the night. And Henry? Well, he was really pissed off. Claimed I had done it on purpose. I let an enemy soldier escape certain death and so on, and I heard about it through the rest of our detail that evening. As I look back on it now, I hope the guy managed to live through that Leyte battle and could tell his grandchildren about the night he was saved because some dumb Yankee had a cold.

We were able to support the infantry directly on a couple of occasions, but generally we were so road-bound we weren't much help for them.

One event stands out in my memory, and thinking of it, even now, makes me wonder at the foolishness, and yes, bravery, we all saw during our days of combat. Our platoon was on a narrow road, and by a miracle it wasn't too muddy. We came to a clearing, and as we drove through it I noticed that very deep ditches had been dug on each side. So deep and wide, in fact, a tank could not cross them. There were four tanks in our platoon that day, and we were number three in the column.

As the first tank got to the far edge of the clearing, the Japanese rushed us. They came out of the jungle on all sides, carrying mines attached to long bamboo poles. Before any of us could react, the tracks had been blown off of the lead tank and also off the last tank. We were stuck right here, and while I couldn't speak for anyone else, I was stunned. I just couldn't believe that real Japanese soldiers, guys who were intent on killing us right now, were in plain view and swarming all over our tanks. As a driver there was nothing I could do except watch this unbelievable attack. We couldn't leave the trail because of the ditches. Now we were being swarmed, and enemy soldiers were jumping onto the tanks trying to get at us.

There seemed to be an endless number of them, but we later estimated their strength at around twenty or so. We all started shooting them off of each other's tanks by using our .30-caliber coax guns. My buddy Couch was in the tank ahead of me, and I felt helpless because, as a driver, there wasn't much I could do except watch. Right in the middle of things, a Japanese officer jumped up onto the back of Couch's tank, and as the turret began to traverse in our direction (in order to shoot the Japs off our tank), the officer began hacking away at the machine gun barrel with his two-handed sword! After about three or four whacks he got it turned a bit sideways, but the blade snapped off about a foot below the hilt. That's when my gunner, Anderson, shot him off Couch's tank.

The radio was filled with yells from first one tank, then another. One of the commanders got the impression that the rest of us were pulling out, leaving him alone. He had a marvelous cussing vocabulary, and under any other circumstances it would have been a real pleasure to listen in.

Of course, none of us left . . . we couldn't. The enemy officer had selected this spot wisely, and all we could do was what we were doing. That is, kill all of them before they were able to take us out with their satchel charges. I sat frozen, and it was certainly the most frightening episode of the campaign thus far. This had to come out right or our lives were over.

The noise was deafening, gunfire, radio chatter, the intercom, and all the while our tank engine rumbling in tune with the whole nasty mess. The attack couldn't have lasted more than a few minutes, but it seemed an eternity.

After the firing stopped, I just sat there in my seat, reluctant to get out but afraid to stay inside. Time had ceased to exist. When we all dismounted and looked around, I grabbed that sword. It was my one big souvenir. We found several satchel charges, and thinking back on our demolitions class, I shuddered to think what could have happened if things had gone a little bit the other away. Several Jap soldiers, still alive, were found in the ditches among the dead, and they were quickly dispatched by our crews.

It was standard operating procedure throughout the island that anything that moved at night was the enemy and to be shot. A daily password and countersign were issued, but no one ever used them. See something move? Shoot it and identify it as friend or foe when it got daylight. Which brings us to another sad event.

Private Kamp, the company drinker, had strayed out of our area one day in search of booze. The Filipinos made an alcoholic drink out of rice, and it was murder! Five Islands gin tasted like velvet after this stuff.

It was after dark, and a guy on guard duty under his tank saw a shadowy figure approaching. He yelled the challenge and waited for the password. Only some incoherent muttering came back, and the person kept on advancing. Private Kamp was shot and killed.

We young, smart guys had twisted our testimonies around so Kamp could walk free from his hearing back on the big island of Hawaii. Turns out, we weren't as smart as we thought we were.

The fighting continued to move ahead slowly, but move it did and in the process it left us behind. While the powers that be were trying to figure out what to do with us, our "encampment" began to take on the look of a permanent installation. Some of our Filipino friends volunteered to build us bamboo shelters, which was welcome news after sleeping and living in mud holes for many days and nights. Our little home was built in a day, and it was an eye-opener to watch those guys at work.

Four large bamboo poles, four or five inches in diameter and about six feet long, were cut and planted in the ground at each corner. Next, four more of the same diameter were installed horizontally between the corners and lashed in place above ground level. These served as the outer edges of the floor, which was built from those same large bamboo trunks. The method was simple and effective and done in a way I would never have guessed. "Flat" bamboo boards about twelve inches wide were laced to the floor joists, and soon we had our entire floor finished. A series of poles was installed for the roof rafters, and our tank tarp was laced down over them as a roof.

The floor was about eighteen inches off the ground, and even though there was no siding, our little open-air shelter was a magnificent structure and kept us dry, or as dry as was possible under the circumstances.

Payment for all this was nothing. None of the builders would take anything for their work. We offered them some of our rations, but they proved to be not very palatable to them. I gave one of the men some pieces of a chocolate bar and he spit it out. He did like the hard candy that came in our K rations though.

Their diet seemed to be basically rice, corn, and camote, which looked and tasted very much like our sweet potatoes. They also had chickens, but I think those were saved for only special occasions.

We had a lot of excitement one night in one of our most chilling and frightening episodes. We had all just settled down for the evening when we heard movement off to the side. The mess sergeant's "hut" was across from us, and we knew that the cooks had even less enemy contact than we'd had. Soon the movement sounded closer and, peering into the darkness, I could just make out a carabao. These water buffalo were used mostly for plowing fields and hauling wagons; in general it was the workhorse of a Filipino family. They were worked until they died of old age and, I suspect, were probably then eaten. Water buffalo were very sensitive to the smell of soldiers, which we had found out early on. As the poor thing came closer, our intrepid mess sergeant stepped out of his hut, raised his Thompson, aimed, and screamed . . . not shouted or yelled, but screamed, "Halt . . . halt!"

The carabao was above such nonsense and came steadily on, and the mess sergeant, near hysteria, screamed once more, "Halt, you son of a bitch!" and pulled the trigger. At that, the beast broke into a run and ran straight through our area with the mess sergeant burning up the air with his submachine gun. Needless to say, the carabao escaped without a scratch, and fortunately, we did too. The mess sergeant was to bear the brunt of jokes about his marksmanship for the rest of the campaign.

PART FOUR

Fire Support

20

A few days later we moved our position up closer to the infantry, but we were still too far back to be of much help. We'd been in our new location a short while when I was informed that Henry and I were to assist a sergeant from a nearby artillery unit. He was going to survey our platoons' guns into the fire control center of the artillery. It was an interesting project and seemed to be a lot like the surveying I had seen done in civilian life.

Henry and I took turns walking out ahead and holding the striped pole steady while the surveyor took sights. We eventually worked our way to the fire control center, and the location of our platoon was marked on their map. We were told that the mark was exactly where our number one gun was located, and during a fire mission it would be used to direct all four guns to the target.

Yep, we were going to be providing indirect fire under control of the artillery. The sergeant accompanied us back to our outfit and, looking at the far mountain, pointed out a huge, white, dead tree. That was to be our aiming point, or base stake. All adjustments would start from there. The next step involved installing a sound-powered phone between us and the fire control guys, and another to each of the guns. We were also given a radio tuned to the artillery's frequency.

Henry, another guy from our platoon, and I were assigned to the phone tent and told exactly how to answer the phone and what to do if a fire mission was called. Our four-tank platoon was designated Easy Battery.

I was on duty when it happened the first time. The phone

rang and I answered, "Easy Battery." The guy on the other end said, "Fire mission."

I blew a whistle and waited. On another sound-powered phone, the guns checked in. "Number one gun, ready." "Number two gun, ready," and so on, until all four guns were reported ready.

Incidentally, I was holding a phone to each ear, one to our guns and one to fire control. "Easy Battery ready!" I hollered into the artillery's phone. "All guns, on aiming point [I repeated the instructions into both phones], right five mills, elevation quadrant reading 23."

All guns complied and reported ready.

I told the guy on the phone that all guns were ready.

He said, "Number one gun only, one round, white phosphorus."

I relayed, and then told him number one gun was ready.

He replied, "Fire one round for effect."

I told the number one gun to fire one round for effect and they did so.

I yelled into the artillery phone, "On the way, Easy." I heard him say, "On the way, Easy" on the radio to the FO (forward observer), and the FO repeated it back, "On the way, Easy."

In a short while the FO radioed back and adjusted fire, but only with our number one gun. As each correction was given, all four guns followed suit but didn't fire. When all was ready, fire control ordered, "All guns, four rounds HE. Fire when ready." When all four guns fired, I yelled, "On the way, Easy," and in a bit I heard the FO radio back that we had hit the target smack on.

It was, or had been, a group of Japanese soldiers we had caught in the open. It had taken no more than three or four minutes from start to finish. None of us were able to see the target, of course, or even see where we were hitting, but the entire mission was received very well. At least we were finally able to help the infantry. Up to then, we couldn't get the tanks close enough do them much good. All in all it was very interesting work but, without seeing the target and what we did to it, seemed to lack something.

21

At Easy Battery, duties were shifted around so that everyone could get a hand in. After a bit I was able to get off the fire control job and see something besides the inside of the pyramidal tent we were set up in.

Some of the guys were wandering around the general vicinity looking for souvenirs, and it seemed like a good idea to me. I contacted Couch and Henry, and we decided to form our own little search party and "find something really great." OW gave permission for us to leave the area and added that we should "be careful." Advice like that, in the middle of battle during WW II, seems to me, in retrospect, pretty obvious. Only problem was, he should have understood that we were all a little too young, a little too inexperienced, and a little too nutty to heed any advice that made sense. But, just to be extra careful, we took our Thompsons along for the ride, which, as it turned out, wasn't all that far down the road.

We left around midday, and after walking along the muddy trail we came to a clearing that had a long building situated in the middle of it. It was not a Filipino-built unit, and looked more like it came from a plywood kit. It sat on the usual stilts, which kept it about three feet above the ground, and appeared to be a schoolroom of some sort. There was no sign that any fighting had taken place around it, but even so, we approached very cautiously. This was, after all, our first possible contact with the enemy while we were on foot. I can say without fear of contradiction that, right then, I would rather have been inside old Cutthroats, buttoned up. We didn't know if there were a jillion Japs inside the building waiting for us, or maybe it was mined. As a small, huddled group of three fearless Yanks, we edged our shaky way toward it, keeping a close look over our shoulders on the outer fringes of the clearing. Just in case this was some sort of elaborate trap.

We were soon close to the steps, and after looking for mines, booby traps, and the like, we ventured up onto the long porch that ran lengthwise across the front of the building. Looking through a window opening, we saw that the place was empty. Empty of any bad guys, but oh boy, we had found our souvenirs . . . in spades! About half of the floor was covered with straw sleeping mats, and what a welcome sight. They were thirty inches wide, about five and a half feet long, and looked to be maybe three or four inches thick. Each of us picked up four of them, two under each arm, and back to our area we went, triumphant hunters returning!

Back at our tank we quickly removed old raincoats, ponchos, and other miscellaneous things we had laid down into the hole in an always failing effort to sleep dry and comfortable. Mud is soft, all right, but after very few hours it gets compacted, and there just is no way to sleep comfortably on or in it. These mats were the answer, and we praised the entire Japanese empire for their invention.

I was so happy with our find I could hardly wait until night came and we could all bed down to a nice dry, comfortable evening. For a change.

Night came, and into our hole we all crawled, settling down on our mats and honestly feeling like this was it. And it was. Up until midnight or so, and then it happened. Itching, scratching, cussing, all of the above, plus a few more. The mats were infested with lice. Lice or fleas, I couldn't tell the difference, but they were everywhere. Everywhere there was hair, that is. Heads, armpits, crotches, you name it and we had it. And we could do nothing, absolutely nothing about it until daylight. We didn't dare get out of the hole or our friendly neighbors in the next tank over would cure all of our ills, permanently.

From heroes to bad guys, Henry and I suffered the slings and arrows of all the outrageous comments our (former) good buddies made. And they made plenty. We tried the famed government's insect repellent, which was supposed to keep mosquitoes away but actually attracted them. It also melted the plastic faces on our wristwatches and would set fire to a bucket of water if not handled carefully. And it did absolutely no good at all. Looking back on it, I think the repellent might have just infuriated the bugs, because, imagination or not, they were biting and itching at an ever-increasing rate and showed no signs of slowing down.

Come dawn and we were out of the hole and headed for the makeshift shower at the end of the company area. An aircraft belly tank hoisted up on a wooden crutch affair did the trick, and we all took turns washing the things off, using every brand of soap we could lay hands on including the good old yellow GI stuff. We washed. And washed some more. But they didn't go away that easily, plus we had to come up with clothes other than those we had worn last night. Our old B bags had been brought up to the area a few days before, so each of us grabbed pants and jackets out of them and got rid of the old stuff by passing them along to an ever-present Filipino girl who would wash them for pennies.

I can't remember how many days of this routine we went through, but eventually we settled back to the good old mud-hole and the good old insect repellent, and things sort of returned to normal. Oh, we continued to itch and scratch. But I think by then it was all just a matter of habit. Of course, habits are sometimes hard to break, and scratching can be so soothing when the urge strikes. Which seemed to be most of the time.

22

After the "mat fiasco" had settled down, the three of us, that is Couch, Henry, and I, decided to try again. No, not for mats this time, but real, genuine war trophies and souvenirs. The kind that you hang on the wall. Definitely not something to sleep on. OW was reluctant to give us permission this time, and I can't say as I blamed him after looking back at our last little souvenir trip. So, I approached Captain Garner and asked if it would be all right. He wanted to know where we were intending to go and how long we were going to be gone. After a short discussion he told me it would be okay, but to report to him as soon as we got back to the company area. And, above all, "Be careful." That out of the way, we got our gear together and set off. Each of us was carrying only our Thompsons and a bag of ammo in clips for them. We hooked up with a couple of Filipino scouts. I saw that one was armed with the usual short machete that all the males on the island carried, and the other had an ancient, rusty Springfield .30-06 army rifle. The kind I had learned to shoot when I first enlisted in the National Guard.

I should comment here on the machetes. Most had a twelve-inch blade, a wood handle, and a sheath or scabbard of native design. Others were just tied to the belt. This was primarily a farming island, and most all of the males carried the little short-bladed *shundung* as a utility tool and used it in a variety of ways. Both of our scouts assured us that they knew where we could find "plenty of Japanese souvenirs, sir," and we were eager to go.

We hadn't walked more than fifteen minutes and were passing through a small collection of houses when all of a

sudden, about sixty or seventy yards up ahead, we saw a
Japanese soldier running for his life, pursued by several
Filipino men, all of them waving their machetes. I brought
my tommy up to my shoulder, flicked off the safety (I had set
it on single fire), and then decided that he was now out of
range for the .45-caliber gun.

I turned to the scout, grabbed his Springfield, and handed
him my Thompson to hold. The Springfield has a folding
rear sight that stands upright when ready, and a small sliding
bar with a peep sight hole is used to set the various ranges.
When it is in the folded down position, I seem to recall that it
was set on "battle sights" of 513 yards. Why such an odd distance I don't know, but remembering that, I eased my sight
picture down to his waist and figured the trajectory would
catch him just right. He was then about a hundred yards
away.

As I took up the trigger slack, he disappeared under a
cloud of Filipinos, all hacking away at him. We ran toward
the group, hollering at them to stop. A moment ago I was
ready to shoot him, and now I wanted them to stop cutting
him. When we got there, he was facedown and gone. He had
deep slashes everywhere, neck, head, shoulders, arms, legs,
back, everywhere. The frenzy had died and everyone was
just standing, looking. I guessed he was a sniper who had
been hiding up in one of the trees the past few days. There
was nothing more we could do.

He had no ID on him, nothing to indicate his unit or for
that matter even his rank. Where his weapon was no one
knew. He'd probably hidden it somewhere, figuring it would
just slow him down when he ran. I can't imagine why he
hadn't waited until night to make his move, unless he had
seen the three of us approaching and thought he had been
spotted. At any rate, there was nothing we could do, so we
left. The small crowd of Filipinos also began to slowly drift
away, leaving this solitary soldier alone in the middle of a
small clearing.

Somehow I felt ashamed, and though I didn't say anything
about it, I wondered how the others felt. Particularly the guys
who had wielded the machetes.

I turned to the scout and handed him his rifle, but he wouldn't take it. Turns out he figured we had traded. He was going to keep my Thompson! I told him that it belonged to the U.S. Army and I was just holding it for them. It took some pleading, several threats, and eye-to-eye glaring, and finally we traded back. He sort of sulked after that, but I couldn't care less. Nobody was going to get my Thompson. At least not while I was still alive.

23

We continued past the small collection of houses and found the road to the mountains a few hundred yards past the buildings. The "road" was the usual mess. Mud in all varieties, from almost completely liquid to clay. It took a lot of strength just to walk, jumping and skirting the worst portions of it while taking advantage of it in order to stay out of the rice paddies and the heavy growth that was starting to appear. We were on the edge of the mountainous jungle vegetation, and while it didn't particularly bother us as long as we stayed to the road, it also made us targets to anyone who wanted to watch and wait. But walking up this way was the only choice we had. None of us felt like charging through the undergrowth, slashing away with machetes, and in the process making enough noise to alert friend and foe alike for miles around.

We were passed every once in awhile by a small tracked vehicle called a Weasel. Not much larger than a jeep, I had heard of them and it looked to me like an excellent design. I'd also heard that because of its light weight and wide tracks, it put less pounds per square inch on the ground than a fully equipped infantryman! These vehicles and the

Filipino carabaos as well as individuals on foot were about the only ways to get ammo, food, and supplies up to our soldiers, and the wounded and dead back to the rear.

With every step I took, I appreciated more and more what our infantrymen were going through. We were carrying only our Thompsons with ammo and a pistol belt with a canteen or two hanging on it. And still we were exhausted. The combination of heat and humidity was almost unbearable, and I honestly don't think you could have paid men enough to undergo it all. Only the fact that they were soldiers and a war was ongoing could energize anyone to move in those conditions.

After a while we came to and crossed a small stream about a quarter mile past the edge of the jungle. As we walked, we went into a single file. The path was that narrow, and once again, with the growth on both sides, we had no other choice. The stream was cool, and even though it was waist-deep running water, it was not fast and gave us no problems in crossing to the other side. We made our way along, both scouts up ahead of the three of us.

In a little less than a couple of hundred yards we came upon a small clearing to our right. It was about fifteen or twenty feet across and sort of a shallow, bowl-shaped depression. We walked into it and I saw a half of a coconut husk lying on the ground. A slender wisp of smoke was coming from it, and for a moment I just stood and looked at it. It had no meaning for me at all. A Japanese army cloth raincoat was folded and lying next to the smoldering husk.

One of our scouts became visibly agitated. He was excited to the point where he almost danced as he called to us. "Sir, they are all around us!" As he spoke, he lifted one edge of the coat and felt under it . . . he could feel that it was still warm from the soldier who had been lying on it moments before. It hit us all about the same time . . . we were standing in a group, in a clearing, and somewhere around us were enemy soldiers. Armed enemy soldiers!

Being the coward that I am, I took the lead and started back down the trail, heading in the direction we had come from. I had my Thompson in my right hand, set for full automatic and off safety. Couch and Henry were right behind, also watching each side of the trail and ready to fight if necessary. During the excitement our brave scouts had disappeared. Maybe they were smarter than I had given them credit for!

As I ran, I kept my eyes looking ahead on the trail and also to my right, in case the ambushers (that's what I now thought of them as) were ready to pop up and kill us. We reached the stream in short order, and for what it's worth, I felt like we were now safe. I waded halfway across, bent over at the waist, and began to drink. The water was cool and tasted delicious. My mouth was very dry from the excitement and the run. Couch and Henry joined me, and as I finished drinking I straightened up and looked around. Just upstream from us about twenty yards, half in, half out of the water were several dead Japanese, their bodies swollen from the heat and decay. I stopped drinking and passed the word to my two buddies. We continued on back down the mountain via the mud road, through the village, and eventually back to our tank.

I searched out Captain Garner and told him that we were back. I also told him about the clearing and the Japanese that we hadn't seen, but we knew that they were there. I didn't mention the dead ones in the stream and also skipped the machete episode in the nearby village. That night I ran the day's events over in my mind and marveled that we hadn't been killed. We were so green, so innocent in the ways of combat on foot. Don't forget stupid, I reminded myself. And, our so-called scouts had done nothing other than lead us into the situation, albeit innocently. I concluded my thoughts that night by remembering that old saying, "Sometimes it's better to be lucky than right." "Or smart," I added.

24

We returned to the routine of camp. That is, doing all the details necessary to keep self and equipment going. Our tanks continued to do indirect firing for the artillery, and aside from that the company activities were nil. We still were on alert at night, still kept guard from sundown to sunup. Every once in awhile someone down the line would see a bush move and open up on it, joined by half the army on the island, it sometimes seemed. But, that was about it.

A few days had gone by since our jungle walk, and as the experience began to slightly fade, our confidence slightly increased. And so, as one might expect of young, not-too-bright guys, we decided to give it another go. Another walk up the muddy road, guided once again by the intrepid Filipino scouts, and armed to the teeth with our trusty submachine guns, looking for trouble. Yeah, right. Once again I contacted Captain Garner and was once more granted an okay to do a little looking around. I also had to promise to "Be careful." Which I did. The trip up the muddy trail hadn't changed; if anything it had gotten worse. The traffic up and down had practically destroyed it, but it was the only access to this part of the mountains and so it continued to be used. Had to be used, no choice.

We managed to get up to the edge of the jungle again and crossed the same stream. I don't remember if the Japanese bodies were still there or not. Maybe they were and I didn't want to look. We passed the small, bowl-shaped depression where the smoldering coconut husk had been, and this time, of course, the raincoat was gone and no coconut husk, smoldering or otherwise.

Our two scouts were up front a few yards, and the three of us watched both sides of the trail. After a bit we came to an area where the growth cleared up somewhat and we could see several yards ahead. The undergrowth had been cleaned out, and about the only things growing were the ever-present palm trees. Suddenly the Scouts began to yell and point up ahead. Couch, Henry, and I spread out slightly, and I had my gun ready to fire but didn't see anything. They opened up, firing straight ahead, and it was then I saw movement. A Japanese soldier was running from the right-hand edge of the clearing toward the left. I fired a few rounds at him as he disappeared behind some of the trees. Firing stopped, and we began a very very slow and cautious advance. As we got to the edge of where we had seen movement, we came to a halt.

Directly to the left was a sight I will never forget as long as I live. It was a shelter, all bamboo, about ten or twelve feet square, open all around, with no side walls. The floor was about a yard off the ground, and the four corner bamboo posts supported a thatched roof. Piled on the floor were the bodies of Japanese soldiers. There must have been fifty or sixty of them, and in all stages of decomposition. Most of them had bloated and swelled because of the heat. Open, gaping wounds were evident everywhere, flies were all over the place, maggots could be seen on all of them, and the smell was indescribable. Some of the bodies were under the floor on the ground, but most were simply piled one on top of another. It was apparently some sort of collection point, perhaps for the purpose of identification or for a later burial. We had no real clue. I recall that Couch was standing to my left and Henry was to my right as we three stood there, silently, looking. Suddenly a "body" right at our feet, facedown, arched his back and gave out a horrible groan. Couch and Henry both began blazing away with their Thompsons, and I just stood there. I knew that there wasn't any use in shooting the guy again . . . he was in the process of giving off his final noises, and my two Tigers had just made sure that the noises were truly final.

After looking around a bit, we called it a day and started

back. Our scouts had disappeared at the first shot, and who could blame them?

When we emerged from the jungle, we found ourselves standing on a dirt road that ran parallel to the growth of the jungle. A coconut was lying in the road, and one of us, I don't remember who, took a few shots at it. About two minutes later an army patrol came around the bend, led by a lieutenant. He asked us if we had been doing any firing and we told him no. Of course not. He asked us where we were from, and we told him our outfit was stationed down below the mountain and we were just "looking around." He warned us not to go into the jungle. "Everything from this road north is enemy territory and very dangerous. Stay out of it." We assured him that we had no intention of doing anything except returning to our outfit. We then parted company with him and his men and started our slipping, sliding, weary way back to our beloved tanks.

I found Captain Garner in the orderly tent and showed him on the map where the Japanese bodies were. I forgot to mention our contact with the army patrol, not that it was important. We were back, in one piece, and had been "careful" as I had promised. And that's all that mattered, I guess.

25

A day or so later the three of us decided to go on "one more patrol." We were still looking for souvenirs and to date had come up empty-handed. Surely our luck was bound to change (how little we knew).

Once again I contacted Captain Garner, and once again he okayed us and asked that we be careful. Looking back I can only conclude that he had his fingers crossed and was saying a small prayer for us under his breath, or had decided that we were a bunch of nuts and maybe we'd learn a lesson one of these times. Regardless, he was a nice guy and a fine officer. I think that he would have liked to join us, but his responsibilities kept him back with his men.

This time we went without scouts. Just Couch, Henry, and myself. About the only thing we were sure of was that we wanted to try an area different from where we had been going. About all we'd found so far was sleeping mats (and we didn't want to think about them anymore), a Japanese cloth raincoat, and a smoldering coconut husk. Not much to take home for the folks to admire. I did have my broken Japanese samurai sword, but lusted after something more. Our route was the same as always, but after we reached the edge of the jungle, we went to the right, following the road toward our infantry's positions.

After a bit we came upon a large group of GIs. It was the 3d Battalion of the 383d Regiment of the 96th Infantry Division . . . our "parent unit." Our Thompsons caused a lot of interest, and we had several offers to buy them, but most of it was good-natured joking. I think. Finally, a sergeant asked what we were doing up there, and we told him that we were just looking around, maybe find some souvenirs. He told us that he was taking a recon patrol out in a few minutes and he'd be glad to have the Thompsons along with him. That maybe we'd even find some souvenirs. Sounded good to us and we agreed. He said there was another patrol leaving at the same time and it would be going a slightly different direction than his, a few hundred yards to the right. He suggested that Henry go with it, and so it was agreed. The purpose of that was to "distribute" our tommy guns between the two patrols.

We soon formed up in a column and began our entry into the bad guy's territory. At the edge of the battalion's area there was a trip wire about ankle high, and we were told to be sure and step over it. It was common practice to hang empty C-ration cans on wire along with a few pebbles inside. These make good alarms at night when someone brushes against them. Other devices involved taping a grenade to a short post and attaching the trip wire to the pull ring on the grenade. Instead of a rattle with that one, you got a loud bang and maybe a few yells.

Because of the heavy jungle, we were forced to walk single file along a path. It was drizzling, the heat was stifling, and due to the oppressive humidity, it seemed as though we could never get a full lung's worth of oxygen.

I felt almost giddy with excitement. Here we were, walking along a jungle path, on a reconnaissance patrol, in a combat zone. There were eight of us, and even though we were small in number, I felt very confident and secure. I was the last man in the column. Couch was up front, the second man from the lead. Our patrol sergeant was placing his automatic weapons on the flanks, just like good sense and the book tells it.

We had been walking slowly for perhaps twenty minutes when the line came to a halt. Word was passed back in whispers that there was a clearing just ahead, and the Japs were dug in on the far side of it. We were to move forward and form a rough skirmish line, but were not to fire until we got the patrol leader's signal or were fired on first.

The man ahead of me was a big guy, an American Indian. His name was Gabriel, and he was the BAR (Browning automatic rifle) man. And a good guy to stay close to, I figured. I knew the BAR's capability because as a former infantryman, I'd had the chance to fire it on the combat range and had a world of respect for it . . . and the men who were equipped with it. It used the same .30-caliber bullets as our M-1 rifles and light machine guns, but the BAR clips held twenty rounds, and when the folding bipod was used and the shoulder plate in place, the weapon became a mini–machine gun.

As we moved into the clearing and at the same time formed into a rough line, "Gabe" and I got behind a fallen log. It was about a foot and a half thick and gave us fairly good cover, or so we thought. As I got down on the mud and grass, shots suddenly rang out and the fight was on. Gabriel began to sweep the front with his BAR while I held my fire, waiting to see a target. I then heard Couch's Thompson cut loose on the far end of the line, and at about the same time I saw a Jap's head pop up out of a hole about fifty or sixty feet ahead.

I drew a bead on the spot and waited. He was in a spider hole. The Japs would dig a fairly deep hole and crouch down in it with their rifle at the ready. Usually the hole would be at the base of a banana tree or something similar, and a branch or limb would be pulled down to cover their face while they looked out through a slit torn in a leaf. Gabriel cut down the banana tree in front of us with one sweep of his gun, and I kept my eye on the base of it. Pretty soon the Jap popped up again and I fired a single shot at him. He dropped back down and didn't come back up.

I raked the area where Gabriel was firing, then pieces of our log began to fly up between and around us like sawdust being tossed by the handful. The wood was rotted and offered only slight concealment and absolutely no cover. Protection was zero.

I saw an enemy soldier jump to his feet and run toward the edge of the jungle, and I fired a single shot at him as he disappeared into the undergrowth alongside a large tree. It looked like he suddenly dived for safety, but I wasn't sure if it was a dive or him feeling the impact of my .45-caliber slug. Bullets were now flying in both directions, and there wasn't any kidding about it, we were in a real fight for survival. I was probably out of my head at the time, but I felt no fear, only an intense awareness of our situation and everything that was going on. I felt very much alive.

In the midst of the shooting I felt a sudden burning sensation in my left forearm. "I've been hit," I hollered at Gabriel. He just nodded and kept pouring fire into the area ahead of us. I slid back a bit and peeled my jacket sleeve up in order to see how badly I'd been hit. I saw in a glance that it was my *friend* who had done the damage. Gabriel's BAR ejected empties to his right, which meant that they were pouring out onto my arm every time he fired. I hadn't noticed it before until one of the cartridges had somehow gotten up inside my sleeve. Talk about hot . . . ! Anyway, I hollered at him and explained the situation. He just grinned, nodded, and kept on shooting up a storm.

I had a chance to fire at a couple of more Japs positioned across the small circle of grass and low bush. I wasn't positive, but thought I'd hit them. At least one of them, anyway. During the firing, I was using up ammunition at a very fast rate, but in the excitement that was exactly what I wanted, lotsa firepower. Both Couch and I were using the twenty-round clips rather than the thirty-round jobs. The problem with the thirty-round units was they were so long, it was necessary to hold the gun and your head, up very high. Too high for comfort. Our twenty-round clips allowed us to keep the gun fairly low, and our heads fairly protected, and still have a good supply of ammo. The big problem, of course, was the high cyclic rate of fire our guns had.

I was almost out of ammo. I'd been firing mostly on full auto, and the gun had been going through clips like crazy. I yelled to Couch that I was almost out and was switching to single fire. He hollered back and said he was in the same situation. About that time, the fight was over, fortunately for us because otherwise we would have become spectators rather than participants. Our men began to move around, looking over the situation. One of them called me, and I went to see what he wanted. The first Jap I had spotted was still in his hole, dead with a single shot right through the front of his helmet. From the size of the entry hole it was obviously from my Thompson. The guy who had called to me grabbed hold of the brim of the helmet, and with the leather chin strap still in place he hauled the body halfway up out of the hole. As the head bent back, it looked like the helmet was filled with gray cottage cheese . . . a real mess.

The body was laid back so the upper half was bent backward at the waist. The G. I. rummaged around, finally unbuttoned a shirt pocket, and found a small plastic box. He opened it up and there was a bar of soap inside. The infantryman said that it was my kill, so the box was mine. I told him that he could have it. I was disgusted now. I noticed another bunch of our men wandering around, and I yelled for

them to check out the area alongside the big tree at the edge
of the clearing. Sure enough, they found a dead Jap there. I
asked where he had been hit and they said one shot, right between the shoulder blades. He had been my second hit. I
didn't try to track down any more . . . the fight had left me
sort of deflated. I found Couch counting his kills, too . . . between us I guess we'd been some help to the patrol. I found
the sergeant and told him that we'd have to return to our battalion to get more .45 ammo, but we'd rejoin them if they
were going to be here for a spell. He said they'd be there for
another fifteen or twenty minutes . . . so away we went,
Couch and I, headed for the battalion, and more ammunition.

Couch and I moved out down the same trail we had come
up on, and I knew that the battalion area was just a short distance away. We could get the ammo and be back in no time.
After a few minutes' walk we came to a small clearing. Right
in the middle of it was a large shell hole. As we walked over
to it, I looked down the trail in the direction we were going
and saw one of C Company's men, George Leet, coming toward us. Leet was a big guy, around six-foot-one, and fairly
heavy. With his blond, almost white hair, he really stood out
among all the green vegetation. He had an M-1 carbine with
him. In a fight I think I'd rather have a sackful of rocks. The
trigger pull was tough, and fine shooting just could not be
done with it. Also, the safety and magazine-release buttons
were located alongside each other, and one infantryman I
talked with told me that in the heat of battle he had raised up
to shoot a Jap and when he thought he was taking the safety
off, he had dropped the magazine from his weapon instead!

A note here about Leet. He was a quiet, nice guy, respect-
ful, and did whatever was asked of him. The problem was,
he was not the brightest star in the heavens, and for all his
good intentions, it scared the hell out of me to see him wandering around up here by himself. I said to him, "Leet, this is
very dangerous country. Couch and I just left an infantry patrol, and a bunch of Japanese were killed. I really think you
should go back with us and not go on up ahead." Before he
could answer, somewhere behind us in the jungle, a machine
gun cut loose on us.

Without thinking or anyone saying a word, all three of us ended up at the bottom of that shell hole, crouched as low as we could, and all the while that blasted machine gun kept firing, full auto. I looked up at the edge of the hole, and the dirt and mud were jumping from all the bullets impacting. The gun sounded exactly like our .30-caliber, and for a moment I thought one of the other patrols had mistaken us for the enemy and was firing on us. I yelled at the top of my voice, "Hold your fire . . . we're K Company" (the company whose patrol we had been with). No response, just more firing. I hollered again, "Hold your fucking fire, we're USA." Nothing but more of the same.

Finally it stopped. We weren't sure what was going to happen next. It was a cinch now that it wasn't friendly fire. And I realized, as did Couch and probably Leet, too, that the guy with the gun could just walk over to the hole and finish us off while we crouched at the bottom of it. All of a sudden Couch said, "I've been hit!" I looked at him and he pointed at a bullet hole in his pants leg. It had gone through the fabric and never touched him! The hole was about an inch, and no more, below where no guy ever wants to get hit. Talk about singing in a high falsetto! We laugh at it now, but we didn't then.

Leet said something about being "hit, too." Couch and I looked at him, and sure enough he had been shot through the back fleshy part of the thigh. He didn't seem to be in any pain right then, and the bleeding wasn't too fierce, but shot he was, and we had to get the hell out of Dodge. Now I told Couch I'd take the lead, he'd bring up the rear, and we'd put Leet between us. I figured I'd have a better chance if I piled out of the hole in a big-ass hurry, before our trigger-happy "friend" was ready for us. I put my Thompson on "full auto" and "fire," and got ready to make a dash for it. As I tensed, ready to jump, I caught myself up short and stopped, like the first time I jumped off the high-dive platform at our local swimming pool. I was getting ready to try it again when Couch yelled at me, "Hey, if you aren't gonna go, let me . . . I'll do it." Bless his heart. Anyway, that did it for me, and I got ready. "Okay, here we go," I yelled. And with that, I

scrambled up the slope of the hole ready to do or die. I figured we were going to be met with a hail of gunfire, however, there was nothing but silence. I thought to myself that
the son of a bitch had probably fired everything he had at us
and had taken off.

It was drizzling, and the path had a lot of slick grass and
weeds growing on it. As I sailed down the line, I slipped and
fell flat on my fanny, slid, dug my heels in, and came right
back up on my feet, still going a hundred miles an hour. Or
so it seemed. Leet was right behind me, and Couch behind
him. I don't think we ran three or four minutes before we
came to the battalion area. We stepped very carefully over
the perimeter trip wire and yelled for the medics. Once we
got someone to take care of Leet, I got hold of somebody
with a radio and passed the word to our recon patrol sergeant
that we'd been ambushed and weren't even considering
coming back to his group. But I cautioned him to watch out
for the guy with the machine gun. He okayed the message
and thanked us for our help.

Days later, I came across some of the guys who had been
on "our" patrol. I asked about the sergeant and was told that
he had lost his right hand because of a defective grenade.
Our grenades had a three-second delay after the spoon handle was released. In close-quarter fights, the Japanese would
often throw our grenades back at us before they exploded. So
it became common practice for U.S. soldiers to pull the ring
and allow the handle to snap free, count one or two seconds,
and then toss the grenade. Doing that assured that it would
explode almost as soon as it arrived at the target. Apparently,
the grenade our patrol sergeant used had a defective fuse and
as soon as the handle was released, it exploded, taking off
his right hand and a portion of his hip. It was also common
practice to hold the grenade down by the side and slightly to
the rear in case something like a premature explosion happened.

When Couch and I finally made our weary way back to our
company area, I reported in to Captain Garner. I told him
about Leet, and about Couch's bullet hole. He raised his eye-

brows quite a bit at my news, but I guess there wasn't much new and/or different about what had happened to us. The trials of encounters were happening all over the island.

Later, back at my tank, I found a cut in the left side of my fatigue jacket. I couldn't tell for sure if it was from a bullet or torn along the way, but it didn't really matter. I wasn't bleeding, and that's what counted. Maybe old Gabriel had had something to do with it, I don't know. I do know that I felt very lucky that night, as I lay in our hole alongside of old #60 . . . with nothing but the mosquitoes to fight.

26

Something entirely unexpected took place sometime during the next week. The majority of the original Southern National Guard members, including the first sergeant and his brother, were rotated back to the States on a new points system. I never did find out how many points were necessary or how you earned a point, but I did know that those guys had been away from the States for many a month, and if anyone was due for a break, it was certainly them.

About then I received a very high honor, one that even today as I write this makes me very proud. It happened suddenly, with a runner dropping by our tank and telling me that Captain Garner wanted to see me at the orderly tent, pronto.

He was waiting for me, and as soon as I reported, he asked me how I felt about receiving a field commission.

"You mean me, sir?"

"Yes, Sergeant . . . would you be interested?"

"Yes, sure . . . I've never thought about it, but . . . yeah, I think I'd like that."

"I thought you might. I've forwarded your name, and a truck will be here within the next half hour to take you to the promotion board. I've requested that you be assigned back here to my company. Is that okay with you?"

"Absolutely, sir . . . I look forward to it." I sort of laughed, and then said, "It wasn't too very long ago that I asked you to take my stripes, and now you're getting me promoted!"

"Well, I thought of that," and he laughed, too, "but, I won't be promoting you . . . just recommending you. I understand that there are, I believe, nineteen men, including yourself, from the 96th Division who have been put up for field commissions at this time. Nineteen out of sixteen thousand men is not bad, Sergeant."

Within the next half hour I managed to get together a halfway decent uniform, shaved, and was up waiting by the orderly tent when the truck arrived. It was full of infantry guys, all of them sergeants, and you could see that they had all been in combat. Something about the way they held themselves, looked at you, just a feeling I got. They accepted me very well, even if I was a no-good tanker, and it looked like we were all going to get along just fine. Soon we pulled up in front of the field hospital. We were told that we'd receive a quick physical and to return to the truck as soon as we were free. One of the guys muttered, "Watch out for the shrink. . . . They have one that will check us out, to see how nutty we all really are, I heard."

I followed along from one doctor to the next and all seemed to be going well. And then I came to the last one. He was the guy who would take my blood pressure reading. I've always had problems with this procedure. As soon as the cuff is installed, my blood pressure goes sky-high. I think it's because I'm afraid it'll do just that, go sky-high, and then I'll fail it. And that, of course, does make it run well above where it should be. Plus, I hadn't run across the shrink yet, so I just "knew" that this guy was it. I told him that my reading was going to be high, and sure enough, it was. He said he'd leave the cuff on and we'd "chat a bit" and then take another reading. Okay, here it comes, I said to myself.

"Aren't those tanks kind of close . . . I mean, do you ever

feel trapped in them?" he asked me. He could see on my paperwork that I was from a tank outfit.

"Oh, no problem, sir. It's just another vehicle as far as I'm concerned. Just a mechanical device to drive around in."

He and I chatted along like that for a while, and finally he took my blood pressure again. It was still high, but it had dropped enough for him to tell me that everything was okay, and he wished me luck.

When I got outside, everyone was waiting. I told them that I'd been held up while the shrink yakked away at me. They all laughed and told me that there was no shrink; apparently the blood pressure guy was just curious. Sure had me fooled.

We arrived at the beach, and an old first sergeant told us to take a seat under a canvas shelter, just the roof, no sides, that had been set up for us. About sixty feet away was a similar shelter. There was a long table there, with several officers sitting around it, and one of them sat at the head. Soon one of the sergeants in our group was called, and he walked over, saluted, and sat down. He was there about fifteen minutes, stood up, saluted, and came back to the group. Because the officers were watching us, none of us questioned our man, but it was easy to see that he was feeling very good about things. Guess he made it okay.

After several others had gone through the interview, my name was called. I walked over, saluted, and said, "Dick, Robert C., reporting as ordered, sir." This was directed at the man at the head of the table, a full colonel, and he didn't look very friendly, either. I wondered if he knew any of the other full colonels that I had met. Nah, not possible.

I was told to be seated, and the interview began. It was conducted almost 100 percent by the colonel. There were six or seven other officers present, mostly majors and a couple of light colonels.

"I see by your service record that you have had infantry experience."

"Yes, sir. I was in the 40th Infantry Division, 160th Regiment, K Company, sir."

"Did you happen to know an officer by the name of William Zeller?" William B. Zeller. We called him Wild Bill

Zeller, and he was a gung-ho, all-out fighting man's officer, and a damn good one, too. I smiled.

"Yes, sir, I know Major Zeller very well, sir."

"It's now Colonel Zeller," he informed me.

I smiled again, nodded, and said, "He's a good officer, sir, and I'm certain his promotion was a well-deserved one."

"And, you were an infantry platoon sergeant. Is that correct?"

"Yes, sir, that's correct."

"How did you happen to end up in an armored unit, Sergeant?"

"Sir, I wanted to attend OCS, armored, and I felt that a solid background in a tank company would benefit both the service as well as myself. When I inquired regarding a transfer, the tank company had no openings other than private. So, I requested a transfer in grade of private in order to complete the transfer and become a member of that company."

"Hmmm. Sergeant, do you know what 'the estimate of a situation' is?" This was an infantry question, as far as I knew, never having come across it in any other context.

"Yes, sir. The estimate of a situation is essentially a tool used in the field, prior to engaging a potential enemy force. It consists of gathering information, intelligence if you will, of your opposition. Information that would cover potential strength, reserve strength and its location, location of any supplies, medical facilities, flanks of the enemy, location and number of automatic weapons, things of that nature. After receiving all this information, the person in command can then make a decision on how or even if an attack should proceed."

He looked around the table, but there were no other questions by anyone, and I felt that a huge load had been lifted off my shoulders. It was then that he lowered the boom.

"Sergeant, your commanding officer has requested that you be assigned back to your old outfit under his command. That is an unusual request. Would this be a problem for you?"

"No, sir. No problem at all."

"I see. Well, Sergeant, we'll commission you as an infantry officer. . . ."

"Sir, I had many opportunities to go to OCS infantry, and didn't. My interest and most recent background is in armor."

"Ah. No problem, Sergeant, we'll commission you as an infantry officer and assign you to armored."

I knew, and he knew that I knew that once my basic commission came through as an infantry officer, it would always remain that way no matter where I went or how long I stayed. I knew also that we were getting ready for the next battle, and though I didn't have a clue as to where it might be, I knew that I wanted to fight it in my tank. I took a deep breath and killed myself with my next statement.

"Ah . . . Colonel, my interest is in armor. My CO has recommended me for a commission in armor. I understand what you're saying . . . that even though I would be commissioned as an infantry officer, I would be assigned back to my outfit. . . ."

"That's correct, Sergeant."

"Well, sir, if I can't be commissioned as an officer in the armored force, I'd rather not accept a commission in the infantry."

The colonel got the same look on his face that most of the other colonels seemed to have gotten. At least the ones I'd had contact with. He was so pissed off he could hardly sputter, "That's all, Sergeant. You'll be hearing from us."

We all knew that another battle was shaping up, and the thought of being in the middle of it on foot really turned me off. I had found a niche in the tanks, and didn't want to take any chances of missing combat in one of the monsters. Besides, I felt that I'd be a better tank officer than I would an infantry lieutenant. When the truck dropped me off back at the company, Captain Garner had already gotten the word. No commission for me. He wanted to know what had happened, and I told him the whole story. He got almost as upset as the colonel had, but not at me, at the colonel. He told me he was sorry, he thought I would have been a good officer. I thanked him for his recommendation and belief in me, and that was the end of my days as an "almost commissioned officer."

27

Several days were spent policing up our area. During the earlier part of our time on the island we had been mostly concerned with doing all those things that would keep us alive, and everything else got low priority. Now that the fighting had moved on up into the mountains and we were more or less an "artillery unit," we were a bit more relaxed around camp, and it was showing.

At an inspection of our personal weapons, we lined up in front of an officer and he inspected each weapon as the man stepped forward. I drew Captain Garner's line and dreaded what I knew had to happen. Somehow or other the brass brushes and cleaning equipment for our Thompsons had been lost. Henry and I were the only ones in the tank who had actually fired our Thompsons, and so OW had not worried too much when I told him I couldn't find the cleaning equipment for the .45s.

When I got to the head of the line, I handed the captain my tommy gun. It had eight notches I had carved in the stock, one for each "confirmed" kill. Henry, Couch, and I had a little race going, and as far as I knew, we were all in a tie. The captain looked at the stock, looked up at me, and asked, "Sergeant, what are these notches for?" The young punk in me had to show off, and so I said loudly, "Well, Captain, there aren't any rabbits on this island as far as I know." This drew a laugh from some of my buddies nearby, and Captain Garner just gave me a very brief smile. He then ruined my day. Hell, he ruined his day. He slid the bolt open, tilted the gun up, and looked through the barrel. I knew what he was looking at . . . rust.

He lowered the gun, slowly, gave me a long, hard look, and handed it back to me. "I don't want to hear any excuses. None at all. Nothing you say can justify letting your weapon get in this condition. Now, take it down to the rice paddy and fire a few rounds through it, then clean it as you are supposed to, and then I want to see what it looks like. If you've allowed the barrel to pit, I assure you, Sergeant, you're in for some big trouble. From me. Any questions?" I was so embarrassed I could only shake my head. I did fire the rust out of it, and while it wasn't pitted, it would've been in short order. How to go from a smart-ass to a stupid rookie in one easy step.

Our "living quarters" came under scrutiny next. They consisted, for the most part, of a long shallow hole dug alongside the tank. Most of the tankers had dug their holes about two feet deep and wide enough for the crewmen to lay alongside each other, from one end to the other. Once the hole had been dug to their satisfaction, the tank's tarp was secured along the edge of the tank deck and stretched downward at an angle and staked into the ground. It was quite a different arrangement from the one we used when we were up near enemy activity, and I had to smile as I thought back about the first one we dug, and I'm not talking about that first night at the beach. The "combat" hole came a day or two later, and was so amazing, I still have to grin and shake my head.

As we approached our infantry's positions, we would look for an area where we could safely get out of our tanks and refuel and reload ammo before bedding down for the night. Obviously this would not be in plain sight of the Japanese, but was close enough for them to become aware of us in short order.

At the lead, the captain's tank peeled off the road and drove around the perimeter of the clearing, making a wide circle. Our little tank convoy followed while he continued his circling, until all of the tanks were now driving along behind the tank ahead, and the captain was just behind the last tank, ours. In other words, we were now one large circle of vehicles. Once all the tanks were in that formation, the captain halted his tank, which resulted in all of us stopping. Each tank then turned and faced outward, just like the old covered wagon days when they circled them for protection against the Indians.

Once we had the tank aligned so it pointed outward from the circle, we drove it forward several feet and stopped. The crew then began digging a hole between the marks left in the dirt by the tracks. Once the hole had been dug to our satisfaction, the tank was then reversed back over it and we were, more or less, set for the night. With a five-man crew, we posted two men on guard at the head of the hole, from sundown to midnight. They woke the next two, and those men guarded from midnight to dawn. This schedule was rotated and allowed the fifth man a night off. Anderson and I used to pull guard together, and we split the shift with one of us dozing while the other stayed on alert. Halfway through the shift we would change duties. If we took the first shift, that is sundown to midnight, we'd both take a good look at the area in front of our tank noting all bushes, trees, and the like. It wouldn't be dark for even an hour when "it" would start.

Me: (whispering) "There's something moving up in front of us."

Whispering back to me: "Bob, that's that bush we saw before it got dark."

"No, that bush is more to the left. This thing moved, I tell you." We watch for a spell, and I don't see it move anymore. I realize that I'm just a bit jumpy.

"You're right, Jim, it isn't moving . . . go back to sleep."

"No, the thing *is* moving, I've been watching it close. . . . It's moving all right."

And so it would go. We'd talk each other into and out of shooting a bush or two during the night's watch. Always, when we woke the next two guys, we'd tell them that "we think that there's something out front moving around once in awhile." After we crawled back to the rear of the hole, we'd lay there for a while and listen to the two guys on guard go through the same routine we had been going through. "Yeah, it moved. . . . No, it's not moving." And so it went.

One night I saw something that really was moving, took a bead on it, and fired. From the howling, we found out that it was a dog I had shot at . . . and missed, but scared the hell out of. The next morning Captain Garner came over and asked, "Who was doing the promiscuous firing last night?" I explained the circumstances, and he left, warning us against creating further incidents. That night, a Thompson cut loose from Garner's tank. Next morning I wandered over and asked who was doing the promiscuous firing last night. Of course it had been Garner. I welcomed him to the club, and he just laughed and said something about bushes.

28

An ongoing and tremendous amount of loading and unloading was happening back at the beach. Our infantry, fighting in the mountains, required daily supplies, as did the rest of the island's troops. And, while all that was happening, U.S. troops hit Luzon, the main island of the Philippines, which meant that a good portion of equipment and other essentials now on Leyte and not immediately needed here would have to be reloaded and shipped there.

All that unloading and loading and reloading needed manpower, and lots of it. Initially when we were on the line, we could not take the time to help out with work details such as these. But now . . . well, only a small part of the company was involved in the indirect fire missions, so we had time on our hands and were needed. Work details were everywhere. And naturally, Anderson and I got swept up in the feverish need for strong backs and weak minds. We seemed a natural for both categories.

As it turned out, it was one of the best things that happened to us during our stay on Leyte. Our work detail was loaded onto trucks and taken to the beach at around 11:30 in the evening. Our shift started at midnight and ran until eight the next morning. We would then have the rest of the day off, and once again report back at midnight.

Jim was not a happy camper and quick to say so. I wasn't very happy myself, and between the two of us we spouted off enough to satisfy ourselves, but that's about all. Didn't do a bit of good, but at the time it felt like something we "had" to do.

The beach was a total mess. Boxes and cartons and cans and you name it were piled, stacked, and otherwise stored along the beach for as far as I could see in the darkness. Lights were kept at a minimum because the Japs still liked to fly over once in awhile and, even though there wasn't a whole lot of bombing going on, no one wanted to take a chance.

Big LSTs were pulled up onto the beach with their bow doors opened up. A long line of unloading equipment was placed at the bow, and crates were slid down tracks on rollers. A box placed on those rollers would almost unload itself due to the slant of the track. At the bottom end, a man would pick up a carton and take it to wherever it was to be stacked, then return to continue the process.

As we were stacking cartons, I couldn't help but notice a large pile of cardboard boxes stacked nearby. The pile was covered over by huge tarps, but I could make out the stenciled words on the sides of the cartons . . . some kind of fruit.

I mentioned this to Jim, and we both eyeballed the pile as we went by on the next stacking trip. Yep, canned fruit. We'd been living on dry K rations for so long, anything like canned fruit made us almost weak with desire. On the next trip, I stacked my box on the pile it was intended for and stepped over in the darkness to the "fruit section." I lifted up the tarp and dropped down under it. It was dark but not so dark that I couldn't make out all the goodies around me. A moment later I was joined by Jim. Using our K-bar knives, we opened up a box and got out a #10 can of sliced peaches. Blessing the folks who had designed and supplied us with the K-bar, we got the can open and proceeded to feast.

After eating ourselves full, we worked our way even farther under the tarp and went to sleep. One of the best things about this work detail was that at the beach there were no mosquitoes. The ocean breeze kept them inland. About 7:30 in the morning Jim and I rejoined the detail, finished up, and rode back to our company area. Happy as could be. No more cussing.

Reflecting back on it, I tend to think that it was a pretty shabby thing to have done . . . duck out on our buddies who were busy helping the war effort. But realistically, there were so many men involved they were getting in each other's way. Our absence was, if anything, beneficial to the whole situation, I kept telling myself, and of course, those peaches really did hit the spot.

29

Right when you least expect it, something new or different always seems to pop up. For example, we were informed one day that tank #60 was going to have a flamethrower installed in it. None of us knew very much about these things, and none of us were very happy with the idea. But what are you going to do when you're told that it'll be installed? Right . . . they installed it, anyway.

The napalm tank was located just to the right of the assistant driver's seat, on a shelf where the 75mm ammunition had formerly been stored. We were given a mini-course on the theory and operation of the weapon, and it seemed simple enough. Essentially, pressurized napalm was run through a hose to a valve controlled by a trigger, then to a pipe. The pipe was inserted through the swivel hole where the .30-caliber bow machine gun usually was installed. When the operator was ready to "fire," a toggle switch was flipped, which energized a spark plug at the end of the pipe. When the switch was thrown and the trigger squeezed, the napalm would be forced out of the tube and would ignite as it passed by the spark plug.

As a safety measure, a hole was drilled through the armor just to the right of where the new "gun" was located. Passing through the hole was quarter-inch copper tubing that ran down the front of the armor, curved around, and went back up alongside where the "gun" was. The end was pinched shut, and small holes had been drilled all along the tubing. The inner end of the tubing was connected to a CO_2 fire extinguisher. This arrangement was called a "snuffer" and was there in case the tank caught on fire.

The biggest disadvantage to the operator was lack of vision. When the flamethrower was actuated, the only thing that could be seen through the periscope was fire. For that reason, the operator was encouraged to use it in short bursts. Open the valve, throw the switch, aim, and give it a burst. Pause, then another burst. The flamethrower's greatest effect was not burning people . . . but burning air. If the enemy was holed up inside a cave or emplacement and couldn't be got at easily, the flamethrower would burn all the oxygen and the victims would die from suffocation.

Some of the tanks in the battalion had been set up for really serious flamethrower work. The breechblocks were removed from the 75mm gun and the flamethrower hoses and tubing were passed through the entire length of the barrel. A very large container of napalm was installed inside the tank. Outwardly these vehicles looked like regular Shermans, but their operation was vastly different. They could throw a burst of flame an amazing distance and were welcomed by the infantry. Watching them at work, I could certainly understand why they were so effective. All in all, it was, to me, a distasteful way to fight a war, but who's to say what's okay and what isn't when it comes to defeating the other guys?

Naturally we discussed the pros and cons of using #60; where and when was the big topic. The answer to that would be played out in a very surprising way.

30

While the Leyte battle was coming to a conclusion, the one on nearby Luzon Island was just getting under way. I had heard that my old infantry outfit, the 160th Infantry Regiment, 40th Infantry Division, was among those units involved. If I had stayed with them, I would just now be getting my feet wet. Instead, as a tanker, I'm now an "old" combat vet of a couple of months. With the news of the 160th's fighting, I also received a V-mail from my old first sergeant, John Clement. My high school friend Joe Mason led my old platoon up a jungle trail and was ambushed. He was killed. I could only think of Helen, his wife, and Brenda, his baby daughter who he had never seen, and his mother, who I had known for years.

I think that the total evil of war hit me then more than at any other time. It was the first time since I had been in combat that I had shed tears . . . and I did then. I could only wonder if it would have been any different if I'd stayed with my old company, but common sense told me there was no way to figure something like that. I realized that up until now combat had been a grand adventure for me. Now I realized it was a distasteful necessity. And the sooner it was over, the better. I also realized that the news of Joe's death was something that other families all over the world had been and were still going through, constantly; news of deaths or of seriously wounded husbands, sons, fathers, brothers, friends.

Looking around at some of the friends I now had made me doubly aware of the dangers of our day-to-day life. I could only wonder what lay in store for us, because it was obvious that our division was preparing for another battle. And you didn't have to be a member of the joint chiefs of staff to realize that there weren't all that many targets left. Formosa and Japan loomed large on the horizon, and I could only shudder at the thought of hitting either.

In other news, some of the old-timers were being rotated back to the States on a new points system. The first sergeant and his brother left, along with a large number of other noncommissioned officers. Captain Garner also left the outfit, and I was sorry to see him go. In my opinion, he had done well commanding the company, especially in light of the fact that it was the first time in combat for all of us.

Capt. A. A. Todd replaced Garner, and he impressed all of us with his professional attitude, his knowledge, and especially his concern for his men. We also got ourselves a new first sergeant. Can't remember his first name, but his last name was Mundy. He was a Regular Army man and planned to stay in after the war. He, too, was not only very knowledgeable, but kept his eye on all of us, sort of like a mother hen . . . make that a rooster. A good man.

Christmas came and went with nothing special happening except for a few packages that came through, filled with a fine powderlike substance that was finally identified as cookie dust. The crumbs had just plain rubbed into dust. Some items came through okay, but we all mostly looked forward to getting packages as a sort of proof that we were still in favor back home. The contents, as important as they were, really became secondary.

On New Year's Eve I was sick. I had what seemed to me a combination of dengue fever and a very bad cold that had settled in my chest. I was lying in the hole, shivering one minute and burning up the next, when the firing started.

None of us had remembered that it was New Year's Eve, but some guys down the line certainly had, and as they began firing, everyone joined in. I lay there, too weak to get up and defend myself. I thought, from the magnitude of the gunfire, a major push had been launched by the Japanese, and frankly, I was at the point where I didn't much care. Anderson came over and asked how I was doing, and I told him, "I've been better . . . and what the hell is all the firing about?"

"Hey, Bob, it's New Year's Eve . . . some of the guys down the line felt like celebrating, I guess." As I lay there listening to the gunshots, shivering and half out of my mind, I suddenly realized that I'd felt like this before on other New Year's Eves, back in civilian life. . . . Small world, like they say.

My tank, #60, passing by a unit from the 96th Infantry. *Photo courtesy of the U. S. Army Signal Corps, taken on October 20, 1944, Leyte, Philippines.*

Company tank #28 bogged down in the mud on Leyte, Philippines. The terrain plus the rains made tank movement almost impossible. *Photo courtesy of the U. S. Army Signal Corps.*

Approaching the beach at Okinawa. Our tank was an LCM (landing craft, mechanized). *Photo by the author.*

The landing craft were unable to land us very close to shore because of a shallow coral shelf that extended several hundred yards out. *Photo by Elden Davenport.*

My tank, #60, is in the background; a dead Japanese soldier is in the foreground. *Photo by Elden Davenport.*

Our platoon passing by a village destroyed by artillery. *Photo by Elden Davenport.*

Passing through an infantry unit. *Photo by the author.*

Same tank, different angles. Notice that the turret has been moved sideways by the force of the explosion. *Photos by the author.*

Same tank, different angles. Notice that the bottom of the hull has been blown outward, probably due to the ammunition inside burning and exploding after it was hit. *Photos by the author.*

Lieutenant Schulter's tank after it had been knocked out by a Japanese 47mm antitank gun. Note the hole at the bottom of the white star on the side. Also note the non-penetrating hits at the front of the hull. *Photo by the author.*

The 47mm antitank gun that knocked out Lieutenant Schulter's tank (photo taken after the gun was destroyed). *Photo by the author.*

PART FIVE

We Leave Leyte, Headed North

31

Our fleet pulled out of Leyte on March 25. I remember the date because I was thinking that Christmas was only nine months away. A small joke I kept to myself. As we turned northward, our convoy began to pick up more ships. A day or two later we could see every kind of ship built, or so it seemed, and there looked to be hundreds. And that's not an exaggeration. In every direction, all the way to the horizon, there were ships in our group. It was both reassuring and at the same time a little unsettling. A lot of help is always good, but we must be going to where a lot of help would really be a big necessity. And, that's sort of . . . did I say unsettling? Yeah, that's a good word for it. I felt really unsettled.

As we proceeded, the weather began to deteriorate. By the third day we were in a full-fledged typhoon. The old flat-bottomed LSD 5 rolled and plunged like never before. With eighteen medium tanks in the belly for ballast, I figured we would not roll too much, but that was wishful thinking on my part. On the fourth day the sky cleared somewhat, and even though the sea was churned up and all the ships were rolling, we could see that the worst was over.

It was then that we learned our destination . . . the Ryukyu Islands group. Specifically, Okinawa Island. We were told that the island was only about 350 miles from the Japanese mainland, and that the fight ahead was going to be a tough one. The island was approximately sixty miles long and at its widest, eighteen miles. Enemy strength was estimated to be sixty thousand plus. Reinforcements from the Japanese mainland were always a consideration, and our navy and airpower would be extremely important in protecting us once we were ashore.

The main forces would consist of the 1st and 6th Marine Divisions, and the army's 7th, 77th, and 96th Divisions. The army's 27th Division and the Marine's 2d Division were to be held in "floating reserve." The 81st Army Division was held at New Caledonia, also as a reserve unit. All army and Marine divisions had seen combat before, and this was reassuring. We were informed that our total invasion troops would number over 150,000.

Although we weren't aware of it at the time, the navy had been bombarding the island for days, softening up key areas ashore.

The battle plan, as it affected us personally, seemed like a good one. The 1st and 6th Marine Divisions plus the army's 7th and 96th Divisions would land, abreast, on the island's west coast. The Marines would cut straight across the island and turn northward. The army's divisions would cut straight across the island and turn south. The northern portion was much larger in area, and at the time we wondered why we had gotten the small end. But, not to worry . . . the light would dawn soon enough, and we'd find that there were plenty enough of the bad guys to go around.

As our ships arrived off the island, the navy's bombardment was unimaginable. Ships of every size and shape seemed to have large deck guns, and all of them were firing. I was told by one of the navy officers aboard our ship that the navy had been shelling Okinawa for more than a week. "Destructive bombardment" he called it. I wondered if there was any other kind, but didn't ask. Something else I learned that day: The 77th Army Division had attacked and taken over all of the key, smaller islands that surrounded Okinawa, thus assuring that those enemy troops would not do us any mischief while we were engaged with the main target.

It was Sunday. It was also April 1 . . . April Fools' Day. And it was Easter Sunday, too. But, most important to us, it was the day we landed on Okinawa.

We were scheduled to begin landing operations at 0830, with heavy gunfire from the navy starting at 0530 . . . twenty minutes before dawn. This most impressive fire support came from 10 battleships, 9 cruisers, 23 destroyers, and 177 gunships. Targeting the beaches, they fired 44,852 rounds of 5-inch or *larger* shells, 33,000 rockets, and 22,500 mortar shells.* This was the heaviest concentration of naval gunfire *ever* to support a landing of troops! This was also the largest land, sea, and air invasion in world history, including the Allied invasion of Normandy.

Standing on the deck of LSD 5, we watched and marveled at the sight and sounds. At 0745, carrier-based planes hit the beaches and trenches with napalm. By 0815, small boats were circling, waiting for the signal to begin landing operations. At 0830 they began, with the amphibious tanks going in first, then troops from the Marine 1st and 6th Divisions abreast with the army 7th and 96th Divisions making their assault landings, followed closely by the tanks.

While we were circling offshore in our LCM, we passed by and under the large deck guns of one of the navy's big warships. Just as we were even with it, the guns fired, and I honestly thought we'd been hit! My God, what a noise. I couldn't begin to imagine what it must have sounded like at the receiving end.

The commander and loader's hatches were open, and all of us sat topside on the tank as we chugged along in the LCM. Over to our right, one of our company's tanks was paralleling our course and most of its crew was also topside. We all waved at each other as we motored along. A large coral shelf projected out from our beach landing areas, and our LCMs had to drop their ramps and kick us out while at least a half mile from shore. All of our tanks had the deep-water wading stacks installed and had been waterproofed around hatches and any "important" openings.

Once the LCMs unloaded us, we all followed, single file, toward the beach. There was the distinct possibility of running into either underwater mines or a large shell hole in the coral as a result of bombing by aircraft. I didn't see it hap-

*Roy E. Appleman, *Okinawa: The Last Battle* (Center of Military History, U.S. Army, 1948; repr., New York: Barnes & Noble Books, 1995), 69.

pen, but the crew that had been running parallel to us did hit a shell hole and capsized. They went into the water upside down, and our reports said that the driver drowned. Other reports said that the entire crew perished, but I wasn't able to confirm that.

As we approached shore, I could see a large opening in the huge seawall. Built of coral, I could only guess at its dimensions. It appeared to be at least twenty feet thick at the base, tapering to around fifteen feet thick at the top. It was about twenty feet high from base to top. All in all a magnificent piece of construction. With the extended coral shelf, I imagine that during a typhoon in the China Sea, winds and ocean would sweep across the shallow water and hit shore with a tremendous amount of destructive force. The seawall had been built to protect, and I had no doubt that it did its job very well.

As I drove us forward and over the bottom portion of the wall opening, I couldn't help but notice the large number of people around us. There were quite a number of photographers, both still and movie type. After the Leyte landing and seeing MPs on the beach, nothing was going to be too new and different, but the sight of the MPs, directing inbound traffic made me proud of them. It also made me feel a little safer. Nothing is more anticipatory, I don't think, than the thought of making a landing on an unfriendly beach. After the terrific shelling the navy had laid down for us, I feared that we'd find a lot of enemy soldiers, dug in and waiting just for us. But not a sign of any could I see.

As with Leyte, our tank had an unusual mission. We were to find and drive up a fairly narrow dirt road for approximately one mile. It ran uphill, toward a mountain range. We were to then stop and sit there, in plain sight, and wait. We were told that there was one particular defense gun, a sort of coastal gun, that the navy wanted to be sure had been taken out. Apparently it was one of those that appears, fires, and then drops out of sight. We were to be the tempting target. We were assured that the gun position would be under close scrutiny at all times, and at the first appearance of the gun, they, the navy, would be pre-aimed on it and take it out. Yeah, right.

Well, we sat there for about half an hour and nothing happened except a goat wandered by. And that was it. Oh, one thing I didn't mention. On the way up, we came across an unexploded shell lying in the road. It looked to be about ten inches in diameter, but not being familiar with that particular size, it was difficult to make an accurate guess. I had edged over as far as I could when we went by . . . and now we would have to drive by it again. I had heard that a so-called dud could be beat on with a sledgehammer and not go off. A minute later a fly lands on it and *boom!* Anyway, we did drive by, very slowly and carefully. We radioed and reported it, and considered it taken care of.

All of us were in disbelief over the total lack of opposition by the Japanese. We had not heard a single shot fired by them, and the longer they delayed in opposing us, the more of our forces would pour ashore. The lack of any enemy seemed almost scary. What's going on, what do they have up their sleeves? Sixty thousand enemy soldiers and not a single rifle shot fired? Some of the guys thought it was a good sign, that our intelligence people had made a mistake and the island was going to be a walk in the park. But most of us just wondered and waited.

I kind of guessed that just maybe all the Japs were up north and the Marines could take care of them for us. What's that called? Oh, yeah . . . wishful thinking.

32

The rest of the first day and on into the next left us still wondering what was going on. There was an occasional shot fired somewhere, but as far as organized resistance goes, we ran up against none. We heard that the Marine troops in the north were moving along with some resistance, but nothing that slowed them up very much. As with any operation like theirs, a lot of time has to be spent making sure that an area is completely clear of the enemy before going on. Some stragglers would inevitably be left, but significant resistance was gone.

About the second day we discovered that we had a real cowboy in our midst. A small Okinawa horse wandered into our area, and we all gathered around to inspect this marvel. I made the announcement that very few people knew this, but Couch had been born and raised on a horse ranch and was a genuine cowboy. That was, of course, a flat-out lie, but, hey, he could always sue me. There then began a group effort to have Couch ride this little guy, and good sport that he is, he approached it. Albeit somewhat cautiously, approach it he did. If it had been me in his shoes, I would have run the other way.

At any rate, with no bridle or saddle, Couch suddenly grabbed the mane and swung aboard the poor thing. Cheered on by our shouts, he gave the beast a little kick in the ribs and *whoosh!* They were off! The unfortunate part was, they were headed straight toward the Japanese lines! Away they went with Couch hollering at the top of his lungs, "Whoa . . . whoa . . . *whoa* you son of a bitch!" At that moment the horse dug his hooves in and came to as fast a stop as any I've ever observed.

Although I didn't see it, Couch claimed he pulled his .45 on the poor critter and was going to blast away if necessary. Apparently, according to Couch, the horse recognized the sound of the slide as it was pulled and released. We were all laughing, Couch included, and I just had to say that I didn't think that "whoa" meant too much to a horse that knew only Japanese. Couch said, "I might not speak Japanese, but that horse sure as hell knew the sound of a Colt .45." Yep, we'd had a gen-u-wine cowpoke in our group all this time and didn't know it. As we walked away, I asked Couch to tell me about life on a horse ranch. He just rolled his eyes and I figured I'd done enough for the day. Besides, he had the Colt .45. I didn't

We learned by late afternoon that the 7th and 96th Divisions had completed their first movement phase and had linked flanks at the middle of our operations zone. The swing south now presented to the enemy a solid front, with the 96th on the right flank, and the line now extended across the island with the 7th's left flank on the eastern side. The 96th had encountered scattered resistance, and a couple of tanks were lost to mines. The best we could figure was they were A Company tanks, and from what we understood, there were no serious casualties.

We now began, for the first time since we had been in combat, to mesh with the foot soldiers and act as a true tank/infantry team. Unlike Leyte, where there was either pure jungle that made it totally unworkable for tanks or mud and rain that made movement by heavy equipment if not an impossibility, then a near one, Okinawa had numerous valleys and flat areas where tanks could maneuver easily.

The Japanese had occupied the island since the 1800s and had been in the process of preparing it for a defensive battle for many years. The people of Okinawa were farmers and considered an inferior race by the Japanese. They were used by the Japanese primarily as slave labor in building roads, caves, and similar military installations.

The southern part of the island, the area where most of the fighting was to take place, was almost an ideal situation for defense. It consisted of a series of valleys intersected by ridges and steep hills. The Japanese not only honeycombed the high ground with emplacements, but also designed and built caves so that they commanded the reverse slopes. What this amounted to was that an attacking force would have to fight to gain control of the ridge or high ground, and once there were forced to defend their backs as they started down the reverse slope, headed for the next set of ridges. It amounted to a fight front and rear all at the same time.

Initially we were unaware of this situation, and the Japanese inflicted heavy losses on our troops after high ground had been won. Movement downslope turned out to be, in many cases, more dangerous than the initial fight to gain the high points of the ridge or hill in the first place. Fierce fighting to gain the top of a ridge more often than not left our troops dangerously undermanned due to the high casualty rate suffered during the attack. Subsequent downslope advancement with the remaining small group was an open invitation for the Japanese to attack with great force, including the use of artillery and mortars.

The ridges had been dug out to the point where the Japanese could ride out the heaviest bombings, and when the shelling had been lifted, pop up ready to resume fighting, usually with little or no loss of men. Air bombardment as well as shelling by the navy's heavy guns did little to overcome this situation. American troops had few options left, but they used them well. One was a direct assault by tanks, which resulted in either eliminating the enemy troops or in sealing the caves in such a way as to render them out of action. Another way was to use flamethrowers, either the small, portable backpack units the infantry had or flamethrower tanks. The last viable way to gain control was the tried-and-true method used by infantrymen the world over: direct assault by foot soldiers using hand grenades and hand-carried demolitions. The last method, it goes without saying, was the bloodiest and most dangerous, and was to be avoided if alternate means could be used.

33

The days began to settle down to a routine, if you can call having people trying to kill you before you killed them "routine." Our "normal" day began right at daybreak with a hurried cup of coffee. Anderson was our designated cook, and he would fire up the little one-burner gasoline stove and heat water for us. The mixing of the powdered "coffee" was up to each of us, and while most of us took our java black, some added K-ration powdered milk and sugar. After breakfast I usually grabbed a can of C rations, meat and beans, to be eaten sometime during the day as my lunch. This was the only C ration that I liked.

As it began to get light, we loaded up the tank with whatever we felt we might need during the day. Shovels were a popular item. They were used to dig our hole for the night position, and we also had to bring them along in case we got bogged down somewhere along the line.

Our first move would be to bring the tanks up as close to the infantry as we could without being too blatant about it. We generally sat behind a small knoll or hillock, and waited. As soon as the infantry shoved off, we were on notice. The Japanese were resisting to the point where they had to be killed to the last man before our infantry could move past them. Generally speaking, the enemy machine gun and mortar fire would be so intense as to pin down our troops, and this is where we came in. A radio call from them brought us to the scene, and we would blast and machine gun caves and emplacements to the point where our GIs could move up toward their target. Again, generally speaking, our role as mobile artillery would last only until the Japanese could bring their heavy guns to bear on us. When that happened, we were no longer a help to our infantry, we were a big, fat deficit. Heavy artillery and mortars would rain down on us and the infantry alongside us. We were then told thanks, but no thanks, just get the hell out. Which we were always glad to do. Sometimes the shelling would follow us, and oftentimes it would continue blasting the initial target area where we had been and where our infantrymen still were.

Before we left Leyte, a telephone had been installed on the outside of each tank at the left rear corner of the hull. It was a weatherproof metal box about the size of a shoe box with a hinged lid, and inside was a handset and a switch. Inside the tank was another handset, installed between the driver and assistant driver/bow gunner positions. When an infantryman wanted to talk to us, he would open the box and hit the switch, which turned on a small red light inside the tank. Pick up the phone and you had the outside world on the line.

One day we were sitting on a dirt road, shelling some positions about a hundred feet or so ahead of us. The infantry officer in charge of the platoon had crawled up on the deck and was leaning against the rear of the turret, talking to OW and directing us to the targets. Suddenly the red light came on. I grabbed the handset and said, "Hello." One of the infantrymen had decided to chat with us while we were busy knocking out some bad guys down the road. We talked for a while, exchanging the names of our hometowns, stuff like that.

Then I heard some heavy-duty explosions to our rear and asked him, "Is that ours or theirs?" He said he thought it was the Japs. I asked him where he was standing. He told me that he was crouched directly behind our tank. I said, "If I get the word to get outta here, I will probably back straight back, so watch yourself." He gave me a "Roger," and we started to talk again. About that time another explosion hit, and this one was closer. Anticipating OW, I shoved the clutch in and slid the gearshift lever over to reverse. About that time OW told me to "back up, now." I dropped the clutch and gave it full power. As we were backing out, I looked through my periscope for the guy I had been talking to. I saw him all right; he was crouched at the left side of the road and wear-

ing a big grin. No wonder. In his upraised hand he was holding our telephone, severed cord and all!

Like everyone else on the island, our workweek was seven
days long, and every day was more or less a repeat of the
day(s) before. When we were called on to help, I could see
the pinned-down soldiers, watching us, waiting for us to
knock down and out some of the weaponry that was holding
them up. Many a thumbs up was given as we drove by, and
many a wave-off when the big guns of the Japs began to register hits in the area.

One morning we received a hurry-up call to assist some
troops that had advanced up a small valley, only to run head-
long into the usual dug-in enemy machine gun emplacements. As we approached the area, we had to first drive
across a cornfield. Looking ahead, I couldn't see anything
like a firefight going on. Matter of fact, I couldn't see anyone, or anything, other than corn. Suddenly we were at the
edge of the field, and about a hundred feet below us was a
platoon of GIs spread out in a skirmish line. Interspersed
among them were a couple of our platoon's tanks.

We had to drive down a very steep slope to get to those
men, who now were pinned down. Staying in first gear and
riding down on compression, we got down to the flat ground
fairly easily. We pulled up on line with the other tanks of our
platoon, and Anderson began laying in some 75mm fire on
caves in the face of the ridge up ahead. We had been firing at
the enemy positions for about ten minutes when all of a sudden we were in the middle of some of the biggest explosions
I had ever seen fired against us. I swiveled my periscope over
just as the tank on our left flank was covered with dirt and
smoke from a near miss. The explosion caused a tower of
debris to shoot up above the tank, perhaps seventy-five feet
in the air.

Other rounds from the same big gun or companion guns
began falling around us, and the infantry was waving us off.
We were only too glad to accommodate them. OW told me to
come straight back, which I did. I figured he was going to
have us back up the steep slope we had come down. Later,
thinking about it, I realized that because of the extreme angle

of the tank, my commander was unable to see much of anything other than sky. About halfway up the slope he gave me
a command that chilled the hell out of me: "Left lateral. Left
lateral!"

I obeyed immediately because I couldn't see a thing except the scene below us, and I'd seen enough of that to last
me the rest of the day. As I pulled on the left lateral, the tank
backed around to the left, and when we were broadside on
the slope, OW had me ". . . stop, then forward and hard right
lateral!" He was trying to get us turned around so we could
go back up the slope nose first. Talk about white-knuckle
time. That was it, because the tank was now rocking ever so
slightly, wanting to roll over to the left. I couldn't believe the
position we were in!

As I started forward, giving it a hard right lateral, the left
track began to make a very loud popping sound. I mean really loud. The entire weight of the tank was being shoved
against the track as we were in the process of going ahead
and turning at the same time. First I thought we were going to
roll over, then I was afraid we'd not only throw a track, but
even worse, break it. I finally got the tank turned and headed
straight up the slope.

It was then that I became aware that the Jap artillery or
heavy mortar was tracking us. As we arrived at the top of the
slope and began our trip across the cornfield, the left track
kept popping and the Japs kept trying to hit us.
Unbelievable! I couldn't accept that heavy artillery was actually tracking and trying to hit us, but they were! And, while
we didn't git hit, they were doing a good enough job that we
didn't dare stop.

As we got across the field, I saw a small collection of
buildings up ahead, and as soon as I could, I turned down a
narrow street and stopped. Their forward observer had lost
sight of us and could no longer direct the firing. No more artillery . . . just us and the houses around us.

Later we had our maintenance sergeant take a look and he
suggested installing a new track, which he had brought up to
us and which we did indeed install. And, yes, that cured

things. Even after all these years I still think about us on the side of that slope, the tank trying to roll to the left, the artillery banging away, the tracks popping, and all that on one of our good days! I try to not think about the bad ones . . . any more than I have to, that is.

34

About the middle of the month, someone remembered that old #60 had a mini-flamethrower installed, and why not use it? A day or two after this momentous discovery, we got the call, and it was one of the many things about Okinawa that I still remember . . . vividly. And every once in awhile, try to forget.

We were doing our usual great job of waiting for a call, and as usual we received one. The infantry had a cave full of Japs that was giving them nothing but trouble and wanted a flamethrower tank to take care of the situation. OW informed us on the intercom while I was getting Cutthroats into gear and on our way. I had forgotten the contraption, to be honest about it. Maybe it was some sort of subconscious wish. I just plain didn't like the idea of setting folks on fire much, as I wished they were all out of here.

Anyway, we arrived at the scene and were directed by radio to a rather large cave. We could see nothing about it that was very formidable, just a yawning hole in the side of a cliff. I pulled our tank up to the entrance and there we sat, about twenty feet from the front door, so to speak. As the driver, I sat in the left side of the tank, and I could watch the assistant driver/bow gunner/flamethrower operator do his magic. He began twisting valves, arranging the flamethrower nozzle and hose, checking the spark plug switch, and doing all the mysterious things those guys do.

Once he had all his paraphernalia in place and was ready, I shifted my view from the inside of the tank to the outside. I could now watch through my periscope. I zeroed in on the end of the nozzle, waiting for the flame to be thrown. Our fearless operator squeezed the nozzle trigger and, as I watched, fire came out the end of the nozzle . . . and sort of dribbled down onto the front of the tank!

In a flash I knew that the operator was unaware of the situation, because all he could see was flame. Matter of fact, that was all I could see. Keeping my cool, I took a deep breath and screamed hysterically and as loudly as any movie Tarzan ever did, "Fire . . . fire . . . I mean, this son of a bitch is on fire . . . !" There was a microsecond of dead calm. No one spoke. Then the intercom erupted with all sorts of great advice. Mainly, "Put that fire out!" In a moment of clarity I remembered the snuffer. I hollered, "Squeeze the snuffer . . . the snuffer . . . the goddamn fire extinguisher, for God's sake!" Our lowlife assistant driver, the guy who had set us on fire, the one who humiliated us in front of our very own troops, finally did actuate the snuffer and, yes, the fire was put out . . . just like the book said it would be. But can you imagine what the Japanese were thinking? "This American tank pulled up in front of our cave and set itself on fire! What will those crazy Yankees do next?"

Finally things quieted down and calm reigned once more. I informed OW that the flamethrower unit on our tank was not to be used ever again. Ever, never. No way. I mean, day-to-day survival was tough enough, why make things worse by setting ourselves on fire? OW agreed, and the subject was never brought up again. Back at our bivouac area, we found the problem was that the pressure had slowly leaked out of the napalm tank, and only enough air remained to push the stuff out in a slow dribble. I wondered, does any of this make sense? Nope, but we did confuse the enemy, and that's worth something, right?

35

We received a call from the infantry requesting immediate help not only for themselves, but for a couple of our tanks, too. We were not too far away and, following directions, we came to a dirt road that ran through a low ridge. A cut had been made through the ridge, and it was on the other side where our help was needed. The cut was narrow, with just enough room for our tank to get through comfortably. The distance from the entrance to the exit of the cut was about a hundred feet.

As we got into it, I saw something lying in the middle of our path. I stopped and took a close look. It was an Okinawan woman, and strapped on her back in a sort of knapsack fashion was an infant. The baby was crying for all it was worth, and the woman was unconscious and apparently in shock. She had her eyes closed and was shaking violently. About the time I was going to tell OW that I didn't think we could get by her, we received another call . . . we were wanted now! He told me we would miss her if we were careful and kept as far to the right as we could.

I eased the tank far over to the right, which meant that the right track was riding up on the sloping bank of the cut. Driving slowly and as carefully as I could, we eased by. After we had passed her, I could no longer see the woman and child. I asked OW if he could see them and how they were. He said that we had missed them and that they were still there, just as they were when we first saw them. Don't worry about it, he said.

As we pulled out of the cut and onto the flat ground ahead,

I saw two of our tanks from the 2d Platoon. They were firing toward a low ridge, and the infantry was scattered over a fairly large area. As I pulled ahead, I saw a deep trench . . . a tank trap. I asked OW what he thought. Because of his height and angle he could see it better than I could. He said it looked fairly narrow and that we could get across it okay. It was only six or seven feet across as I recall, and we did manage to get to the other side with no problem. Once there, we joined up with the other two tanks and poured a lot of 75mm cannon fire into enemy positions.

Later in the afternoon, the infantry moved up, and we now found, much to our delight, that we were in a rear area rather than ahead of the lines.

We started back to our bivouac area and had to, once again, go through the cut in the ridge. As we got close to the woman with the baby, I could see that she had suffered massive injuries. I couldn't tell if it was from our tank or some other vehicle. It could have been from ours, and I was very unhappy with OW. I had relied on him to guide me around her. He told me that our infantry had been pinned down and needed us as soon as we could get to them. We had had no choice. My brain told me that he was absolutely correct, but my emotions took a beating. The baby was still alive and crying up a storm. Stopping in the middle of the cut and getting out would have been a certain invitation to the Japs to swarm us using their now-famous satchel charges and mines. As it was, we radioed our company, and a medic with an infantry team was dispatched to the location.

There are a lot of things to not like about combat. Killing and injuring innocent civilians tops my list of inhumanity to man.

36

The infantry, God love 'em, had the toughest job of all. It doesn't matter what country's infantry we are talking about, they are the backbone of a combat operation. Always have been, always will be. And it doesn't matter if they're Marines or Army, the guy with the rifle is THE man.

As big a target as we were in the Sherman tank, we still had some comfort in that small-arms fire didn't bother us. Of course, we had "other stuff" shot at us, but all in all we had a better deal than the infantrymen, hands down.

But in spite of all that wonderful armor, that great protective shell we moved around in or under, our company was still getting its fair share of casualties. We started the campaign in what must have been the regular manner as far as finding out who had gotten hit, how badly, and all the details. We were now at the point where brief comments were made and accepted without further discussion or details. Example, "Sergeant Doe's tank got hit today. . . ."

"Oh . . . how did they make out?"

"The gunner, Smith I think it was, got it pretty bad, the rest of them made it out okay. I think."

"What did they get hit with?"

"47mm I heard."

"Yeah, that'll do it all right."

That generally ended the discussion regarding Sergeant Doe and his crew. It wasn't that we didn't care about those guys. It was that it had become so commonplace, it was a non–news item. Once we heard about any death or injuries, that pretty much was it. What was also "it," but not discussed, was the hard fact that our own odds were getting more narrow every day. The percentages had gotten to the point where it would have been a safer bet that we'd get hit than not. And that's a rotten way to greet each day, knowing that you can't phone the boss and say you won't be in to work today . . . you might have the flu or something. Too many guys depending on us, and us depending on them. And so it went. With that in mind, knowing that it's tough enough to stay in one piece with the enemy looking down a gun barrel at you, what makes it really tough is when you come under "friendly fire" . . . or *are* the "friendly fire-er."

That's what happened to us one fine morning. We were called by an infantry platoon leader and requested to drive down into a fairly small, bowl-shaped valley. And, yes, take out some enemy machine guns that didn't want to cooperate with our war effort.

It appeared that the slope into the valley was too steep for us, so we decided to drive parallel to it for a short distance where it seemed to shallow out, and we could go down it there. The plan was that once we got to the bottom of the bowl, we'd turn left and sweep back up the valley, taking out any resistance we came across. The infantry was to hold its position at the top edge of the slope until it appeared safe, or at least safer, to move down and into the flat floor of the depression.

All planning completed, we started off. At this point something should be understood about the view from the turret. While the driver is steering the tank, making small turns and corrections according to the demands of the terrain, the commander and gunner are, generally, on the watch for targets. So, here we are, the driver driving straight or nearly so, and the commander and gunner traversing the turret back and forth, at the same time looking around through their respective periscopes. Oftentimes they would move their periscopes in opposite directions to the travel of the turret. Or, indeed, each other. So now we have a situation where each crewman is looking in a direction none of the others are!

As a result, a gunner or commander can very easily "lose

the true direction of travel" under certain circumstances. In the turret they might be totally unaware that the driver has had to make a rather sharp turn at one point to avoid some obstacle. If the gunner or commander is looking at a particular object such as a suspicious cave, then as the tank is turned, he corrects his vision by keeping the periscope or gun sight on his original point. And, perhaps be completely unaware that the tank is now traveling in a totally different direction. In other words, he is "lost."

That essentially is what happened to us that morning. As we got to the point where we turned left down into the bowl, I had found it necessary to make several adjustments in direction along the way. And the turret had been moving back and forth all that time. As a result, when I made the turn down into the bowl, our infantry wrongly decided it was time for them to also move on down in anticipation of us clearing the way in a short time. Our gunner, looking through his periscope, saw a platoon-sized group of soldiers moving across his front and, knowing that our troops were to hold their position until we were finished with our mission, he and the commander decided that the soldiers they saw on the move were the enemy. They were far enough away so their bowl-shaped helmets looked Japanese. He cut loose on them with the .30-caliber coaxially mounted machine gun. As soon as I heard the gun firing I looked to the left and saw what was happening. I yelled on the intercom to "cease fire . . . cease fire! Those are our men!" We stopped firing, and all I could think of was thank the Good Lord we hadn't fired our 75mm cannon into them. And, also, that they hadn't returned fire with a bazooka.

We never did learn how many or if any casualties resulted from that situation. I know that the infantrymen had hit the ground immediately, and it appeared from our position that the fire probably went over them. I also know that the situation was completely understandable.

Once down into that bowl-shaped valley it began to rain pretty hard, and after mopping up, we found that we couldn't drive back up out of the place. The tracks would just slip and slide on the wet grass and mud, and we were sort of like a bunch of ants trying to climb out of a slippery-sided coffee cup. In the middle of all that, the Japs began to rain mortar fire down on us. I remember parking the tank on the side of the slope and waiting.

Across the way was an infantry squad hugging the ground where the steep slope and the flat area met. As I watched, I saw them suddenly bury their faces in the mud and I knew we had a round incoming. And as soon as it hit, everyone raised their faces up, looking around. Soon, they buried their faces in the mud again, and I yelled on the intercom. "Incoming!" We couldn't hear any of the stuff above the idling engine noise, so watching the guys on the ground at least gave us some idea of what was happening. Finally, one of the tanks radioed and said that they had found a section of the slope that we could drive up and get out. One by one our platoon left those guys. I must say that while the shelling was going on, I would much rather have been with them. A Sherman makes one helluva big target.

37

By mid-April we were running into heavily defended areas. The Japanese troops were there to "do or die" and they made us pay dearly for every foot of ground we took. The frequent use of mines, and especially their 47mm anti-tank guns, accounted for a significant number of our tank platoon, and the rest of our company was being hit just as hard. The result: five-tank platoons now made do with two or three vehicles.

One morning we were told that our tank would be the reserve for the day. The 1st and 2d Platoons would be on the line and on call . . . and, lucky us, we'd hang back in reserve, relaxing. But, we had momentarily forgotten that the reserve platoon was always called on if one of the other two got in trouble.

The reserve unit that day consisted of two tanks, ours and one other, with the third tank left behind at company headquarters in case it was needed elsewhere before we got back. If we did indeed, get back.

Blissfully ignorant of the future, but knowing that it wouldn't be all that great, it didn't take very long before the call came in. 2d Platoon had gotten hold of more than it could handle, and could we please give them a hand?

Following their directions, our two "reserve" tanks drove to a small village that had been taken over by our infantry just that morning. In the middle of a narrow street, bounded on both sides by a stone wall, was a U.S. half-track, on fire. It was sitting at an angle so that there was some room, but not quite enough to allow us to get by without hitting it. The right front wheel on the half-track had been hit and was bowed under, and the entire nose of the vehicle was canted down and to the right. Unable to drive past the thing, I did what every Sherman driver loves to do. I drove over it! *Crunch, Snap,* and we were over and by, fire and all. OW told me on the intercom that "the low corner of it is even lower now."

A short block farther on we came to the end of the walled street and paused, looking out over a valley that appeared to be about three-quarters of a mile across. The road we were sitting on went down a slope, then leveled off, then went up a slope into the next village. About halfway out there, sitting alongside the road, was one of the 2d Platoon's tanks, also on fire. We learned that the other two tanks of the platoon had gone on and entered the village, where they had run into a mined area. Their tracks had been blown off, and there they sat, immobilized, with the crews still in them, and no infantry around. No U.S. Army infantry, that is. So, being the good old reserve unit, all we had to do was cross the valley with a good chance we would get hit by mortar and/or artillery fire, enter the village, find the two disabled tanks, get the guys out of them, turn around, and make a run for it across that wretched valley, all the time avoiding enemy fire. Piece of cake.

We found out that infantry had accompanied the tanks but withdrew back to the safety of the village because of the intense resistance put up by the Japanese.

So here we were, a two-tank reserve unit going to rescue two other tanks and doing so without infantry support. The gunfire was just too much for a foot soldier to survive very long, and because we intended to be in and out as fast as we could, the presence of troopers would, hopefully, not be absolutely necessary. We hoped their absence would not ruin the party, but you never know.

As we drove down the slope and approached the burning tank, I saw someone standing by it, watching us. I found out later that he was the driver, Larson. His hair was gone, most of his clothing had been burned off, and what I first thought was cloth hanging from his arms on closer inspection turned out to be flesh. He was burned so badly I didn't recognize him. He was the only crew member I could see, and I didn't know if anyone else was still inside or not. If they were, they were dead, that was for sure.

We continued on without meeting any enemy fire. No mortar, artillery, not even small-arms fire. All was quiet. Too quiet. I felt like we were driving into a trap of some sort, and I think the rest of the crew felt that way, too.

I drove up the short slope and into the small collection of houses. OW told me to look for a vacant lot to the right just past the first few buildings. As I poked along, slowly, Anderson kept the turret moving back and forth, looking for targets. Then OW and I saw them at the same time. Across the small field were the two tanks, side by side, both port side tracks blown off. OW told me to follow the track marks because the field had been mined. We would operate on the theory that if a tank had already rolled over the ground and nothing had blown up, then following the tracks should be fairly safe. And, that's what I did. The following reserve tank pulled up on the right side of the second tank and proceeded to pick up that crew via their escape hatch.

I pulled up on the left side of the first tank, and we dropped our escape hatch. It didn't take long to get the three men out of their tank and into ours, and we were ready to go. Two of that crew had already taken off on foot and were trying to get back by avoiding the road, which seemed to be targeted by the Japanese. The crewmen figured that going wide to the flanks would see them safely back.

OW watched through his periscope and gave me steering directions so that we could back out over the same track marks we had followed coming in. Once out of the field, I got the tank turned around, ready for the dash back across the valley. Our second reserve tank had already gotten out and was ready to roll ahead of us. As it started down the slope and onto the flat portion of the valley, it drew some heavy fire. What it was we couldn't tell exactly, but it was heavy enough to know that if they got hit, it would probably disable them. As we waited our turn, we realized that whatever it was that was firing at the first tank would soon be firing at us. When our turn came, I got old #60 going as fast as the engine governor would allow, probably all of twenty-two miles per hour. As I drove us out, Anderson kept the turret turned to cover our backside.

There were several explosions off to our right flank and I had to assume that they were meant for us, but none came close enough to cause us any real concern.

Safely across the valley and up into the village, we stopped and off-loaded the rescued tank crew. We then turned around and headed back to the tank sitting alongside the road that was still on fire. When we got there we learned that the burned driver had been picked up, but we found another crewman who was still alive.

A few days later I was talking with our medical officer and he told me that the driver, Larson, had passed away as a result of his burns.

Back at our bivouac area, I told OW that if we never drew the reserve spot again, it'd be too damn soon for me. Anderson said, "Amen." OW just sort of rolled his eyes. He was getting real good at that. Hey, lotsa practice, I guess.

For that day's action, OW was awarded the Silver Star, but we all felt that it was "just another day" for old #60.

38

A word or two here about the use of mortars and artillery by the Japanese. During the Leyte campaign we hadn't had to contend with either. At least not to any great extent. Okinawa was completely different. Not only did the enemy prove himself an expert in the use of these weapons, he also proved to our satisfaction that he had a lot of ammo stored and available.

A mortar or artillery strike could occur at any time. It didn't matter if it was fire directed against our troops during a daylight move or harassing fire at night, the Japs were only too eager to show us their capabilities.

One thing we soon noticed was the flare signals. At the close of the day, as we all were sitting around talking, smoking a last cigarette, and drinking that last cup of coffee before darkness closed in, sometimes a yellow parachute flare would appear high overhead. This was a signal used by the Japanese to alert their own troops that the immediate vicinity would soon see mortar and/or artillery fire. In other words, it meant: Get out . . . this is an intended impact zone.

One day just before sundown, *pop* went a parachute flare. We all looked up and, sure enough, it was a yellow one and right above us. From past experience we knew we had another five or ten minutes before the artillery said "hello," so we all got up very leisurely and began preparations for crawling under the tank for the night. All of us except Jim Anderson. He sat watching the flare for a moment and then said, "I'm gonna get that silk chute. Fern [his wife] can make a blouse out of it for my daughter." With that, he jumped up, grabbed a shovel, and away he went, running toward where it looked as if the flare, still burning, would land.

As luck and the wind would have it, the flare drifted slowly by the headquarters tank, where several officers stood watching the show. As it got lower, it became apparent to all of us that the burning magnesium was dropping almost straight down into our 75mm ammunition storage dump. Jim put on the brakes. All thoughts of a silk blouse for his daughter were now gone, and replaced by the fact that a "situation" was developing, and he was right at ground zero, so to speak. The flare landed, and yes, it landed right in the middle of the ammo dump. Our 75mm shells were shipped encased in cardboard tubes, three packed together in a cloverleaf configuration. The cardboard, or whatever the stuff was, had been treated so as to make it water-resistant, and I guess that's what made it burn so slowly as the flare lay there, bright fire and white smoke marking its location.

The time for watching and wondering was past, and Jim, armed with his trusty shovel, jumped into the battle, throwing dirt onto the fire. He was in a most dangerous situation, and he knew it. All he could think of was getting that fire out before we all went up in one big blast. A couple dozen or so shovelfuls of dirt brought things under control. It was then that all of us realized we had just stood there, doing nothing except watching while a brave man did what he felt had to be done. What had started out as a lark ended up being a most serious yet happy situation. Happy for all of us that Anderson knew when to not back down. A brave move by a gutsy guy. For his actions that day, Anderson was awarded the Soldier's Medal. If I'd had anything to say about it, he would have also gotten a chrome-plated shovel. Suitably engraved.

39

The Sherman was, after all, nothing more or less than a mobile artillery piece. In the European war zone, tank-to-tank fights were not uncommon, and despite all its limitations and faults, the Sherman gave an excellent accounting of itself. But here in the Pacific, it was valued as a piece of direct-fire artillery that could be moved about in support of the infantry. This was especially true on Okinawa.

One day the infantry contacted us and requested that we rendezvous with them near a very deep gorge. When we arrived, an infantry second lieutenant told us that they had to go some distance to the flank, drop down into the bottom of the canyon, and then assault the opposite face of it in order to gain the high ground where the enemy forces were dug in. Could we help him?

There were two tanks in our platoon that day, and we decided to drive up to the middle of the high ground, overlooking the canyon, and direct our fire across toward the far lip. As we prepared to move out, our second tank threw a track, and that left us as a force of one to do the job. Everyone in our battalion was well aware that we all were supporting the infantry, and having seen our troops in action, we needed no further incentive to do the best job we could. And so, with only half of our original two-tank platoon, we set out to "do the job."

We began firing as requested by the infantry officer and at first directed most of our attention to the center portion of the ridge across the way. We then began to work from the right flank toward the middle, and on to the left flank. We fired just about everything we had except the armor piercing.

When we got to the bottom of the ammunition pile, OW radioed our other tank, and they told us they were having trouble getting the track back on, but to come on down and they would off-load their ammo into our tank. We did just that, and by late afternoon we had fired two full tank loads of 75mm shells into that ridge. The infantry shoved off after we shot our last round and made its way down into the bottom of the canyon and up to the other side. A few days later I saw the infantry officer and asked him if we had done him any good. He grinned and said that they hardly fired a shot. The top of the ridge had been "swept clean." This was a rare case of the Japs not being dug in at all, or not deep enough in their caves as they usually were.

Who did all the work that day? Anderson and Roy Greenup our fearless gunner and loader, me, my assistant driver, and OW just sort of became an audience of three while they did all the work. Of course later, back at our bivouac area, all of us had to pitch in and reload old #60 with 75 ammo. As I recall, our capacity was something under a hundred rounds, but that's the maximum load. I don't think we always carried the full set, which tended to vary somewhat depending upon availability at any particular time. With all of us working together each evening—refueling the tank using five-gallon cans, cleaning the 75mm gun (a two-man job), and resupplying ammo—I guess it wasn't a free ride after all. But the three of us agreed that it was nice watching two experts at work.

40

We rumbled along, somewhere between Tombstone Ridge behind us and Kakazu Ridge up ahead. The last thought on my mind was antitank fire.

I was just behind our platoon leader's tank, keeping a close watch for mines. Suddenly a shell blew a hole in the dirt in front of us.

"OW, did you see that?"

"What . . . see what?"

"Something just hit the ground between the lieutenant's tank and us . . . !"

"You sure?"

"Hell yes I'm sure, I was looking at the ground when it hit. We might be drawing fire."

OW got on the radio.

"I told the lieutenant, and he says it was probably a stray round."

"Yeah, you mean like nobody would dare fire at us on purpose, right?"

"Well, that's what he said. What am I supposed to do?"

We were going down the road in answer to the infantry's request that we sweep a small valley. They had been held up by enemy fire, and it looked like a job for tanks. There were two of our tanks that day, Lieutenant Schluter's and us. Schluter was a small-statured man, soft-spoken, and a Regular Army enlistee. He had started army life as a private in the horse cavalry in Texas, patrolling the Texas/Mexico border. From horses to tanks was a large step in the early days of mechanization. He was a nice guy and well liked by his fellow officers as well as the men he commanded.

As we were driving into the valley, with a small ridge at our left, the infantry was just on the reverse side of the ridge, waiting for us to show up. After a bit the lieutenant turned left, and as we followed, I could see that we were now driving past the low ridge and down the right-hand edge of the valley. Schluter's plan, as requested by the infantry, was to drive to the far end of the small basin, turn left, cross it, and then drive back alongside the far edge of the bowl. Meantime, we would take care of anything we observed.

We reached the far end of the valley and Schluter turned left, driving across the base of it. What he hadn't noticed, and no one else had either, was that midway across the end of the valley was an intersecting gully, where, we discovered to our total astonishment, the Japanese had put one of their 47mm rapid-fire antitank guns along with a machine gun unit to protect the AT gun crew.

We were following close behind Schluter's tank. Too close, really, but the situation thus far didn't seem too dangerous. As his tank came broadside to the gully on his right, it suddenly seemed to be coming apart. I stopped the tank and looked with amazement. The first thing that caught my eye was the tank's tow cable. It was flying through the air, stretched out straight as a string. It was so straight that I thought at first it was his antenna! All of us carried the tow cable hooked to the front left clevis pin. Schluter's driver had tried to turn the tank toward the gun and took a hit on the clevis pin, which sheared it off. I steered our tank to give Anderson a clear shot at this guy. The 47mm was at the end of the draw, and the only way we were going to be able to fire at him was to pull up almost directly in front of him. As soon as the nose of my tank poked into his view, the antitank gunner fired a couple of shots right in front of us, into the dirt. When they hit, I realized that that was what I'd seen earlier in the day. I backed us up a couple of feet, and we fired smoke into the ground between our tank and Schluter's in order to cover him.

By this time his driver had gotten the tank turned around so that it presented its left side to the Japanese, who began to pour fire into it. Some of the crew got out and began to run back down into the valley. I guess in the confusion they didn't realize that we were sitting right there a few feet away, waiting to pick them up.

Our tank was shielded by Schluter's, but there was no way we could get at the antitank gun without poking our nose into its line of fire. That would have ended up with us in the same situation as Schluter's tank—knocked out.

OW called for me to back up and "get the hell outta here!" Which I did, gladly. We drove back to the other end of the valley, and it was an easy shot from there to take out the little 47mm gun.

As an aside, the 47mm rapid-fire antitank gun was a wonderful weapon. It could be fired in an almost semiautomatic mode. That is, as fast as the gunner could pull the lanyard, the weapon would spout them off faster than one of us could say, "We're hit, let's get out of this thing . . . now!"

I didn't get a chance to examine Lieutenant Schluter's tank closely at a later time, but did manage to get a photo of it. We were told that it had been hit by eleven shots and that nine had penetrated. Recalling that day, I would estimate that all eleven shots had been fired within a span of seconds. To actually witness that, right in front of us no more than twenty feet away, was a sight I'll not soon forget.

41

When they designed the Sherman, little regard was given to crew comfort. By that I mean there was no air-conditioning, no fridge, easy chair, none of those little intimate touches that make a tank a home. One of the most important items that had been left out was . . . you guessed it . . . a place to, well, wee-wee. As you must know, we tankers didn't actually say "wee-wee." But to keep it clean and simple, that's what we'll use.

Usually, one of the last things we crewmen did before mounting up on the tank was relieve ourselves. Our days were long, stretching from an hour or so after sunup until an hour or so before sundown. Those hours in-between were spent sitting in our respective seats, and that was about it. No walking around to stretch the old leg muscles. And absolutely no wee-weeing inside the tank. With one exception. An empty 75mm cannon shell could be used and then tossed out of the turret's pistol port. The receiving and handling, and eventually opening the port and tossing, was all handled by the loader. An unsung hero if ever there was one. As the rest of us were wont to say, "Better he than me."

One day our tank had been sitting behind some cover, waiting for a request from the infantry. We'd been there about an hour or so when I had the urge to go. I began to think of other things, figuring the feeling would go away. But it didn't, of course, it just got worse, as in unbearable.

We hadn't been involved with the enemy yet that morning, and I wasn't sure if we had any of the invaluable empty shell cases up in the turret. Using the intercom, I called our gunner, Anderson.

"Jim . . . ah . . . do we have an empty shell case up there? I really could use one right about now."

"Just a minute."

I heard the *r r r r r r* as the turret was traversed, and then the gun was elevated to a random angle. I heard the *clunk-snap* of the breechblock as it closed. And I damn sure heard the roar of the 75mm's BOOOOOOM as our gun was fired. Then I was told that an empty shell casing was all mine. It was handed down, hot and still smoking. Matter of fact, Anderson said, "Be very careful of that, it's pretty hot . . . if you know what I mean. Heh, heh."

Well, I made sure that I was damn careful in its use, and as I handed it back up the turret to our loader, I asked if anybody knew how much one of those 75mm shells cost.

"Yeah, I heard they cost $18.75, same as a twenty-five-dollar war bond."

I thought for a moment and said, "Well, I just wish I could thank whoever bought that particular war bond. It meant the world to me."

One of the wise guys in the crew said, "I don't think that is quite what was in their mind when the War Department urged us all to 'buy bonds and support the war effort.'"

I said, "I don't care what they had in mind, it's just damn nice to know that we have a way to do what we have to do from time to time, even at $18.75 a wee-wee."

42

Sometimes it seemed as though bad things happened in bunches. Or lumps. Such was a day that none of us would soon forget.

It started with the Japanese artillery trying to show off. Those guys didn't have to prove anything to anyone on the island. Soon after we landed it became apparent that there was more than enough artillery here, that the Japs were excellent shots, and that their ammo supply seemed to be endless. To make the entire situation even worse, they had occupied the island for such a long time, planning, installing, and in every way preparing for us to invade them, it's no wonder they were so successful with their big guns.

All of which leads me to what happened to an otherwise fine evening.

We had not been under our tank very long, still talking in whispers as was our custom. Whispering was preferred to talking at regular volume because we didn't want to attract the attention of any Japanese infiltrators. Of which there were aplenty. Anyhow, as we lay there, whispering, we heard incoming. It was loud, and when it hit, we knew that the night was going to be a long one. The impact area was just past us a hundred feet or so. Way too close, for sure. No one said anything when suddenly two more rounds hit. The impact zone was moving away from us, thankfully, but where it was moving to gave us all chills. Directly ahead was our ammo dump, and alongside that our fuel dump. I figured a full colonel must have decided on locating the two dumps that close together, because that's where the intended target was, and that's what they hit.

Once they registered one or two shells on target, all hell cut loose. I don't know how many shells rained down on that area, but after the first few, the resultant fire and explosions made further shelling unnecessary.

The underside of the tank was lit up like it was daylight outside. None of us moved, not knowing if the impact area might shift over to us next or what.

Finally Anderson raised his head up and watched the show for awhile.

"Bob," he said, "you ought to get your camera out and get some pictures of this."

"Jim, first of all, I don't have my camera with me. It's inside the tank, where I think I might like to be. And second, I don't usually bring the camera to bed with me at night. There's so little to photograph then."

He just looked at me for a second, then turned his attention back to the light show. Finally I couldn't stand it any longer and raised up just high enough to see what was taking place. Fifty-five-gallon steel drums holding aviation gasoline were burning, and every once in awhile one would fly up into the night sky, leaving a trail of fire behind it like a giant skyrocket. It really was an awesome sight. Mixed in with the "skyrockets" were colorful explosions deep within the fire itself; blues, yellows, and reds mostly.

"Jim, my camera is in my musette bag, right alongside my seat. If you'd like to get it for me, I'd be happy to take some photos." He said some colorful army words that I really didn't recognize, but understood them to mean that he wasn't interested in moving from where he was.

"Chicken," I said.

"Right," he replied.

The next day we moved out, assisting the infantry as usual and in general doing what we regularly did during the daylight hours. There was a lot of talk about the little show we had witnessed the night before. The general consensus was that the ammo and fuel would soon be replaced as we knew that the amount of material being unloaded on the beach was more than enough to keep us going.

As it turned out, we didn't move about much that day. We did roll through a few places where the Japs had made some stubborn stands. Evidence of the fight was everywhere, including more than a few enemy bodies.

It was an impossibility to bury the enemy soldiers individually. As the heat made it imperative that this disposal be done as soon as possible, it was common practice to bulldoze a large hole and push the enemy bodies into it. A decomposing corpse, bloated in the sun to the point where it had burst open, would be covered with maggots and flies. The stench was overwhelming, and it is a smell that cannot be gotten used to. As I write this all these years later, I can vividly remember it. Burial was the only answer. But because the front lines sometimes didn't move ahead very fast, and dozers couldn't come up to do the job while fighting was ongoing, the landscape would be littered with more bodies than we'd like to see.

It was difficult to open up a can of meat and beans and begin eating while the flies from nearby corpses landed on our faces, our lips, and on the food we were trying to eat.

We came back to our camp and put the tank over the same hole we had used last night. After refueling and resupplying the tank with ammo, we cleaned the guns and prepared our dinner. As sundown approached, we did all the last-minute things we had to do and one by one crawled under old #60, prepared to spend another night watching and waiting for whatever might want to visit us there in the darkness.

As soon as we got settled, it became apparent that somewhere along the line we had run over somebody. A Jap soldier. A Jap that was dead and had been for several days. We could smell him. Parts of him must have been stuck in the tracks.

Being the driver, I at once became the villain.

I was informed by the other four members of our formerly happy crew that I was the lowest of lowlifes . . . ever. I was the worst thing that had ever happened to anyone, and so on and on into the night. Well, they refused to believe me when I told them that I hadn't run over this guy on purpose, and that I hated the smell just as much as they did, maybe even more. Of course, that didn't mean a thing to my pals, and so there we five lay, mumbling, cursing, trying not to breathe, and wishing for daylight to arrive soon so we could get out from under and get away from the tracks.

Just to let us know that they played no favorites, the Japanese artillery decided to say "hello" to our tank company again that night. And, oh yes, shells were falling all over the place. The noise was earth-shattering, screaming as if the shells were headed right under our tank, looking for us. But what really made it memorable was what happened right in the middle of all that.

A shell landed very close, the ground shuddered, dirt was flung, and something hit me on the side of the face. Hard. I mean it hurt. I lay there for an instant, then realized that I had no feeling in the cheek and jaw area, at all. I reached a trembling hand up to feel. It was sticky, and as I pushed on it I couldn't feel anything. Oh, my God, I whispered that I'd been hit. Somebody asked me where, and I said the left side of my face.

Someone reached over and gently felt along my head and chin . . . and began to giggle. The giggle soon turned into full-fledged laughter, and I must say I was dumbfounded to think that one of my dear friends would react in such a rotten-assed way.

"You think it's funny? You bastard," I hissed, still running my fingers over my wound. It was still numb, and no pain . . . yet.

"Ahhh . . . Bob, try feeling your face again, and this time scrape off some of that mud." That was followed by more hysterical laughter. I could hear him saying something to the rest of the guys and they, too, began laughing. Hell's bells, the shelling was still going on, the dead Jap still stunk, my face was ripped off, and these characters were having a ball.

At my expense. I gingerly scraped at my face and brought out a handful of mud! I knew at once what had happened. A slab of that mud had been shaken loose by the nearby impact of shells, and had fallen about a foot or more to land on the side of my face. I was so relieved that I forgave them, more or less, and joined in, more or less, with their laughter (you have to be a good sport or they eat you alive every chance they get).

After a while the shelling stopped and everything quieted down. We lay there silently, and finally one of the guys said, "I hope you aren't too mad at us for laughing. It really was funny, ya know."

I lay there a minute and then said, "Oh, I don't mind a little humor now and then. Especially if it's the other guy I'm laughing at."

"You're not planning on getting even with us or anything, are you?"

"Well, that's what I'm considering now. You know, there's a lot of dead Japs lying around, and I am the driver, you know, and I could just . . ."

I knew that I had found the perfect weapon, and none of these guys were gonna fool with me. No siree, not as long as I was doing the driving. I took a deep "stinky" breath, smiled, and went to sleep.

43

April 30 is a day that I'll always remember for several reasons. It marked thirty straight days on the line for us, and it also meant that we were going to be relieved at noon. Until that morning we'd not heard anything about getting a rest, and as a matter of fact, we all had sort of resigned ourselves to seeing the war go on and on until either we had killed all of them or they had killed all of us. From personal observation, at this point it appeared to be a close race.

We'd had replacements come in who lasted only a few days and then, just like that, they were gone. Either wounded or killed.

One second lieutenant was killed his first day with us. He insisted on riding with the hatch open and his head out. Shrapnel from a mortar did the job.

So many of our company had left, we began to get the feeling that there wasn't any end to all of this. Couch had been hit by the recoil of his own 75mm cannon. His tank had been engaging an enemy cave, and as he was preparing to re-load, the tank hit a hole and threw him forward. At the same time the gunner fired his gun. All things combined to catch Couch on the head as that breech moved back twenty-one inches in recoil. He was evacuated to the hospital and later returned to combat duty on Okinawa until the war's end.

Personally, I had gotten to the point where I "knew" that sooner or later I was going to get hit. The only question left in my mind was how bad would it be? Looking back on it all, it's difficult to realize how psychologically and emotionally messed up we were. When I arrived at the point where I *knew* that I was going to get it, my nerves were just about shot. I think I was hanging on more by force of habit than anything else. And I think the rest of the crew were pretty much in the same state. OW was no exception. He went to the field hospital on the beach to be checked out. He couldn't keep food down, and he was vomiting blood every once in awhile.

On the twenty-ninth we were told that at noon on the thir-tieth we would be replaced by fresh troops and tanks and given a ten-day rest and resupply period. That afternoon we got our new tank commander, Lieutenant Bomax, temporar-ily replacing OW. It was to be his first battle action, and he was looking forward to being with us. We had a reputation of being a lucky tank. Knock on wood, somebody.

That night I listened to Anderson and Bomax comparing notes on their daughters. It turned out that both of the young gals were about the same age and, of course, photos were hauled out of wallets and compared. Their whispered conversation went on for several hours that night, and I felt good for them.

Next day we moved out to some cover just behind the infantry, as usual, and waited. Captain Todd had gone to the rear to prepare our bivouac area, and the company had been left in charge of Lieutenant Finian. As we sat and watched, fresh infantrymen relieved the combat-weary 96th Division Deadeyes, one man at a time, foxhole by foxhole. Amazingly, even though the Japanese could see all of this going on, not a shot was fired. It looked to be an almost routine maneuver.

Suddenly our radio crackled and Bomax gave me the command to move out. We were ordered up ahead of the lines and moved in close to the base of a fairly high ridge. The infantry continued to be replaced, and still no firing was taking place.

And then it happened. Lieutenant Finian ordered us to begin firing into caves and emplacements on the ridge face. I couldn't figure out what was happening, but hell, orders are orders. So Anderson began firing. Off to our right was another tank, commanded by Sgt. Hoyt Boggs, and he too began firing into the caves. I remembered that Boggs, a very likable guy, hailed from Alabama.

Anyway, we sat there and shelled the ridge, and suddenly I heard heavy enemy mortar or artillery fire exploding to the rear of us. I knew from past experience that we would soon be ordered out of the area, so I grabbed the shift lever with my right hand, preparing to go into reverse as soon as I got the word from Bomax.

Right at that moment, we were hit. I didn't hear or feel anything. I can only assume that the concussion overrode my hearing and feeling. I only knew that something had happened, but didn't know what. It was all very strange, and I'd not felt anything like this before. I looked back up into the turret and saw someone's foot disappearing out of the commander's open hatch. I had been out of it long enough for three people to get out of the turret! Everywhere I looked, it was as if I had red goggles on. I'd guessed it had something to do with the concussion.

I looked to my right, and my assistant driver, Kahn, was frantically jerking at the hatch lever. He yelled that we were on fire and that the hatch was jammed. Dust in the air was so thick it almost obscured my vision. I realized that the concussion had blown the dust up from all the nooks and crannies, and that it wasn't smoke from a fire. I yelled at him to calm down, that there was no fire. He stopped for an instant and then reached up and pulled the lever back and opened his hatch. And just like that, he was gone. I was alone in a tank in front of the lines, and as far as I could tell still in one piece. I wasn't frightened, and I don't know why I wasn't. Probably not enough good sense to fully understand the situation.

The engine was still running, and I tried to get it into gear. When I moved the shift lever into the gear slot, I could hear and feel a tremendous noise of gears clashing. I was sure that we had been hit on the back deck, and something in the shift mechanism was messed up, too. I tried several times to get it into gear, but always with the same negative result. It was almost as though the shift lever was locked out of the transmission or the clutch was knocked out, or maybe both.

About this time I became aware of a voice. It was Anderson. He and Bomax were crouched down alongside the front left drive sprocket, yelling at me to get out. I hollered back and told them I'd be right out. I reached over and got hold of my Thompson. Every morning I very carefully laid it down into the space behind the dash panel. It fit well there. Today it seemed stuck. I yanked and pulled, but it wouldn't move. I realized that I was doing the same thing Kahn had been doing, getting in too big a hurry. Anderson was yelling again, and after one more unsuccessful yank, I decide to hell with it, I'd better get out before the Japs hit us again.

I knew that with all the hatches open, my chances of getting out unhurt were slim to none. I had opened my hatch about the same time Kahn had finally opened his, and now decided to get out while I could. I stood up and as I did my head was jerked backward. I had forgotten to unplug my helmet intercom cord. At the same time a bullet whizzed by, striking the edge of the hatch just about where my head had been!

I dropped back down onto the seat and then very carefully unplugged the intercom cord, grabbed the hatch opening with both hands, and using a combination of hands and arms plus some mighty strong pushes from my legs, propelled myself up and out of the hatch opening. I landed in a heap in the dirt and scrambled around to the side where Anderson and Bomax were crouched. The air was full of small-arms fire. The dry branchlike snap of the bullets as they passed by was very unnerving, to say the least.

I yelled, "We'd better get the hell out of here. Those guys are bound and determined to get us." The lieutenant disagreed and said that the gunfire was all from our own troops covering us. I knew from experience that whenever any of us fired at the enemy, they always fired back. I also knew that regardless of who was firing, it was too close for comfort.

Without further conversation, I took off on a dead run. Anderson came right after me, and I'm not sure what the lieutenant did. As I ran, I zigzagged and even fell down a couple of times. The falling down was not deliberate. It was a case of me wanting to go faster than my legs could keep up. I was frantic. A very unheroic-like figure.

I looked up ahead and saw a small depression in the ground. Good. I'll just slide into that and see what happens. I slid headfirst and as soon as I stopped, I turned around so that I was facing the enemy. Anderson came crashing down into the hole and crawled up alongside me.

I yelled, "Why the hell are you following me?"

He said, "You've been in the infantry. I figured you'd know what to do."

I yelled back, "All I know is to try to get as far away in as short a time as I can."

About that time, bullets started hitting the dirt around our hole, some very close. Friendly fire my ass. I looked around and saw Boggs's tank headed back. He must have been in first gear because they were moving very slowly. I jumped up and ran to the front of it, waving my hands for them to stop. They did, and I motioned for the escape hatch to be dropped. While I crouched there, Anderson and Lieutenant Bomax joined me. The hatch dropped, and because of the amount of small-arms fire around us, I said that I was going to run around to the rear and slide under the tank and on up to the escape hatch. I didn't trust getting in front of the tank.

The tank was stopped alongside a small ridge, maybe fourteen feet high, and I thought some of the rifle fire had been coming from there. Again the lieutenant disagreed, saying that the Japs weren't firing at us, it was all our own troops firing at the enemy. He said he was going to crawl under the tank from the front. I didn't want to waste any more time discussing the situation and ran to the rear, slid under the tank, wiggled my way to the open hatch, and in I went. Anderson was right behind me. I got up through the hatch and went on up into the turret basket to make room for Anderson and Bomax.

I sat on the turret floor because there wasn't much room to sit anywhere else. My head was directly behind the breech-block of the 75mm. I knew that the recoil of that gun was twenty-one inches, and I guessed that my head was just about . . . yeah, twenty-one inches away. I glanced down through the turret struts and saw Anderson looking into the escape hatch. I yelled and asked what the holdup was. He hollered back that Bomax had been fatally hit in the back as he crawled under the tank. Bomax had slid under the front and was a couple of feet short of the hatch opening when he was hit. Anderson said he was trying to get hold of him to drag him into the tank.

About that time the 75mm cannon began to elevate. I asked Boggs what was going on, and he said there was a Jap on the ridge just above us. He said the guy had a satchel charge that was so heavy he couldn't lift it. He was trying to drag it over to the edge so he could drop it on us!

"Well, don't fire that 75mm," I yelled, "the recoil will get me for sure." Okay, they were going to fire the .30-caliber coaxially mounted machine gun at him. The gunner punched the firing button and, so help me, it fired once and jammed! Boggs then opened his hatch and began firing at the guy with his .45 pistol. While he was doing that, I unstrapped his Thompson from under the lip of the radio and handed it up to him after he fired the last shot from his handgun.

All this time Anderson was trying to haul Bomax's body up to the hatch so he could get him in, but the weight was just too much, considering the lousy position he had to be in when looking down into that hatch opening. There wasn't enough room around the hatch opening to kneel on, just a small area where your feet could be placed. Imagine standing on the lip of an opening and bending over at the waist because there is no place to put your knees. Then try to reach down a foot or so below the level of your feet and drag 185 pounds or so up into the tank. I don't think there was anyone I ever ran across who could have done it, and yet Jim tried. And tried some more.

Finally he yelled up at me that he just couldn't get Bomax into the tank. In the meantime, Boggs got his man, but we didn't know who else would come up and try to finish the job with the satchel charge.

I heard Captain Todd calling us on the radio, and I grabbed the mike and answered him. Boggs had his hands full right then. I gave Todd the situation and told him that we should probably get out of here or we'd lose another tank. He wanted Anderson to double-check Bomax; he didn't want to leave him, and we didn't, either. But it wasn't a case of what we wanted to do, it was what we had to do. Boggs would rip off a few shots once in awhile, Anderson would strain and pull to no avail, and I finally radioed Captain Todd and told him we had just about had it. He then told us, very reluctantly, to move on out.

I told him that #60 was still sitting, all hatches open, engine running . . . a perfect thing for the Japs to crawl into tonight. He ordered it destroyed by other tanks, and informed me that the infantry would recover the lieuenant's body as soon as it was dark. I silently thanked our dear Lord that Bomax would not be left behind.

The captain was waiting for us just behind the hill, and after thanking Boggs for the lift, Anderson and I walked over to his jeep. He told us to get in, he'd give us a ride back. Anderson got in first, in the middle, and I sat on the outside. We were all in the front of the jeep. As we started off, Anderson suddenly said that he couldn't feel his legs. I asked him if he'd been hit, and he said he didn't know. I felt both of his legs and didn't find any evidence of a gunshot. He was shaking all over, and I knew that the terrible thing we had just gone through was getting to both of us. I put my arm around his shoulder, and he began to quietly sob. I knew that he blamed himself for not being able to get Bomax into the tank, but there just wasn't any way he could have done anything other than what he did.

The captain let me off at the old bivouac area, and he and Anderson drove on. I walked over to the hole where old #60 had been that night, looked at some of our gear there, and sat down. Out of nowhere Kahn appeared. He had run back to the rear and gotten a ride to our area. Our commander killed, our gunner out of it for the time being, and our loader, Roy Greenup, was only the Good Lord knew where. Kahn said that Greenup was okay, that he was back talking with some of the infantry when he last saw him. And so here we sat, Kahn and me. I kept running the day over and over in my mind, wondering what we could have done differently so it would have ended up a bit better than it did.

What a dismal sight. What a lousy way to end our first thirty days of fighting. My nerves were so shot I was shaking all over. I went over to our company medic at his foxhole. I guess I hoped he could give me something for my nerves but all he could come up with was what we called green pills, a super aspirin.

About that time Japanese mortar fire began landing in our area. I looked around and realized that with old #60 gone, I had nothing to crawl under. Then I saw a tank from our reserve platoon nearby. I started a fast run toward it. Just as I got close I could see some guys under it, but I didn't slow up a bit. *Wham,* I hit the front opening at full speed and slid right through the middle of a poker game! Cards flew and curses were rained down on me as the mortar shells kept on landing. Finally all was quiet and I crawled out from under the tank. At the front of it was someone's duffel bag, full of shrapnel holes.

A really lousy way to end the first thirty days!

PART SIX

New Tanks, New Men, Old Fears

44

Just the idea that we didn't have to think about going up on the line tomorrow, or the next day . . . or any day until ten of them had passed by, was a tremendous lift for our spirits. But before we could start relaxing, we had work to do.

Our few remaining tanks were driven to a collection area and left there. And, sitting right before us, waiting, were eighteen almost brand-new Sherman M4's. This tank had the new 500-horsepower, liquid-cooled, Ford V-8 engine, and the performance difference between it and the old 385-horsepower Continental was unbelievable. The tank was still slow and cumbersome, but it was so much better than our old one, we felt like we had found a new toy under the Christmas tree.

It was a brief drive to our new rest area, so my hands-on experience was short-lived. Still, all in all, I was very encouraged by our beloved, updated monster.

With the tanks parked all in a row at our new home, most of the crews dug sleeping holes alongside of them. The Japanese were miles from where we were, but old habits die hard, and we had learned that the enemy didn't necessarily always play by the rules.

We had hot showers, hot chow, and even movies. The movie theater was the outdoor type, and seating consisted of palm tree trunks laid down in rows. But no one was complaining. Old hands were quick to tell us to bring a poncho along in case of rain. We found that the information was good, because it was almost guaranteed that showers would hit sometime during the movie. We were told that Japanese stragglers would sometimes sneak into the chow lines and even sit through a movie with no one being the wiser. Jumpy as we all were, this was an added incentive to keep on the alert.

Matter of fact, the first night we were at our new quarters, someone in an adjacent outfit cut loose with a rifle, and soon the whole place was lit up with small-arms firing. It was a false alarm, but hey, a guy can't be too careful.

The first morning was wonderful. No orders to go anywhere or do anything. Other than clean up our tanks, check the ammo supply, look over the engine, and, well, get ready for what was going to happen in nine more days.

I had been giving that a whole lot of thought, going back up on line that is, and the more I thought about it, the more nervous and shook up I got. I was certain that my nerves wouldn't be able to stand up under much more, but I really didn't know what I could do about it. Then, out of the blue, Anderson gave me the answer, or, at first I thought he had. I saw him walking toward our tank, stopping once in awhile to talk with someone. Finally he got to me. And he wasted no time in coming to the point.

"Bob, Captain Todd told me I'd had enough, and I'm not going back up in the tank. He's assigned me to maintenance, and I know that I and Sergeant Smith over there can get along just fine."

"Hey, partner, I'm happy for you. What did you say to Todd when he said that. Was he mad about us losing the lieutenant or what?"

"No, I just told him we'd done the best we could, and he said not to worry about it, that he understood completely."

"Well, good enough. I'm gonna find him and tell him that I really don't think I can do it again, either, Jim. My nerves are totally shot." We talked a bit more and then he left. As I watched him walk away, I felt like I had just lost my best friend.

I started to look for Captain Todd. I was going to grovel, cry, get hysterical, or whatever it would take, but I wanted him to know that I was all through. I just plain had had it. I honestly had serious doubts about my ability to continue.

At every tank I came to, I asked if they had seen the captain. I left a message with everyone that if they saw him, to tell him I wanted to talk with him. After about twenty minutes of this I saw him down the line, walking my way. As we came together, I said, "Good morning, sir." He returned the greeting and said, "I've been looking for you."

"Well," I said, "I've been looking for you, too, sir."

"Okay," he said, "you go first."

"No, mine can wait. What is it, sir?"

"Well, I want you to take command of number 57. I know you'll do a fine job."

I stood there looking at him and realized what a spot he was in. He had to get his company ready to go back on line, and it was going to be filled with troops who had never seen combat before. He was going to need all the help he could get.

"So, Sergeant, what is it you wanted to see me about?"

"Ahhh . . . it was nothing, sir. Just an idea I had, but thinking it over, I know it's no good."

"You sure? I'm right here, and if there's anything bothering you, now's the time." He grinned as he spoke.

"Oh, yeah, I'm sure, sir, no problem . . . and thank you for your confidence."

"Should have been done a long time ago. Carry on." He smiled, and we both went our separate ways. And me . . . I went back to #57, sat down alongside it, and tried to make sense out of what I'd just done to myself. I looked around and saw that three new men were sitting in the hole, their gear stacked alongside them, all of them looking at me with a sort of lost sheep expression. Talk about the blind leading the blind.

"My name is Dick, and I'm the commander of this tank. You are now crew members of it. I'll get you assigned in a minute, but for now I just want you to understand that this is *your* tank, number 57, and I'm the boss. You'll do as I tell you, and maybe we'll all get out of this mess alive. But no guarantees. Any questions? No? Great . . . now let's find out what we have here and go from there."

45

One of my new guys trained at Fort Knox and had actually driven tanks before. Not in combat, but, heck, any idiot knows that the tank drives no differently in combat than it does at any other time. Right? Right. He confessed that he had "driven one only a short distance, like maybe a quarter of a mile or so." I told him not to worry, that we'd give him some on-the-job training.

One of the other men also trained at Knox, but he wasn't any more into things than the first guy. Happily, they all had a general idea of the tank's layout, and I asked them their preferences for position. No one had any great desire to be anything special except, maybe, alive. So that's the way I assigned them. The one who had driven a quarter of a mile got the driver's slot, and the other two flipped for assistant driver and loader.

My new gunner was a former loader from the 2d Platoon, and he was as happy as anyone under these circumstances would be. Which is to say not real happy, but accepting it all with grace. I knew from the past experiences he had had that he was someone I could count on.

Here I was, the guy who couldn't go it anymore. The fellow who was gonna grovel in the dirt and cry until the captain removed him from combat duty. Yep, here I was with four other guys who were just as keyed up as I was, and all of them counting on me to pull them through. I kept wondering, who was going to pull me through?

One of the first things we did was decide on a name for our new tank. We had several good suggestions and finally

settled on COME 'N GET IT. We painted the name on each
sponson near the nose, and we painted IT on the 75mm gun
barrel.

Despite the fact that we were behind the lines and supposedly there were no enemy soldiers about, our crew, like most
of the others, still pulled guard duty at our own tank each
night. We no longer slept under the tank, and only one person
was needed to be awake for guard. Fortunately, we didn't get
much rain while we were there, so that was one thing we
didn't have to deal with.

The days went by slowly at first, then seemed to pick up
speed as the end of our R&R approached. I pulled guard
duty from midnight to 4:00 a.m., at which time I was relieved by one of the others. I had that time slot on the last
evening . . . the next day we were due to move back up on
the line.

As I sat at the side, near the front of our tank, I began to
feel my nerves giving out. It was all I could do to keep from
breaking down. I just was not able to envision myself going
into the fight again. As I sat there, I made a decision not to
go. I pulled my .45 pistol out of the holster, eased the slide
back, and chambered a round. The gun was now cocked and
needed only slight pressure on the trigger to cause it to fire. I
decided to shoot myself and, come what may, avoid further
combat. I placed the muzzle near my left leg, about midway
between my ankle and my knee, in the fleshy part. I sat there
running the upcoming dialogue through my mind: "I had my
pistol loaded because I was on guard. I thought I heard
something and was going to shoot it and somehow squeezed
the trigger too soon and shot myself in the leg." I knew that
everyone would know what a phony story it was, but I was
at the point where I could face anything except more combat.

I must have sat there for fifteen minutes or more . . . then
dropped the clip, jacked the round out of the chamber, eased
the slide back into position, and wondered if I was too big a
coward to do even this. Somehow, my nerves did quiet down
a bit after that. Maybe it was the fact that I had actually put

the gun to my leg that gave me courage. "Now I know how easy it will be." "I can do it anytime I want." And so on.

Even though I hadn't pulled the trigger, I felt that somehow I'd betrayed my crew and the rest of the outfit for even going as far as I had. I couldn't help but wonder if I was the only one who felt like this. If there were any others, they had my heartfelt sympathy and total understanding.

46

It was May 11, and our ten-day rest and resupply period had come and gone. Seemed like five days. It reminded me of the time we had been sitting behind a little knoll for what seemed hours. I knew that as soon as it was late afternoon, we'd be going back. I got on the intercom and asked Anderson (he had the wristwatch that still worked), "Jamie, what time is it?" A pause, and he said something like, "It's 1623." I sat and sat, and waited, and finally, when I was sure that at least an hour had gone by, I asked him again, "Hey, Anderson, what time is it?"

"It's 1650." Then he added, "Time sure flies when you're doing something you like. Heh, heh." If I could have reached him, I think I would have inflicted great bodily harm. As it was, I just sat and steamed. And Jim just sort of snorted as he tried to keep from laughing out loud.

We were rolling down the usual narrow, chewed up, semi-muddy road. Lieutenant Finian was in the tank ahead of me, and we both were riding with our hatches open. I watched him as he twisted in his hatch opening, looked back at us, and brought the mike to his mouth.

"Ah, Hitchhike Charlie 56 to Hitchhike Charlie 57."

"Go ahead 56."

"Ah . . . 57, have your driver avoid following in my tracks. This road is getting really messed up and will get even worse unless we avoid following like we are. Out."

"Roger 56, wilco. 57 out."

"Commander to driver. I just got a radio call from Bird. He wants us to avoid following in his tracks. I don't know how the hell you're gonna do that, but at least give it a try."

"Hitchhike 57. You are on 'transmit.' 56 out."

I had not switched the radio transmit switch off, and instead of talking to my driver on the intercom, I ended up transmitting on the radio. Oh, boy. I made sure I was on intercom and relayed the message, and without the sarcasm this time.

Bird was a nickname someone had hung on Finian a long time back, and I used it without thinking, almost as though it was his real name. I had no doubt that somewhere along the way I'd pay for that little slip.

We continued on our way, the scenery gradually looking more and more familiar. That is, like a war zone. Small buildings were demolished, trees shattered, shell holes everywhere. Muddy vehicles, muddy, gray-looking men.

Following the convoy, we pulled into a cleared area and immediately threw a track. From long experience, I knew exactly what had happened. As the driver was pulling on one of the steering laterals and the tank was turning, he let up quickly on the throttle. The sudden absence of power to the outside track caused slack to develop and it had jumped a cog or two.

Finian and a couple of other tanks continued on. We dismounted and looked the situation over. I explained to my driver what had happened, or rather why it had happened, and we, the crew, began the weary job of getting our tank back in service. We'd been at it for about fifteen minutes or so when the first sergeant walked over and told me he had a mission for me. I showed him the thrown track (it was on the other side of the tank and he hadn't noticed it). He told me that was okay, the crew could go ahead and get the track back on . . . and that I was to take #60 and go down the narrow road he pointed out. A little way down the road, he said, a second lieutenant from the infantry would stop me, get aboard, and show me some targets that were giving the infantry a bad time.

He said a couple of tanks had arrived on the scene, but they didn't seem to understand exactly what the infantry was requesting. I asked him where OW was; it was his tank, and I knew that he was back from the hospital checkup he'd gotten. The first sergeant said that OW had just received orders to report back to the field hospital at the beach for more tests. I would command #60, a new tank with the old turret numbers.

I walked over to #60 and saw OW getting his personal gear together. I said, "I hear that you're running out on us."

"Oh, no . . . they just want to run a few more tests, I guess. I'll be back here by tomorrow at the latest, I'm sure."

"No, OW, what's happening is they're gonna send you back to the States. And when you get to San Francisco, would you do me a favor?"

He laughed, then said, "What's the favor, Bob?"

"Why, have a drink for me, that's all, OW."

We both laughed, and I got aboard #60 as OW climbed into a waiting jeep. We waved at each other, and I felt suddenly alone. OW gone, Anderson not here, Kahn, I don't know where. And Greenup . . . hey, I found that Roy Greenup was still the gunner on #60. What a wonderful discovery. It felt like a homecoming.

I got my helmet plugged in and told the driver to fire this monster up and follow the dirt road he could see to his right front. We pulled out, and down the road we went. We'd gone several hundred yards when suddenly a man stepped onto the road and signaled for us to stop. It was our infantry officer, and I had him climb on up and join me in the turret. He was very nervous, and I couldn't blame him. Getting inside one of these very noisy, smelly things the first time is an experience. Knowing that there are guys out there who are perfectly capable of blowing you up or setting you on fire in an instant is unsettling, too.

Keeping our heads together, we hollered back and forth.

The mission was simple enough—that I fire tracers into the caves and over the radio tell the two tanks already there that that was the target. Sure, no problem.

As we pulled up, I noticed that the ground was spongy. Not sloppy mud, but very soft. The two tanks, Lieutenant Finian's and Sgt. Ed Metz's, were a short distance away.

According to the officer, the targets were several caves that, I imagined, had the usual machine gun nests in them. Instead of firing tracers, I had Greenup put a few rounds of 75mm into them. As he traversed to the next one, the first one erupted in flame and explosions. We had hit a secondary target, and it looked like a major ammo dump. Or rather it *was* a major ammo dump.

About this time we heard some heavy explosions to our rear. Mr. Japanese artillery wanted to get into the act. As usual. The infantry officer asked me if those were enemy rounds and I told him I thought they were. He said he was getting out. I told him he was crazy, that it was much safer inside. After a couple of more rounds, he thanked me and out he went. Oh, well, to each his own.

Talking with him before he left, I found that we were just outside of Yonabaru. Our infantry had made an advancement early in the morning but they weren't able to hold their new positions. It looked like they were going to pull back.

After the infantry officer took off, I turned my attention back to the caves we had taken care of. About that time Greenup said on the intercom, "Hey, Bob, take a look at this." He leaned over to the side so I could move forward and peer through his gun sight. What I saw raised the hair on my neck. About a hundred yards or so down the valley was a Japanese artillery piece. Several Japs were working on it, and I realized that they were moving it into position to fire it directly at us!

I yelled at Greenup, "How long has that been going on?" He said just a couple of minutes. "Well, hell," I said, "let's take them out. Load white phosphorus and put a couple of rounds of it right in there." I wanted to take care of the gun's personnel and at the same time mark the range to be sure we were on it. We fired two rounds of WP, I then had a round of HE (high-explosive) thrown at it, and closed with AP (armor-piercing) to take care of the gun itself.

I congratulated Roy for keeping a sharp eye out, but asked him to let me know right away when he saw something suspicious after this. He grinned and said he would. About that time Lieutenant Finian radioed me and said we were pulling out and to fire smoke to cover the infantry's withdrawal. As I got ready to order us out of there, I noticed some activity by our infantrymen. A couple of them were alongside my tank, working on a wounded GI.

I radioed Finian and asked him to take a look. I watched as his periscope swiveled my way, and then he said on the radio, "It looks like that guy is done for. Let's get out of here."

"What are we going to do about the wounded man?"

"Leave him," he said.

I thought of Bomax, but then realized we hadn't left him under these same circumstances. Not exactly; when we left him he was dead. This fellow was still alive.

"Okay, Lieutenant, you go ahead and leave. I'm going to give these guys a hand."

I opened up the commander's hatch, unstrapped our first aid kit, and tossed it out in the general direction of where the infantrymen were. I leaned forward and yelled into Greenup's ear, "Tell my mom that I love her." He nodded, and I stuck my head out, ready to go for it. The noise was horrendous. Small-arms fire from both sides made the sounds of a million cracking, snapping dry branches. Explosions from the Japs were not too far off, and the smoke was rolling all around us. It was a scene right out of all of my nightmares. All of them rolled up into one . . . and here I was, wide awake and no way out.

I don't remember getting out of the hatch and down onto the ground. The two infantrymen were huddled over their wounded buddy, and I could see that he was unconscious. He had been hit in the upper right portion of his chest just below the collarbone and above the lung. Blood didn't seem to be bubbling, which would indicate a lung wound. But things were so hectic, this really was not the time to do much else except get him out of here. I opened the first aid kit and grabbed a large compress bandage and handed it to the nearest GI. He slid it under the man's shirt and pressed it against the wound. That was it.

We had to get moving, and right now. I told them to stand fast, and ran around to the front of my tank. I could see the periscopes watching me, and I pointed down below the assistant driver's position and made a downward pushing motion. I wanted the escape hatch opened up. A second or two later, down it dropped, and my heart fell with it. Our tank was sitting on soft ground, and the space between the mud surface and the belly of the tank was just inches. There was no way we could get our wounded friend under there and into the escape hatch. I motioned with my two hands that the space was too small, then gave them the pickup sign.

I went back to the infantrymen and told them the bad news. But I said that I would get up on the rear deck of the tank, and if they could lift him up from the bottom, with me pulling, we should be able to get him onto it and out of here. That sounded good to them, so I got up onto the deck just aft of the turret and spread my legs wide apart so that I could bend way over and grab our victim under the armpits. I guess I was in the same position as a giraffe when it drinks water, legs wide apart and bent over at the waist.

They began hauling him upright and shoved him up to where I could grab hold. As I bent all the way down, my helmet was almost touching the wounded man's head. And then it happened. It felt like someone hit my right foot with a sledgehammer. My foot was literally knocked out from under me, and down we all fell in a heap, right back where we'd started. The pain in my foot was very intense. I sat, holding my shoe, afraid to look. The way it hurt, I was sure that a part of my foot had been blown away. I looked over at Sergeant Metz's tank and could see his periscope pointed my way. I knew he had seen the whole thing. I shook my head and saw him move his periscope from side to side. We were in agreement. This was not a good situation.

Getting up my nerve, what was left of it, I took my hands away and looked at my foot. No hole, no nothing! My boot looked perfectly normal. The pain was still there, but no wound. What the hell had happened? I found out later, when describing it, that the bullet must have hit the armor plate exactly at the edge of my boot, and the concussion from it is what knocked my foot out from under me and inflicted the pain.

But we weren't getting anywhere with me sitting around holding my foot. I motioned to the guys that we should try it again. I told them that I must have been hit by a stray bullet; there was so much ordnance flying around, it had to be that. After all, I thought, who would want to shoot me?

We tried it again, them pushing from below and me pulling at the armpits, and BAM! I got hit again. And again it knocked my leg out from under me, and down the four of us fell. This time I had been hit in the left leg between the ankle and the knee. I had a quick flash of déjà vu, remembering last night and my little episode with my .45 pistol.

The pain was, strangely enough, not as bad as the pain in my foot. Maybe I was getting used to getting hit. Anyway, I didn't have to get shot more than twice to figure out that some Jap sniper had a real good bead on us, and all we had to do for him to get the big target, me, was for us to get back up and do it all over again. Nope, no way, not your Uncle Bob. Twice was enough for me, and I had gotten the message. I told my infantry friends that maybe we should drag this guy around to the other side of the tank and get his fanny onto the deck that way. They agreed, as they too were now very eager to get the hell out.

So, with all three of us shoving and pushing him from below, we got the still-unconscious guy up and onto the other side of the rear deck, and without a word or a wave, the two infantrymen took off, and I couldn't blame them.

And here I was, in the open, surrounded by three tanks and the Japanese army. Hit in two places . . . well, one that showed, and all I had was my trusty .45 pistol and a burning yearning to get back into a tank, any tank, and go where I could no longer hear bullets flying by or hear explosions from enemy mortar and artillery fire. And, as confused as I was right then, one thing was crystal clear . . . I had to do something. There wasn't anyone else who was going to do it for me.

I crawled around to the front of my tank and tried to decide what the hell to do. I was afraid to try crawling up the tank to get into the turret. What a target that would make! And entering through the driver's or assistant driver's hatch would be an awful mess, what with those seats already occupied. I looked over at the nearest tank, Finian's. It was about thirty or forty feet away, just sitting there, waiting for me it seemed. I took a close look at the ground clearance under his tank and it looked, from where I was, like there would be enough room for me to get under it and up inside through their escape hatch.

I didn't know if Finian would understand my hand signals, but I knew that Metz would. I looked over at Metz and pointed at Finian's tank and made the "drop the escape hatch" motion with my hands. His periscope swiveled up and down, as in a nod "yes." I waited a moment or two, and then Metz's periscope gave me another "yes."

In the meantime I had looked around and found a small rock, about the size of a walnut. I had placed it at the pressure point on the back of my leg, under my knee, and tied it there with my handkerchief. I twisted the handkerchief so that I had a makeshift tourniquet. My .45 was in my hand after the two GIs had left, and I had it now, ready to do or die if necessary. I looked over at Finian's tank, took a deep breath, and made a dash for it, although it wasn't exactly a "dash," more of a limping plod, but I made it okay. I had thought for sure that my sniper friend would lay another one on me, but I guess I was out of his firing zone.

I was at the back of the tank, sitting close to the engine bay doors, feeling fairly safe for the first time in a long while. I lay down on the ground and looked toward the front and could see that the escape hatch had dropped. Facedown, I started to crawl under.

The first thing that went wrong was my canteen wedging between me and the belly of the tank. I unhooked my pistol belt and shoved it away from me. Resuming my crawl, I made it a few more feet and then my helmet made contact. The space between the bottom of the tank and the ground was very small, and my helmet was just not going to let me go. I backed up a bit, took my helmet off, and gave it a toss out onto the battlefield. I hated to see it go. We'd been through a lot together and I had definitely decided that I was going to bring it home with me as a souvenir, one way or the other. But it was not to be.

I resumed crawling and the farther under I got, the narrower the space was until, finally, I could go no farther. The hatch opening was just a few feet ahead. As I looked at it, I saw a pair of hands come into view. They were reaching for the hatch handles and I knew what was going to happen next. They could see that the space was very limited and probably figured that perhaps they could move a few feet onto harder ground and get more space. The big problem with that was, when power is applied and a tank first starts out, it sort of settles or squats. I knew that if that happened, I'd be squashed like a bug. I stretched one arm out as far as it would go and managed to get just my fingertips on the edge of the hatch opening. Now they knew I was right there. Frantically, I yelled, "Hold it! Hold it! Don't close the hatch!" I could just barely see the edge of a helmet as the assistant driver tried to look down and back at me.

He hollered, "Hurry up, we've got to get out of here."

I told him, "Give me a second . . . just don't move the tank, for God's sake."

I backed up about a yard or so and began digging a trough in the soft dirt with my hands. As I scooped the dirt away, I kept having visions of the tank smashing down on me. Finally I got to the opening and had one helluva job twisting and bending myself to get through it. When I finally got up inside, the assistant driver reached down and pulled the hatch up. I grabbed the dogs and latched it shut, then hollered to the driver, "Okay, let's get the hell out of here!" He was one of the new men, and this was his introduction to combat. That he was nervous was the understatement of the year. For whatever reason, he just couldn't seem to get the tank in gear. Straddling the transmission case, I yelled at him, I'm quite sure with a near-hysterical note in my voice, "If you can't drive this fucking thing, get out of the way. . . . I'll do it." He hollered back that he would be okay and not to worry. And he finally did get us rolling.

PART SEVEN

My Skipper Gives Me a Medal

(It's a Good Conduct Medal, but What the Hell)

47

We finally pulled up at the medics' position, just behind the infantry's location. I found out later that we were on the edge of the city of Yonabaru. We were not alone. Other tanks had also brought back wounded who were in the process of being off-loaded. Everyone was out of their vehicles and watching the medics at work. I managed to stand up on the assistant driver's seat, but the pain in my leg was starting to really make itself known.

I finally got somebody's attention, and several guys came over and helped unload me. I was laid on a litter and waited my turn. Several officers came over. There was a major, a captain, and a lieutenant. The major and captain were infantrymen; the lieutenant was a medical officer. The major and captain both thanked me for helping their men, and the lieutenant cut open my pants leg. We all took a look at my wound. It was the first time I had seen it, and I was surprised at the small hole. The flesh was pushed up in a sort of mound from the swelling inside. He saw the handkerchief and laughed. "Who did this?" I said that I had. Why? He said that what I had was, in essence, a puncture wound, which was supposed to be encouraged to bleed. "Well," I said, "I didn't know about that. I just didn't want to bleed to death." He patted me on the other leg and said I'd done a nice job.

About that time a familiar face appeared, hovering over me. It was Captain Todd. He had a very serious look on his face, grabbed me by my shoulder, and asked if I was okay. I said yeah, I was fine. To tell the truth, it was just about here that I realized that my wound was going to see me off the line and away from the fighting for a spell. I suddenly felt like a kid on Christmas Day having just found a new bike and a Daisy BB gun under the tree. But I didn't want to let anyone know that this big, tough guy was happy about being out of it for a bit. So I kept my serious expression on my face as I spoke with the captain, but he was such a nice guy I had difficulty not telling him how wonderful it all was.

He leaned down close to me and asked in a low voice, "Is there anything I can do for you?"

In as serious a tone as I could muster, I replied, "Yes, sir. I'd sure like to have a Good Conduct Medal." I meant it as a joke and fully expected him to take it as such. Instead, he straightened up and said, looking me in the eyes, "You've got it, soldier."

Wow, I said to myself, a Good Conduct Medal! Those, of course, were one of the semiautomatic awards given if a man stayed out of trouble for a full year.

I looked around and saw the medic and asked him if they were going to bandage the other side, the exit wound. He looked at me sort of strangely and said, "There ain't no wound on the other side. The bullet's still in there."

"Well, are you guys gonna take it out or what?"

"No, we don't do that here. They'll take you back down to the beach to the field hospital and take it out. You'll probably be off duty for a week or so."

Hot dog. A full week of nothing to do but lay around and heal. I lay there, a happy glow inside, hurting like the devil in my leg, but hey, when added all up I could see that I was way ahead on this one. A full week! Yeehaw!

48

They strapped my litter down on a jeep, along with a couple of other guys, also on litters, and it looked like we might get out of there in pretty good time. The driver had been talking with the medics, and when he came back, I asked him for a drink of water from his canteen. He said he couldn't do that and I asked him, why the hell not? He said that water would make me vomit because I'd just had a morphine shot. I told him my mouth was so dry I could barely speak.

"Please, let me have just a small swallow," I begged.

"Okay, but just wash your mouth out and spit," he told me.

"I promise," I said. I got hold of the canteen and drank almost all of it in one great big chugalug.

He was furious and said, "Now you'll get sick and it'll be my fault." I told him, "Not to worry, I never get sick, and if by chance I do, I won't tell anyone that you gave me a drink of water."

"A drink! Shit, man, you had the whole damn canteenful."

"Well, I think you're making a big deal out of nothing. Oh, and before we leave, why don't you refill your canteen in case one of us gets thirsty?"

He replied with some choice army words. Seemed like he had no sense of humor at all, but aside from me stealing his water, we got along all right. I was the only one on the jeep who felt like talking, and as we drove along, he and I astounded each other with wild-assed tales of the things we'd been through. He was an infantry medic, a breed that I take my hat off to anytime, anywhere. He'd been on the driving detail for about week and was eager to get back to the field. I felt a little guilty about being so happy to get away from the field, but wisely didn't say anything.

As we drove along, I couldn't help but notice how careful our driver was in avoiding any potholes or gullies that would cause the jeep to bounce around. He knew the wounded he had aboard were in enough pain.

The roads, all of them either dirt or mud depending on the weather, were in terrible condition due to the heavy traffic. Finian was right in trying to get us not to tear up the roads as we drove along, but in most cases they were so narrow that we had no choice. After we had driven for quite a while, we came to a halt. The driver got out and went up ahead a little bit and talked with a soldier who appeared to be in charge.

Our driver told me that the next quarter of a mile or so was targeted by Japanese artillery, and they fired at random. There was a guard at each end of the stretch, and each had a walkie-talkie. Traffic would be allowed to proceed in one direction, and the next batch going the other direction would then be allowed to pass. I didn't feel real happy about traveling down a road that was subject to harassing fire, but what are you gonna do, get out and walk?

We got through, and a little farther down the road we were transferred to a Regular Army ambulance. I wished our driver good luck and thanked him again for the water. He grinned and gave me a thumbs up. Nice guy.

49

The ambulance came to a halt, the back doors were flung open, and me and my fellow travelers were placed in a long tent. There was a row of litters on the left and right side of the room. At the far end, a canvas curtain ran from one side to the other. Behind it was the operating room. As the doctors finished with a man, he was brought out of the operating area and placed, still on his litter, on the floor just outside the canvas wall on the right side. In essence, we had one line of men being moved into the surgery area, as the other line was moved out.

Every once in awhile, soldiers would come in and pick up the outgoing litters, closest to the front of the tent, and take them away to other tents on the beach. And, every once in awhile, new wounded were brought in and placed at the start of the row on the left. Incoming and outgoing.

One of the men who was detailed to help out inside the tent came by and asked how I was doing. I told him fine, and could he get me a sheet of paper and a pencil, and an envelope? He brought back some Red Cross stationery and waited until I wrote a short note to my mom. I told her I'd been scratched and the army would probably send her a telegram. And not to worry, it was no big deal and I'd soon be back in good condition. My new friend said he'd mail it for me, and that was a big load off my mind. I didn't know how slow or fast the army's telegram service worked, but I didn't want anyone to be surprised by the delivery of one of them, especially when so many were the bearers of really bad news.

I don't recall how long it took the line to move up to where I was next, but it seemed to move fast. The doctors who were operating amazed me. There they were, ready for the next patient even if they didn't have the slightest idea what that next guy's problem was. I don't know how many hours they put in on this detail each day, but it seems to me that they all deserved a halo. A golden one, at least.

My litter was brought in and placed on a table. A doctor looked at the tag that the medics had attached to me. It read WIA GSW which meant "wounded in action gunshot wound." He removed the bandage that had been put on my wound, looked at it, and as he cleaned it he asked me what outfit I was in. I said, "763d Tank Battalion, sir, attached to the 96th Division."

He said, "You're in the tanks. How the hell did you get a

gunshot wound?" All the while he was probing my wound with a long icepick-looking thing, trying to find the bullet still in there.

I told him that I had "got out of my tank to give a wounded infantryman a hand."

He stopped what he was doing, looked at me, and said, "I don't think I can get the bullet out under these circumstances. I am going to have you evacuated to a general hospital." While he said that he was smiling at me, and I had the feeling that I had just been given a nice present by the doctor. I also had the feeling that he might have been able to find and remove that bullet, but instead decided to get my ragged ass out of combat for a spell. I'm probably wrong, but it's a nice thought and one I still keep close to me.

Wound cleaned and bandaged, bullet still in, I was taken out of the operating room, still on the litter that I had been placed on in the field. I was put down at the back end of the outgoing line. I dozed for a spell, and before I was really aware of the time passing, my litter was picked up, and out of the operating tent we went. I raised my head up enough to get a fair look at our surroundings. Rows of tents, dozens of them it looked like. And, from the quick look, I could see all kinds of ships unloading supplies on the beach. The whole scene was so, well, so huge that I couldn't really comprehend the enormity of it all.

The two guys carrying my litter stopped at the entrance of a tent. One of them said something about "a vacant spot in this one." So, in we went. It was very dark inside, and I couldn't see a thing. On our short trip from the operating tent to this one, I did notice that the day had almost ended. It seemed like the fastest day I had ever experienced, and yet at the same time it seemed hours and hours longer than it should have been.

They set the litter down on top of a GI folding cot and left. For the first time that day I began to realize just how fortunate I really was. Running over the events in my mind made me very nervous. How in the hell I did what I did and not be killed hit me hard.

50

My throbbing leg began to hurt worse than at any time since I was hit. They had given me a shot of morphine, again, but that didn't do much to lessen the pain. It did help me relax and, in a little while, sleep. But the pain never went away. I had always thought that morphine stopped pain.

I had been lying on that litter for a few minutes when someone, the guy next to me, said, "Dick . . . is that you?"

It was OW! Of the hundreds, maybe thousands of guys in tents here at the beach, how the hell did we end up not only in the same tent, but on cots next to each other!

"Yeah, OW, it's me, all right. Your old driver."

"Wha . . . what the hell happened to you?" he asked.

"Well, I tell you, OW, I got to thinking about that drink in San Francisco and decided, what the hell, I'll come along and we can have one or three together."

"Sounds good to me, but come on. What happened?"

"What happened was, for whatever reason, I was put in command of a certain tank number #60. Does that ring a bell, old wise one?"

"Don't tell me that they knocked out our new #60, too!"

"No, they just knocked out the old guy who was crazy enough to get in the dumb thing, and then crazy enough to get out of it."

I said that it was strange. Old and new #60 had had three commanders: OW, Bomax, and me, and, all of us had to leave for one reason or another. I didn't know who would get command then. Maybe Greenup. He certainly could do the job, but I sure hoped he stayed lucky.

As we lay there in the darkness, some pretty impressive groans could be heard in our tent. Neither of us had any idea of the extent of the injuries of the other guys around us, but we both knew that probably all of them were hurting worse than either one of us. My leg had settled down to a steady throb, accompanied with jabs of pure pain at almost regular intervals. I asked OW if his stomach hurt him all the time and he said, "Only when I vomit." An encouraging answer if I ever heard one. He asked me if I was hungry. I suddenly realized that the last time I had eaten was almost twenty-four hours ago! I told OW that, in fact, I was starving. I heard him rustling away in the darkness, and, bless his heart, he handed me something. As I reached over and got hold of it, I heard antiaircraft guns firing. And, they were getting louder and closer. "What the hell is this all about?" I yelled.

OW answered me from the floor . . . "It's just a Jap plane. He flies over every night, and sometimes he drops bombs, but most times he doesn't."

Lying on top of the litter, on top of the cot, I felt like I was on the roof with a spotlight on me. I sure wanted to roll off and get down close to the ground, but the pain was just too much. The noise faded a bit, and I took a bite of whatever OW had handed me. "What is this shit you gave me?"

"It's carrot and pork loaf from a K ration," he answered. And just as suddenly as I had felt hungry, I lost all my yearning for food. I'd had it up to here with K rations, C rations, or anything else even close.

"Getting killed by the Japs is one thing, but getting poisoned by our own government is not gonna get it with me. When the generals and Congress start eating this crap, then I will, too. Until then, forget it."

A voice from somewhere in the tent responded with "You said it, brother," and a couple of other guys joined in. Somehow we made it through the night, and now all we had to do was wait and see what the new day would bring. More Japanese kamikazes attacked that day, but we couldn't see what was going on, and they were all far enough offshore that we had no worries.

After a while one of the guys on beach detail stuck his

head into our tent and said something to the effect that we should get our gear together, as we'd be loaded up soon. I asked OW, "Do you have all your gear together, buddy?" Everybody who wasn't hurting too much started laughing. Somebody said, "I'm naked as a jaybird, but as far as I know, all my stuff's together." That one brought howls of laughter, and even though a few were close to hysteria, it was good to know that as a group we could still find something funny after all that had happened to us.

True to the man's word, the loading detail soon pulled up in front of our tent, and one by one our litters were carried outside and placed inside an ambulance. OW and I shared the same ambulance, and I found myself marveling at the fact that out of the hundreds of soldiers, and all the tents, and all the ambulances, here we were rolling along together.

After a while we arrived at an airfield, and the ambulance drove up alongside a huge airplane and we were carried aboard. Someone said that the plane was a Douglas C-54. All I knew was that ours had four engines, and I couldn't wait to get on.

The litters were stacked from floor to ceiling with about eighteen inches between each one. This arrangement went the full length of the fuselage on both sides and I was situated somewhere in the middle of the mess. The best part of the whole deal was the navy nurses. These were the first white women we had seen since leaving Hawaii in September. What made it nice was they were all wearing great-looking green nylon one-piece flight uniforms. Every one of us who could muster a whistle or call out a "wahoo" did so. The gals were wonderful, and I'm sure they had put up with this sort of thing on every flight.

We no sooner got off the ground than the guy in the litter below me began coming alive. He was Mister Life of the Party himself. At least he was if one of the nurses came within ten feet of him. His gyrations became a bit much because he was constantly banging his knees into the bottom of my litter and with the old leg giving me fits, he wasn't going over too well with me. After a bit of this nonsense, I rolled my head over to the edge of the litter and said, "Soldier, if you don't settle down and stop banging into me, you will find yourself in really big trouble."

He came back with a snappy, "Yeah, says who?"

And I said, "Lieutenant Colonel R. E. Lee, if you're taking names. That suit you, soldier?" Things got real quiet after that, and except for the pain, it was a pretty nice ride from then on.

51

It was dark when we landed at Guam. Ambulances were waiting for us. The ride was very long, and aside from giving us morphine shots once in awhile, there wasn't much the nurses could do for us while we were in flight. There were some very severely wounded men in our group, amputations and the like, and my heart went out to them. My wound seemed so trivial in comparison, but in spite of its minor status, the pain was really intense.

As the men were being removed from the ambulance, one of them started screaming, "Oh, God . . . oh God . . . oh . . ." Another one began laughing. We could tell that the guy laughing was near hysteria, and no matter how hard he tried to control himself, he continued on, almost shrieking.

It didn't take the soldiers on this detail very long to get our ambulance unloaded and the wounded taken to the wards. I guess they were configured according to the severity of their injuries. I was the only one from our ambulance taken to the particular ward I ended up in.

The ward was a fairly long room with beds on both sides. Everyone seemed to be asleep, and it felt strange to be among so many guys who had recently been on Okinawa . . . and were now here, away from the fighting, sleeping between clean sheets, peacefully. That is, no bad guys lurking around in the dark trying to kill us.

I had been lying in bed about ten minutes when in came a nurse. She was so nice, so concerned, that I thought to myself that I must have been taken to the wrong ward. I just didn't feel like I warranted anything special. But the first words out of her mouth made me want to ask her if she was married and, if not, please be mine. She asked me, "Would you like a cup of coffee, soldier?"

"Oh, absolutely, nurse . . . Black will be great!"

She returned in a few minutes with a tray, and on it a large white china cup. Steam was rising out of it, and I could hardly wait. I still had not eaten anything since, when? I couldn't remember for sure, but I did know I was very hungry. I also knew that I wasn't going to ask for anything this late at night.

She held the tray out toward me and I took the cup from it. As I did, I became abruptly aware of my shaking hands. I had to hold onto the cup with both hands. I was shaking so bad I almost spilled the coffee. She smiled, and for whatever reason I was ashamed. "I didn't realize I was such a coward, shaking and all like this." She shook her head and told me that this was so common among "you guys" that no one paid much attention to it anymore. She also told me that in a little while I'd calm down somewhat. She didn't say what she meant by "a little while." Hours, days, what? The coffee was wonderful. Matter of fact, it was the best cup of coffee I have ever had . . . in my life. And I told her so. "Well," she said, "it's not K ration instant if that's what you mean." And she laughed again.

She told me that a ward attendant would be on duty all night and if I needed anything to call out. I desperately wanted her to stay and talk with me. I felt very alone, for the first time in a long, long while. Until now I had been with my tank crew, and we had been more like a family than I could ever have imagined. Now it was just me here. And I suddenly wondered, what had happened to OW? We had been on the same plane but not in the same ambulance. Oh well, I'd track him down later.

That night I slept well, but in bits and pieces. I'd drop off into a deep sleep and then wake suddenly, wondering what was going on, realize where I was, look around, and then drop off to sleep again. I woke up the next morning to an entirely different atmosphere. It was one I immediately felt at home in. That is to say, it was all army. The talk, the hollering between beds from one guy to another. I knew it was going to be an interesting experience.

All of a sudden I was "discovered" by these guys. "Hey, buddy, what outfit you from?" I found later that this was the most important bit of information to be gained from a new-comer. If he was from one of the units that any of our resident wounded were from, then names and incidents were exchanged. When they asked me, I said, "The 763d Tank Battalion, attached to the 96th, the 383d Regiment." There arose an almost 100 percent protest from all of them. "A lousy tanker? Get him out of here," and so on. All of these soldiers were from the infantry. Every one of them. And anyone not from the infantry was an intruder.

I knew exactly why they reacted the way they did. Before the yelling got too far along, however, another voice was heard. "Hey, listen up, you apes. This guy got hit because he got out of his tank and helped get one of you dumb wounded GIs onto the back of his tank and back to the medics. So lay off, he's okay." I didn't know that guy, but he must have been one of those we'd picked up that day.

I heard a couple more "no-good tanker" remarks, but they were now in a good-natured vein, and I felt accepted. A good feeling, I must say. As an ex-infantryman, I knew the pride these soldiers had in their jobs. In truth, theirs was the fight that every other branch supported.

I soon found that the daily routine consisted almost entirely of what was about to happen that morning. This was the time when the doctors would visit each patient and the wounds would be inspected, cleansed, and rebandaged. It was a time to look forward to, or a time of dread, depending on the individual circumstances. I knew that I was very apprehensive, and wasn't looking forward to the visit . . . at all.

All too soon the doctor and nurse arrived at my bedside. I

was asked how I felt and I assured them that I was just fine. All this time the doctor was removing my bandage. He and the nurse peered at it, and he informed me that the bullet was still in there. I admitted that it was and didn't know if I was supposed to feel guilty about it or not. In the meantime the nurse had stuck a thermometer under my tongue and wrote down the reading. The doctor asked me if I was wounded anyplace else. I told him about my foot, and he examined it. He said it appeared to be okay, but that they would X ray it later. I asked him when the bullet would be removed and he informed me, "You're running a low-grade fever, and we won't operate until we get your temperature down to normal."

As he was speaking, the nurse had rolled a piece of one-inch-wide gauze material up into a tube about a quarter of an inch in diameter. The gauze had been coated on both sides with what looked to be Vaseline. After the wound opening was cleaned and had some sort of powder sprinkled on it (I'm guessing it was sulfanilamide), the gauze tube was picked up by forceps and inserted into the wound, sort of like a cork in a bottle. This was to keep it open so it would drain and not heal closed.

I must say that as the tube of gauze was inserted, I experienced the most pain I've ever had in my life. As I tried to shrink back, the doctor told me that the pain was being caused by the tube pressing against the bullet, which in turn was resting against the bone. It didn't hurt any less when he told me that, but at least I knew that I wasn't being too big a sissy about it.

I watched as the doctor, nurse, and ward assistant (we called them "ward boys") continued to make their rounds. I almost wept when I saw one young fellow who had lost both legs. I could only wonder at his future, and I prayed that his family and loved ones would give him the support he was going to need. After wars are over, the heroes are soon forgotten. I knew this. As a youngster, we had a fellow in our family who had been in World War I. I seldom heard anyone talk about him except to say something to the effect that he had been "gassed during the war." And that was it. I wanted to talk with him about his experiences, but I was so young and frightened about talking to him that I never mentioned it. I guess the rest of the family felt the same way.

It soon became apparent that there was a little game being played by the patients and the medical staff. Okinawa was sending so many wounded into the hospital, they were in danger of overfilling the place. As a result, many of those soldiers were being sent directly to hospitals in Hawaii. The doctors here in Guam would try and get the men in the wards healed and back to duty as fast as they could in order to open up more space for more incoming. But the fellows in the ward just plain did not want to go back to their old outfit, and combat, if they could avoid it.

There was one gentleman who, judging by all his antics before the medical staff arrived, was fit as a fiddle. He would visit between beds, carry a paperback book from one guy to another, magazines, things like that. Everyone liked him, including the doctors and nurses, but getting another bed space was a serious and grim business for the staff, and as much as they all seemed to like this fellow, they were intent on getting him out. I watched as they approached his bed. How are you this morning? Oh, I don't feel real great, Doctor. And so it went, each party trying to do their thing. Finally, after inspecting and doing whatever he was supposed to do, the doctor said, "We've come up with something that I'm sure is going to help the healing process. Roll over on your side and let's see your butt." The guy was suddenly apprehensive and asked what was going on. The doctor lifted a towel off of something that was lying on a stainless steel tray. It was a hypodermic needle, the size a horse veterinarian would use. The needle looked as big around as a soda straw. The poor patient slid clear out of bed on the far side from the doctor and said, "Hey, Doc . . . y-y-you're not gonna stick me with that thing, are you? Come on, sir."

The doctor just smiled and began filling the syringe with some kind of colorless liquid, pointed it upward, and squirted a bit of it out of the needle. He turned to his "patient."

"Okay, lay back down and roll onto your side."

"Doctor, listen to me. I'm really much, much better. Matter of fact, I think I'm ready to get outta here. I mean all the way out. Sir. Okay?"

The doctor said, "Well, if you're sure. But, I really think this would help you . . . a lot." All the time this little interlude had been playing itself out, the rest of the guys in the ward had been yelling at the poor guy, giving him advice, the whole bit. He wasn't sure if he was being scammed by the doctor and nurse or what. It was very funny and at the same time very sad. It spoke volumes about the horrors of Okinawa and what it had done to us . . . make us try every trick in the book to keep from being returned to duty.

In all honesty, replacements were flooding into the units on that godforsaken island, and the only thing that was missing by not returning these men was keeping experienced men away from where they were needed and could be used. As for the men, from what I could see, and from my own personal feelings, we were all so uptight, with nerves frayed, it's doubtful how much, if any, value we'd be back in combat.

The daily routine of inspecting my leg, taking my temperature, and redressing it continued. The temperature I was running was, to me, very slight, like a degree or two. But I understood from the doctor and later the nurse that any temperature above normal indicated infection. They just did not want to operate with the danger of an infected wound taking off and getting out of control. As long as I continued to sleep between sheets; eat hot, good food; and not worry when it got dark outside, I was content to hang around and let come what may.

One day I had a surprise visitor: Sgt. Maynard Ware. Maynard had been commander of the tank we passed on the side of the road the day we went up into a small village and evacuated a couple of crews. His driver, Larson, was the fellow who had been so badly burned. After the usual comparison of wounds, I asked him about that day his tank was knocked out. He told me the crew had scattered because of mortar fire and he had run straight out to the flank for quite some distance and then turned and started back toward our lines. In his own words, with a rich Southern drawl, he said, "I came to a little old dirt road and figured that I'd follow it. I knew it was going in the right direction." It had some shallow ruts in it that had been put there during the rain by some vehicles and had hardened after drying out. He said that as he ran, he found that he was almost completely exhausted and began to walk as fast as he could, considering how pooped he was. Suddenly without warning, a machine gun cut loose on him. He said he'd hit the road and tried his damnedest to snuggle down in those little ruts. He said he just lay there while that gun had its say.

I asked, "Were you afraid?"

"Well," he said, with never a trace of a smile, "I can tell you this. You couldn't have driven a nail in my ass with an air compressor." It was nice to hear that I wasn't the only one who was allergic to gunfire.

Another visitor showed up a few days after Ware dropped by. Lt. Carl Schluter, my former platoon leader and victim to one of Japan's best weapons, the little rapid-fire 47mm anti-tank gun. He told me that he scanned the list of new patients the hospital published every day or so, and had made it a habit of visiting the guys as they showed up. After we had chatted a while, he drew closer, looked both ways as if he had something to tell me that he didn't want to get around, and spoke in a low voice.

"You know, Dick, those people are dangerous." I looked at him to be sure that he wasn't joking, and when I saw how serious he was, I told him, "You know, Lieutenant, you and I didn't have to wind up in this place for me to be convinced. I was in on that little secret a long time ago." Carl was my favorite field officer, and it was a delight to sit and listen to him talk about the "old days" in the Regular Army, when he was in the horse cavalry. I rather think that he wished he was still in his old outfit. From the way he described it, I'd have liked to have done a hitch in it myself.

My doctor was a major. I had hopes that he would not turn out to be a full colonel. The Good Lord only knows what that would have ended up like. His hometown area was around San Francisco, California. The folks in San Francisco and

those in the Los Angeles area are always squabbling about
how much better each is than the other. So when I found out
my doctor was from San Francisco, I took the liberty of saying that I was from the good part of the state, the Los
Angeles area. The line was drawn, and we at once began
what turned out to be a very enjoyable relationship. He was a
very nice guy and always had time to stop and chat. Mostly
about how wonderful Frisco was. He hated it when I said
"Frisco."

One day as we were talking, he mentioned that my medical
records were screwed up. "What's wrong with them?"

"Well, for one thing, actually, the only thing, they show
you as a GSW. A gunshot wound."

"So what's wrong with that?"

"According to the X rays, you were hit by shrapnel, not a
bullet."

"That's a bunch of, er, baloney, sir. I was shot. Twice. By
the same guy, sir."

"No, no, you were hit by shrapnel, take my word for it."

"Begging the major's pardon, but that's a bunch of horse
hockey, sir."

"Well, why don't you just put your money where your
mouth is, my friend?"

"Sounds good to me. What do you want to bet?"

The major looked at me, then said, "How about a drink of
whiskey?"

I said, "You're on."

And, he asked, "How are you going to pay off. You don't
have a jug stashed away, do you?"

"No, sir, I don't have a jug stashed away. But, I know that
you are gonna lose, so it doesn't matter about my end of it."
And, I asked, "When are you folks gonna take that bullet out,
if for no other reason than we can settle the bet and I can get
my drink of whiskey?"

"Soon, Sergeant, soon. Just be patient and get your fever
down."

As it turned out, I lay in that bed with the bullet still in my
leg for eighteen days! For eighteen days they would clean the
wound and shove that damned plug into the hole. And, for

eighteen days I was left as limp as a dishrag when they got finished with the "shoving."

Not only did it seem more painful than ever, I thought I could smell it. And, it didn't smell good. On the next morning's visit, I asked the doctor about taking the thing out. I said, "It's starting to stink, and while I can stand the odor, the fact that it does sort of worries me."

He started in about the temperature I was running. I didn't feel like I had a temperature, but I knew that they had valid reasons for doing, or rather not doing, anything right now.

"Look, Doctor, how about this? How about you folks either take it out, or sew me up and leave it in. Will that work?"

He looked at me, then looked at the nurse and said, "Okay, tell you what we'll do. Let's wait a couple of days, and if we can't get that temp to drop a degree or two, we'll go ahead and take the shrapnel out."

"The bullet."

"Whatever."

A couple of days went by, and I don't know if they got the temperature to move or not, but I did get the notice that my operation was scheduled for the next morning. And, I really hate the thought of operations of any kind, minor, major, or in-between. But, regardless, bright and early the next morning I was moved onto a gurney and rolled down several thousand miles of corridors, or so it seemed. Actually, I'd heard that the 204th General Hospital on Guam was, at the time, the largest hospital in the world if you count covered or roofed areas. What made it so big was the outside corridors were all covered, and it wouldn't have surprised me if someone had told me that there were miles of them.

My gurney was left just outside the operating room. Also sitting there was another gurney, and a young-looking guy was on it. He looked over and said hello, and I answered. I asked him, what kind of operation was he getting? He grinned and said that he was having his tonsils taken out. Right away I figured he was a noncombat guy stationed on the island and was having his tonsils removed.

He asked me about my operation, and big-deal me, the great combat soldier, talking to a rear-echelon guy; well, I said, it's just a little bullet I picked up in Okinawa. I said it like I was receiving the Medal of Honor.

I had no sooner awed him (or so I thought) when my doctor came out, stopped, and chatted with this young guy. Then he went to the foot of the man's gurney, looked at a chart hanging there, and—the final blow—he raised the sheet that was over the fellow, and I could see that he had had one leg amputated. I wished I'd had a rock to hide under, anything instead of lying there with egg on my face. The doctor told him it was looking good, and then told me that they'd be ready for me in a couple of minutes. I smiled kind of weakly at the guy and wished him good luck on his tonsils deal.

52

In the operating room two doctors were holding an X ray up to a light, and my doctor says to the other one in a loud stage voice, "Should we take it off there or there?" They both looked at me, waiting for my reaction, so I said, "I really don't care where you take it off just as long as I can put a shoe on it when all is said and done." Well, they thought that was hilarious, and right away I could see that these two were not a professional standup comedy team. I was hoping, however, that they were an outstanding operating team. Oh, yeah. My doctor said, again in a loud stage voice, "As you can see, the *shrapnel* is resting against the bone." I said in an equally loud voice, "*Bullet*, and don't forget the drink."

They gave me a shot of Sodium Pentothal, and I was told to count from ten to one, slowly. I started, "Ten . . . nine . . . eight . . . ," then stopped and said, "I'm still awake." I was afraid that they might start cutting on me while I was still awake, and I sure as hell didn't want that to happen. They assured me that they'd wait, and I asked if I should start at ten again or what. I could hear them having a little consultation, and while they talked I found myself fading away.

I woke up sometime later, back in my own bed in my regular ward. I raised my head up, looked around, and went right back to sleep. I felt great! Later, my friend in the next bed told me that something special had happened. "What did I miss?" I asked. He told me that the nurse from the operating room came back to the ward, accompanying my gurney, and had her hand on the side of it as the ward guys unloaded me into my bed. She stayed for about fifteen minutes, sitting there, and then she left, he told me. He also said that I was talking up a blue streak.

"What was I saying?"

"Oh, something about blue skies, green valleys, poetic stuff like that." I remembered then that there was a nurse in the operating room and I had kidded with her a bit before things got under way. Hmmm. Too bad I can't make that kind of impression on them while I'm in full control of all of my senses.

The next morning my doctor came in along with the operating room nurse, who wasn't bad, incidentally, and he asked me how I was feeling. I told him that I felt better than I had in a long time.

The nurse was holding a tray out in front of her. My doctor reached around, removed the cloth covering, and handed me a shot glass of whiskey. And, a beat-up piece of pure lead. I had been shot with an unjacketed lead bullet, and it had splattered so much when it hit the bone, it resembled shrapnel. But looking at it close, you could see the rifling marks on it. So I got a drink of whiskey and a great souvenir, all at the same time. The doctor smiled, the nurse smiled and patted me on the head, and I smiled. And the guys close enough to hear and see all this, well, they smiled, too.

My leg still hurt, but nothing like it had been. The doctor told me later that there were still quite a few fragments left, but they were all dust-speck size and shouldn't give me any trouble in the future. He had also X-rayed my right foot and found the same small dust-sized specks of lead at the edge of that foot. I guess that when that lead slug hit the armor, it disintegrated and some of the "dust" went through the leather of my shoe. At any rate, my right foot hadn't hurt a half hour after I'd been hit there, so I didn't worry about either the leg or the foot as far as the future went.

A few days after I had been operated on, a new doctor arrived. I mean, new to me. He was totally different from my old one. This guy was all business, and I mean as GI as they come. "All right, soldier, I want you to sit up on the edge of the bed."

I did so, and then he told me to stand on both feet. I gave it a try, but the left leg just wouldn't take it. As soon as the toes of my left foot touched the floor and weight was applied, the cut portion inside began to try to stretch, and I must say the pain was as bad as any I'd had for a long time.

"I can't put any weight on that foot, Doctor."

"Nonsense. Stand up on it and make it stretch."

"Can't do it, sir." I did try again and almost passed out.

"Okay, soldier, we'll see how it goes tomorrow morning. But I can tell you this, you'll put your full weight on it, and soon. I'll see to that."

"Yes sir" (anything to get him out of there). Later the nurse came by and told me that even though it might seem that the doctor was being unreasonable, he was only interested in seeing me walk. I told her I was, too, but hell's bells, I'd only had the bullet out for three days. Let's give it a chance to heal, I told her. She assured me that she knew what I was talking about, but I really did have to work the area that had been injured.

Next morning was a repeat of the first morning. The doctor was really pissed off at me. He said, "If you don't start walking on it, scar tissue will form to the extent that when you finally feel like you can walk without pain, you'll find that you have a permanent limp. And, I don't mean to have that happen."

Well, I'd try, and the pain just wouldn't let me put much weight on my toes when I tried to force my foot out flat on the floor.

After several days, all of them with more or less the same

scenario, the doctor flat-out said to the nurse, "Make a note. No more food to be served to this man." He told me that from then on I'd have to go to the mess hall like everyone else who was fit enough to do so. I asked for some crutches. No, no crutches. He would allow me a cane, and that was it.

The nurses and ward guys continued to feed me at bedside. A day or so later I asked for a set of crutches, and those were given to me. I would use them to go to the head at night rather than bother the ward guys or nurses. I also would hobble to the mess hall at noon. The doctor had not returned, so I wasn't afraid we'd get caught at breakfast or dinner hours, but I felt uneasy about lunchtime. I didn't want to get anyone in trouble with this guy, most of all, me. Also, I took to heart what he had said about developing a permanent limp. So I would stand up on my right foot and, using the crutches, very gingerly set my left foot down on the floor and let it rest there. I still got pain, but it was manageable now.

A week, or maybe two, later, I had a real breakthrough. I was at the hospital library. It was a small wood building and the books were all paperbacks. But when I discovered it, I spent a lot of time there. One day I was sitting at a table in the library and decided to look for another book on the shelf, about six feet away. I got up from the chair and, using my crutches again, moved on over to the shelf. As I stood there, with my left foot off the floor, toes just resting on it, I began to scan through one of the books.

As I read, I slowly became aware that my entire left foot was flat on the floor. Oh boy! I raised it up a tad, then lowered it down. I had some pain, but it was very manageable. Talk about happy. It was truly a wonderful moment for me. As the days passed, I began to use just one crutch under my left armpit. And it wasn't long before I hardly needed it at all. The doctor had been right, I did need to work my leg. But I'd been right, too. I'd had to take a little time. I've always felt that pain is your body's way of telling you that something is wrong. And if you stop doing whatever it is and the pain stops, then you've been sent a message you should listen to.

One day while I was in the chow line, I noticed that the guy

in front of me was from the 184th of the 7th Division. One
of my scouts had left for OCS while I was still an infantryman. Upon graduation he had been assigned duty with the
7th as a second lieutenant. I tapped the guy on the shoulder
and asked him if he knew Lieutenant Freggoli. He told me
that Freg had been killed by a Japanese officer just a couple
of miles from where my own outfit had been on Leyte at the
time. He said the Jap had used his sword and cut Freg up
pretty badly. It turned out that the Japanese had been hiding
in a cemetery and ambushed Freggoli's platoon as it made its
way through the area. It was a very sad moment for me. Al
Freggoli was one of those guys who always seemed to be
smiling. After being commissioned, he arrived in Oahu and
had looked me up at Schofield Barracks. I got a pass for the
day and we had lunch in Honolulu. He laughed when he told
me that he'd had to get his birth certificate when he was in
OCS and found that he had been an adopted child. He wasn't
Italian after all. He had blond hair and blue eyes, "but," he
laughed, "I'm still Italiano all the way through . . . where it
counts."

My mail started to catch up with me, and one day I received a bit of news that really amazed me. It was from my
mom, and she had enclosed a clipping from our local newspaper. I'd been awarded the Bronze Star! She chided me for
not having told her ahead of time, but I hadn't known anything about it. In the same batch of mail, I got a V-mail from
Sgt. Ed Metz. He said among other things that he had put me
in for a Silver Star, but it had been turned down by
Lieutenant Finian. Finian had downgraded it because, he told
Metz, the company's "quota" for Silver Stars had been used
up for the period. Metz said he didn't know that medals were
awarded on a quota basis, and neither did I.

Oh well, me and my big mouth. I assumed (wrongly, I
hoped) that Finian's memory of our little radio talk(s) had
soured him as far as medals for me went. Anyway, it was
nice of Ed to have done that. He'd had a grandstand seat to
the whole mess, and I appreciated the fact that I'd impressed
him enough with my shenanigans to have him do that for me,
put me in for an award. Along these same lines, a few days

later I was awarded the Purple Heart. I had woken up from a nap one afternoon, and my friend alongside said, "Congratulations." I asked, "What for?" And he said, "Look on your bedside table." I did, and there was an oblong leather case. Inside was the Purple Heart! It really was no big deal in this instance . . . everyone in the ward had received one. It turned out that the chaplain had dropped by with it and didn't want to wake me! As a kid I had often dreamed of receiving a medal, which was always awarded in some big-deal ceremony. Now I'd received two: one via a newspaper clipping and the other while I was asleep. Things seemed to continue being strange. But hey, they'd been strange for many months now, I told myself, grinning in spite of it all.

About this time a rumor started making its way through our ward. It supposedly was about a new point system that would allow an honorable discharge from the service. The way it worked, according to the rumor, you would earn one point for each month you had been in the service, an additional point for each month of overseas duty, and one point for each medal earned. The rumored goal was around eighty points. Using the rumor scale, I had more than enough points for a discharge. The whole thing sounded too good to be true. And, as that old saying goes, it if sounds too good, it probably isn't.

I'd been in the service almost four and a half years at that time, with three of it overseas. I'd just gone through Leyte, from October '44 to March '45, and then Okinawa from April 7, '45 to May 11, '45. I was ready to go home, and didn't feel like I was shirking my duty by feeling that way. Without getting dramatic about it, I'd shed my blood and done my time, and outside of getting myself killed, I felt like I'd done about as much as I could. Besides, I honestly didn't think my nerves would hold up in combat anymore.

A couple of days later my original doctor dropped by and we had a chat. Toward the end of our conversation he became quite serious. He asked me, "How many operations have you had?"

"Just two . . . one at the beach and then the one you did here."

He smiled and said, "No, I mean campaigns, battles, you know."

"Oh, well, the answer's still two, sir. Leyte and Okinawa. Why, what's up?"

"Ah . . . this sodium Pentothal that we're using now causes a person to talk their head off. We believe it's got a good side effect in that it allows someone to get a lot of things off their mind and clear their feelings up. Things that they may have been carrying around inside and didn't realize."

"You're telling me that I was blabbing about combat?"

"Oh, yes, you certainly were. I think, from what I heard, that you got wounded just in time. I also think that it wouldn't have been too long before your emotions overran your ability to control them."

"Well, sir, I have to say that I was pretty near the so-called snapping point. I had considered shooting myself to get out of this mess, I'm ashamed to say."

"Don't be ashamed of thoughts. You did hold on. Anyway, how would you like to go home?"

"What does that mean, sir?"

"I mean Stateside duty, get out of this situation over here. I'm not talking about discharging you or anything like that. Just a change of duty."

"Well, that sounds like Christmas to me, sir. But, from what I hear I might get outta here through channels."

"Through channels, what do you mean?"

"There's a rumor floating around that we can get honorable discharges if we have enough points accumulated. Have you heard anything about that?"

"I've heard the rumors, but that's all it is right now . . . Do you want to stick around and take a chance of getting sent back for duty with your old unit, or home, on points?"

"I think I'll stick around, but I do thank you, I really do."

The next guy I tackled was our chaplain. As soon as I saw him come into the ward, I knew that if anyone had heard the straight stuff, it would be him. He worked his way down the line, bed to bed, until he finally arrived at mine. He was a nice guy and everyone liked him. After we got through our "good mornings" and "how are we today," I asked him about those point rumors.

"Yes, I've been hearing more and more about them, but nothing official."

"Well, if you had to guess, what would you say?"

He thought about it and then said, "I think there's something to it. It seems to be getting stronger, and it also gets a bit more detailed each time I hear it."

After he left me, I did a lot of deep thinking. If we were going to be offered discharges based on length of service and medals it seemed to me that the army either had enough men to fill the gaps left by those who left the service, or they figured the war was winding down. In either case, it left me with the feeling that I had better grab this chance, if it was true and not a rumor. Not only was the idea of getting out very attractive, the idea of not going back into combat seemed to me essential at this stage of the game. I knew as sure as I was sitting there, my nerves wouldn't take another round of the same. Thinking of all the ramifications, of all the sides of the idea, I made a decision to try and get myself out of the hospital and into a replacement center . . . and, hope that the rumor proved true.

53

The next morning I told the doctor that I felt I was ready to return to duty, and that little statement caused a mild upset in the morning's rounds. The situation was an interesting one. It was sort of like the doctors against the rest of us. "Us" being the patients. The enormous number of men who were wounded, and still being wounded during the Okinawa battle, had filled all the available beds in the hospital, and the additional injured were being flown on to Honolulu. So, the big emphasis here, aside from seeing that we received the best treatment possible, was to also see us healed and returned to duty. Or at least gotten out of the hospital so our vacant beds would then be open for new arrivals.

The wounded guys in my ward were all the result of combat and, except for me, were all infantry. And, none of us was eager to return back to the hell we had recently left. And so, as they healed, some of them tried to not show it too much, hoping that they would be able to stall for a few more days and maybe delay what really was the inevitable. Anything to stay here with the clean sheets, good food, and peace and quiet. My little statement was, I think, the first that the doctor and nurse had received. They were immediately suspicious. Was I sure that I felt good enough to return to duty? Was my wound healed to the point where I could maneuver around okay? And so on.

I assured them that despite some small amount of pain, things were just great and please mark me for duty. The doctor was the same one who was going to ban food being brought to my bedside, who wouldn't let me have crutches, and now he wasn't at all ready to let go of me without finding out just what the hell was going on here.

The final upshot was that he'd forward my case to a medical review board, and their decision would determine what my future was going to be. A few days later I received my orders: Be at such and such a building at 0900 hours for a review of my medical condition. Came the day and hour and I was there, along with about ten other GIs. None was very happy, and they all seemed to be griping to each other about this next step. As we waited, outside the door, a name would be called out and the man would enter the room, leaving the rest of us to wonder what was going on in there.

After a while my name was called, and in I went. Across the room was a table, and two officers were sitting there with a pile of papers in front of them. I said a silent prayer that one of them was not a full bird colonel, and by golly, neither was. They were both medical officers, and as I walked toward them I became aware of how much I was limping.

They, of course, knew of the ongoing situation about the men not wanting to be marked for duty, and I felt sure they were viewing my slow, limping progress across the room with some suspicion. And, knowing what the deal was, I couldn't blame them.

I arrived in front of them, stood at a half-assed attention, and waited. They gave the papers in front of them their full attention, and finally one of them said, "I see that your healing seems to have progressed very nicely, Sergeant. According to your doctor's report you have regained full use of any injured muscles and ligaments." I hadn't known anything about ligaments, but the way things had felt, I wasn't about to argue the point.

"Yes, sir . . . I feel fine. Ready to go."

"Pull up your pants leg. I want to see the wound area."

I pulled up my pants leg and became very aware of how swollen my leg was, especially around the ankle area. The swelling had prevented me from fully lacing my shoe, and all in all it didn't look good for me. One of them asked me to walk around a bit, which I did, and try as I might, I still limped a bit.

I knew what was going on . . . they were trying to determine if I really was all right, or was I putting on a little show in hopes that they wouldn't mark me for duty? I decided to level with them. "I've heard rumors that there is a new system in place that will grant discharges if a man has enough points based on length of service, time overseas, things like that. If it's true, I know that I have enough points to qualify, and knowing that, I sure would like to be returned to duty and have my points added up. Provided that the rumor is true . . . and, I sure hope it is."

Now it all was clear for them. Big smiles and nods, and then the same one said, "Okay, Sergeant, it appears that you are physically fit. In a day or so you'll receive orders to report to the Replacement Center on Saipan Island. And, good luck to you."

The next day a full set of new fatigues, shoes, the whole works, was issued to me, and now all I had to do was wait.

Hey, I told myself, you're still in the army, and waiting is part of the game. So, I settled down and, well . . . waited.

Next morning about a dozen or so of us piled into a truck and were driven to the airport. It was midmorning, and the sun was as hot as it was going to be all day, that is, near boiling. When we got to the field and unloaded, a sergeant told us to "wait in the green building over there. Your ride will be ready in a few minutes, so don't go anywhere, just stay put."

I picked up my duffel bag and limped over to the green building, entered, and there, in all his glory, sat . . . yep, OW! "Where the hell did you go, what happened to you, anyway?"

He laughed and said that when we had been unloaded from the plane that night, he had somehow been taken to the navy hospital, and there he'd been until this morning.

"The navy! You are such a traitor, OW. How was the food, the nurses, stuff like that? And what's going on with you now, where are you headed, have you heard the rumor about that new points system?"

"The nurses were wonderful, the chow was lousy—they had me on a bland diet because of my ulcer—and, yeah, I had a bleeding ulcer. But, being a combat guy from a tank outfit in a ward full of navy guys, I was unique. All in all it wasn't a bad experience. Better than what I'd left at Okinawa. And, yeah, I've heard that rumor. What do you think about it?"

About that time I saw the sergeant approaching the doorway. He stuck his head inside and yelled for us to get aboard that plane right there, pointing as he said it. We got our gear together, and over to the plane we went. It was a C-47, the old Douglas workhorse, one of the best airplanes ever designed and built.

When we got inside, we found that the "seats" were a long bench that ran the full length of the fuselage on both sides. As we settled down, I noticed the guy who was going to be our pilot. Right away I knew him. "Hey, OW, I know that guy, the pilot."

"How did you end up knowing a Marine pilot?"

"I don't know. Maybe from high school. I just know he looks very familiar." As we talked, the pilot walked our way, entered the cabin, and looked right at me. Oh, boy, he recognizes me, too, I thought.

He paused in front of me and then said, "Buckle your seat belt, soldier." And, he went on up to the cockpit.

"Hey, that was Tyrone Power, the movie star!" OW said to me.

Yeah, no wonder he looked sort of familiar. But, wearing the uniform, dark aviator's glasses, and all, I didn't recognize him for who he really was.

Well, Tyrone was one of my favorite movie stars of the day, but as a pilot he left a lot to be desired. We took off from Guam and flew to the island of Tinian. After several landings—by that I mean we bumped, hopped, and jumped more times than I'd liked—we finally settled down and taxied to a hangar where he picked up some more victims, er, I mean, passengers. From there we flew to Saipan, did a repeat of the last landing, and a grateful planeload of GIs got out under as hot a sun as you're going to find anywhere. What it did lack was rain, and that made it more bearable than Leyte had been. Otherwise, the temperatures were close twins.

We piled into the ever-present trucks and after a few minutes ended up in front of the headquarters tent of the Replacement Center. I can't remember the name or number of the unit, but it was large, and I had the impression that it was the main one on the island. A first sergeant greeted us and told us some good news, and some bad. The good news was that there was, indeed, a points system in effect, and we would be notified of our standing and how we might or might not be affected by it. The bad news was twofold. First, we would have regular duties. That is, physical training in the mornings, police the area, and after breakfast go on whatever detail we had been assigned.

The second bad news was worse. Regardless of our points, if we were slated for discharge, we would have to wait until a man with the same MOS (military occupational specialty) as ours had arrived at the center and was capable of replacing us back at our outfits before we could be processed for shipment home. In other words, OW and I would have to wait until a couple of tank commanders came in before we started looking eastward, toward the States, that is.

When the first sergeant asked if there were any questions, I waited and when none was asked that I wanted more info on, I decided to take the plunge. "Sergeant, what if my MOS doesn't arrive. It's not too common a one." He looked at me, then looked at all of us. "I say again, you will be stationed here at this replacement center until someone with your MOS arrives. Until that happens you will carry on with routine duties that include but are not limited to details about the camp. Any other questions?"

A corporal with a handful of our papers gathered us together, called out names, and led us down a company street. Our new living quarters were the old pyramidal tents. They had wood floors and sides that came up about waist-high. I knew from experience that under this sun, with those canvas roofs, the heat would make things miserable. And I was right.

"Hey, OW, we might be here for a long, long time. Whaddaya think?"

"Need I remind you?"

"Remind me of what?"

"Well, I realize that you're a new guy, but try real hard and think. What is one of the army's favorite games?"

"Oh yeah . . . hurry up and wait." And we both said "wait" at the same time.

PART EIGHT

Homeward Bound

54

Our records were examined and both of us had more than enough points to qualify for discharge, and both of us were eager to get going. But that cotton-pickin' MOS rule kept us on a tight rein. Infantrymen, of which there were jillions it seemed, were being replaced right and left. No problems for them. But tankers, there were none at all. We wondered if they had stopped training them. Maybe we'd end up here, years from now, the only army personnel left on the island, waiting for . . . what was it we were waiting for? It's been so long, I forgot.

Details proved to be like all details at every place in the army I had ever been. We did KP, we hauled trash, we did it all. Rank meant no difference. If you were due for a detail, you did it and rank be damned. Looking back on it, it really was a bad deal. All of the guys in my group were fellows who had been wounded. They were just out of the hospital and not too strong. And just about the time when we all should have been happy about at long last getting back into the world of normalcy, here we were, stuck on work details that came close to being demeaning. At least in my view.

But what put the cap on the whole thing was "the house." I became acquainted with it one day about a week or so after we had gotten to the center. One morning I was told to fall in, get aboard a truck, and that was it. We traveled several miles, always climbing upward. The road was a good one, having been "paved" using crushed rock. I think it was volcanic cinder, which makes an excellent road base.

Finally we arrived, and what a view! We were at one of the highest points on the island, and the scene was spectacular. It was fairly cool up there due to the constant breeze coming in off the ocean. But the thing that caught my eye was the house. Actually it wasn't a house. Not yet, anyway. It was a beautiful rock patio area that surrounded the foundation and partly finished walls. That was our detail for the day— working on the house. When I asked whose house it was, I was told that it belonged to the island commander. I don't know if the guy was army or navy, but the use of enlisted personnel to build his house seemed wrong to me. No one was happy about the situation, but at the same time, none of us was about to make waves when we were waiting for that boat headed home. So . . . we kept our mouths shut and did the detail.

I was talking to one of the guys one day, and he asked me if I liked to read. I told him I sure did, but so far I hadn't been able to find a source of paperbacks. It turned out that he had quite a stack of them saved up and offered to share them with me. My lucky day. I was really into one of them one morning on the way to the mess hall for breakfast, when my friend said he was not going out on a detail that day. Are you sick, I wondered? No, he was going to duck out.

I knew that the only time they called the roll was just before we got aboard the trucks. After that we were not checked on at all. It was very simple, after all. As soon as roll call was over, all we had to do was sort of drift away from the group. I followed his lead, and we ducked down a row of tents. I should mention that our tents were located on a gentle slope, and because the floors were level, that meant the ground sloped away below them at an angle. The space between the underneath part of the floor at one end was quite close, and as the ground sloped away the space became wider. We ducked under one of those wider spaces and crawled back toward the narrow part. Unless someone got down on their hands and knees, we wouldn't be seen. A simple duck down of the head and looking under would not have done it. As it turned out, it was a nice day. Beat the hell out of working on some guy's house.

I had my paperback, and after reading most of it, I napped the rest of the afternoon. After that I kept a candy bar or two handy, and that did the trick for me as far as lunch went. I told OW about it, but he didn't want any part of it. He was concerned that if we got caught, it might affect our getting out of the place somehow. He was probably right, but I went ahead and skipped out a couple of times a week, no harm done. The work on the mountain wasn't all that tough. There were so many guys we were falling all over each other. But it was a detail, and I always enjoyed getting out of them no matter what I had to do.

We, OW and I, continued to sweat it out. Fellows who had arrived after we had were soon replaced and shipped out for home . . . and here we sat, still waiting. In the meantime, writing V-mails had become popular, and we did our duty as far as they were concerned. V-mail was an interesting idea. A single sheet of preprinted paper was used to write your message or letter on. It was addressed by you and handed in, and then photocopied and reduced in size to both save paper, I guess, and to save space. They were used by all the armed forces, and while the photocopy robbed a letter of a personal touch, they were still in our own handwriting . . . it was just very small. When they were folded and delivered by the U.S. Post Office, they were about four by six inches and looked like a regular (small) envelope.

I can't remember how long we were there, but it seemed as though it had been months and months. It hadn't been, but it sure seemed like it.

And then one day it happened. At our morning formation, where the lucky guys' names were called, we heard ours. OW and me. We were actually slated to go out on the next shipment. A couple of tank commanders had arrived, and while we never did see them or get a chance to thank them for being what they were, we did know that they were available and would be headed for our old outfit. And us? Well, we'd be headed for the States. Soon. We hoped.

55

Catching that boat homeward bound wasn't anything like calling up a travel agency, booking passage, and getting a firm schedule for departure. Nope, nothing so easy, but, what was ever easy in the army? Knock that question mark off . . . that wasn't a question, it was a flat-out statement. So, what was ever easy in the army! Not too much, unless it was getting in trouble with full-bird colonels. Now, that is easy. Anyway, we were informed to get our affairs in order, more or less. We were also informed that it would probably be within the next several days, whatever that meant.

At any rate, you couldn't have made either of us mad if you'd stuck us on KP or worse. And naturally, that's what happened, we got KP. But we didn't suffer: We got first dibs on desserts, and we didn't have to travel far to get from our tent to the mess hall. Life was good again. There was a lot of conjecture about the length of the trip. Some of our tentmates said we'd probably make great time because we would be traveling east, and the bad guys were to the west. Made sense to me. As we should have known, we made good time all right. Good if we had been trying for a world record for the slowest passage from Saipan to the States. But the good old point system was working, we had been measured and found fit, and now . . . now we were going home. Or somewhere, anywhere, east of here.

Our departure was not marked by bands playing, confetti streaming over the sides of the ship, people waving, or the ship's horn tooting. We didn't even have a bunch of people standing on the pier hollering "Bon voyage." Matter of fact, I didn't pay too much attention to our leaving except to give a couple of minutes' scrutiny of the shore, just to make sure that we really were moving out. Once satisfied that we were at long, long last on the way, I began looking for my bunk, followed closely by OW.

We found our sleeping area, dropped our barracks bags, and went topside to have a cigarette and enjoy the feeling of being at sea again. The throb of the engines could be easily felt under our feet, and the easy roll soon began as we left the lee of the island. It really was wonderful to not only be on the move, but to know that we were moving, for the first time in a long time, in the right direction . . . east.

The ship's store had just about anything a person would need. Shaving goods, candy bars, cigarettes, writing materials, T-shirts, name it and they probably had it. It was the navy's equivalent to the army's PX. OW and I took stock of our finances and the result was not so good. I had seven or eight dollars and he had about the same. Both of us smoked, and we began wondering if our money would hold out, depending on how long the trip was going to be and when we would get our next payday, things like that. I found the answer, although I must admit it was purely accidental. Poker. Yeah, I got into a little penny ante game just to pass the time and ended up winning a tad over what I'd invested. The game was sort of an ongoing thing, meaning that you could find guys playing most anytime of the day or night. Wait awhile and someone would drop out and you could sit in. Because the stakes were so low, no one was able to lose, or win very much at a sitting. And so it became in truth what it was intended to be when it first started out—entertainment. There were some fairly high-stakes games aboard, but I wasn't that good of a player even if I'd had the money to gamble with. Which I didn't. As it turned out, I was able to keep us in candy bars and smokes for the entire trip. When we finally did arrive at our destination, twenty-seven days after leaving Saipan, I still had around ten bucks in my pocket!

Aside from my occasional poker game, life was easy, simple, and really sort of boring. If it hadn't been a trip that we had all dreamed of for such a long time, we would have been bored out of our minds. As it was, the days sort of blended one into another, and life was good.

We were one day out of Pearl Harbor when the word was flashed around the ship—the war was over! Japan had surrendered. We had heard about the two A-bombs being dropped, but at the time I didn't believe it. Now it looked like maybe it was true. I knew, as did everyone on the ship, that if the war had not ended, it wouldn't have been many months more before the full-scale invasion of the Japanese homeland would begin. From what we had learned of the enemy on Okinawa, we all knew that our losses would have been unbelievably high.

As news of the war's ending sank in, I couldn't help but feel a pang of deep sorrow for all those who had lost their lives. I had lost more comrades than I wanted to think about. And, I had lost my best friend. I knew that when I got home, I would visit and talk with his mother, and his wife, and, thinking ahead, I wondered what in the world I could say that would help ease their pain. Already I was feeling guilty because Joe had been killed, and I came through the whole scrap in as good a shape as I did. And I thought of the thousands upon thousands who, at this moment, were thinking of their husbands, sons, and fathers who would not be coming home.

As we approached our destination, San Francisco, we were told that there would be a detailed inspection of all of our possessions. All explosives, handguns, and souvenirs that had not been cleared by G2 (army intelligence) would be confiscated, and the man who possessed such items would be in deep trouble. Neither OW nor myself had anything close to a souvenir of any sort, let alone anything as sophisticated as a handgun.

When we passed under the Golden Gate Bridge, I looked over to the left, and on the side of a hill, spelled out in large white letters, were the words WELL DONE. It was a navy term, but I knew it was meant for all of us. I, for one, was truly touched seeing that great sign of appreciation for what all of our armed forces had accomplished.

We leaned over the ship's rail, taking in the view of everything around us, and OW said, "Well, I guess this is the last chapter."

"What do you mean, the last chapter?"

"Oh, the war and all. It's been almost like a book, and now that it's over, it seems to me that we're sort of in the last chapter . . . the final scene, so to speak."

Yeah, I thought OW had something there. It had been so unbelievable at times, it now seemed that it had all been a dream. Or maybe nightmare would best describe it. And I told him, "One thing for sure, it truly is the 'last' chapter as far as I'm concerned. No more loud noises and guys with guns looking for me, or anything even close. Yep, the last chapter sounds just about right to me, too."

We were taken off the ship and put on a small vessel that transported us to Angel Island, location of a permanent army post. We were not inspected, and the guys who had tossed souvenirs overboard were pretty much upset. And I can't say that I blamed them.

It was midafternoon, and we were led to a nearby auditorium. After we were seated, a captain gave us a little welcome home speech and ended it in a way that I will never forget. He said, "You fellows arrived here a day earlier than we had anticipated, and we had a wonderful meal planned for you . . . but, of course, it's too late now." Groans were heard all over the place, mine included. We had been living for literally months on GI food and had been dreaming of something good for a change.

He continued, "So you'll just have to make do with our regular chow. When you leave here, you'll go next door to the mess hall. Our menu for tonight is steak, mashed potatoes [not dehydrated, but the real things], gravy, fresh tomatoes, lettuce, milk, rolls, fresh vegetables, salads, and several different soups. Our desserts include pie, cake, and ice cream. Fellows, eat as much as you want, but eat all that you take. Oh, and one thing more. No KP here. You'll notice that the people serving you are POWs, Italian prisoners, who volunteered for this work. They are a bunch of nice guys, so you don't have to worry about protecting your flanks. Have a good meal, and tomorrow . . . no reveille."

I think OW and I had at least one of everything. It was so
wonderful. The contrast of what was happening to us now
compared to only a few weeks ago was, well, almost impossible to realize. Except that it was happening pretty much as
we had been dreaming of it for months now. So I guess
things were playing out like we had hoped for. I was almost
afraid to go to sleep at night for fear I'd wake up in a hole
somewhere with shells exploding and small arms going off
all around me. And rain. Don't forget the rain. Oh, and the
mud, and . . . well, need I go on?

A day or so later OW and I wangled a twelve-hour pass
and went into San Francisco in search of a good restaurant.
The town was full of them, and while I don't recall the name
of the one we finally settled on, it was very nice. Before we
started eating, I proposed a toast. "OW, here's that drink we
promised ourselves . . . and I want to toast all of the crews—
present, past, and future—of old #60. May they always be as
pure in heart as we two." I grinned as I said it, and he raised
his glass and said that he'd drink to that.

Next day I walked down to the little landing where the
shore boat was waiting. OW was headed home to Rumbly,
Maryland, and this was the last time we'd see each other. In
this lifetime, anyway. I guess we both knew it. We started to
shake hands but somehow ended up with a long hug and a
"Take care of yourself, buddy."

He hoisted his duffel bag over his shoulder and walked up
the gangplank and onto the boat. He didn't turn around, but
instead walked around to the far side, behind the small cabin,
out of sight. I was glad that he did . . . I didn't want him seeing me with tears in my eyes . . . to find out what a softy I really am!

We were issued a full set of everything. I couldn't believe
it. We were leaving the service, not entering it. Hey, maybe
I've got this all wrong. Just maybe we're back in and we'll
find out later where we're headed and what's gonna happen.

Then it came time to turn certain things in that the army
felt we should no longer have or need. "All right, men, hand
your dog tags to the corporal as he passes by."

"Sir . . ." I raised my hand. "I don't have any dog tags."

"Well, where are they, soldier?"

"I don't know, sir. I haven't had any for almost a year now."

"Are you with the group that just arrived from the hospital?"

"Yes, sir. But they were missing long before I got to the hospital. Before I got into combat even."

The guy really didn't care for this. I was thanking the Good Lord that he wasn't a full colonel. No telling what would've happened then.

"Soldier, you have to have dog tags. . . ."

"To turn in, sir?"

"That's right. Go over to the north end of the compound, to Warehouse 11, and see the soldier there. He will furnish you with a set. Then return here. Understand?"

"Yes, sir."

And I did. The army said I had to turn in my dog tags, and by golly, I was going to turn in dog tags. I hoped I could find a set with my name and all that other stuff already on them.

The guy at the warehouse stamped me out a set, complete with chains and all. Then he asked me if I'd like a set to take home for a souvenir. Wow, I finally got a souvenir! Anyway, I got the spare set, went back and turned in the first set, and spent the rest of the day wondering why they wanted my old set and what they were going to do with them. I still wonder every once in awhile.

We were ready for the final step. In my case it was a train ride to Southern California, and eventually to San Pedro at the southern edge of Los Angeles. I arrived at Fort MacArthur ready for most anything. And most anything is what I got.

First we received a little welcome home, then we were told how to treat the civilians, what kind of questions to expect, and how to answer them.

In we went to another room where a guy typed out info that went into our service record. Which we didn't get a copy of, incidentally. Then we received our medical exam. I was handed a set of papers, medical forms, and told to follow the painted line on the floor. I did so and came to a doctor who took my papers, checked my eyesight, handed the forms back to me, and told me to continue to follow the line.

Eventually I came to the guy who was going to check my hearing. This was the fellow I really wanted to talk with because my hearing had taken such a beating. I had a high-pitched ringing in my ears all the time. It didn't get any louder, but it never faded away, either. Just a constant noise. I could hear anything as loud as gunshots and loud yelling, and that was darned near it.

When I got to that station, there was another GI waiting. The doctor told us to go to the far end of the room, which was very narrow. At the far end there was a circle painted on the floor. We were told to stand back to back, on the circle, which we did. He then said, "Repeat these numbers after me."

The way we were standing, my right shoulder was toward the doctor and the fellow behind me had his left shoulder toward him. I didn't hear the doctor say a thing, but suddenly the guy behind me started saying numbers, like "twenty-four, sixteen," and so on. We were then told to change places, which would now test our other ear. Same thing. The guy behind me could hear them like a champ. Me . . . nothing.

We walked back to the doctor to get our papers, and I asked him, "What's going to happen now, sir?"

"Happen? What do you mean, soldier?"

"I mean that I didn't pass the test, that my hearing is pretty bad, sir. What will happen now?"

For whatever reason, this seemed to set him off, and he got very angry with me. "What do you want me to do? Send you to the hospital, is that it?"

"Sir, I just got out of a hospital, and I sure don't want to go back to one."

"Well, soldier, there's nothing I can do for you."

And, that was it.

Later that day, after I had turned in a full set of everything, I was handed my honorable discharge papers, my pay plus travel money, and that truly was it. There was no band, no parade, no one shook my hand. Nothing but the main gate of Fort MacArthur to walk through, out into the world of civilians, ice cream, and no artillery looking for me. I hoped. I was in a pair of OD slacks, an OD shirt, overseas cap, issue shoes, and that was it. I might have looked like a soldier on leave, but I had a secret. It was September 22, 1945, and I was a civilian, a civilian, a civilian, yeah, an ex-army . . . ex-GI . . . an ex-by-God-tanker, a genuine certified civilian, and I've got the scars to prove it! Looking over my papers, I saw that I had ten days to register with my local draft board! And I guess that sort of capped it off. I began laughing at the utter stupidity of it. Ex-GIs, soldiers who were discharged, were being given ten days to register! I just hoped that no one was going to hold their breath until I "turned myself in." As it happened, I did drop by the office a couple of weeks later. My tardiness was graciously forgiven.

56

I made my way across the vast Los Angeles area via street-car and local bus, arriving at the central downtown station, where I would catch the bus that would take me on the last leg of my journey.

When we got to the downtown El Monte depot, it had just turned dark, and I wasn't sure how to get from there to where I lived. Then I remembered that there are things called taxis, and that's what I did. Took a taxi home. Not all the way. I had the driver stop at the corner of my street. It was a long block, but I wanted to walk it, to take in my old neighborhood, to see if it looked anything like I had pictured it those many months. I paid my driver, and he refused my tip, wishing me good luck. And I started walking. Limping I should say, be-cause it still hurt, and I still couldn't lace my shoe up all the way because of the swelling. But, hell's bells, all that was minor, I was here, walking, and I didn't have to go anywhere else or do anything that I didn't want to. I was, after all, a civilian now.

Everything looked the same, yet was somehow different. Some of the houses seemed bigger than I remembered, others not so big. Well, it was dark now, maybe my eyes were playing tricks. I kept a sharp eye open for any suspicious-looking bushes, but didn't see movement anywhere. Nothin's ever gonna creep up on me, no way.

Finally, I was standing on the street in front of my house. Lights were on inside, and a car was in the driveway. As I walked by it, I saw that it was an Oldsmobile and knew then that my Uncle Earl and Aunt Ruby had driven down from Las Vegas, where they lived and worked, to be on hand to greet me. I had phoned my mom from Angel Island and told her it would probably be a week or more before I could see her. It had gone much faster than I had guessed, and that was okay by me.

I walked onto the front porch and could hear voices through the screen door. The light from the living room spilled onto the porch like a splash of bright golden paint. I stood in the shadows and looked in. All three of them, my mom, aunt, and uncle, were standing about six or seven feet from me, in a little group, and I figured that my uncle and aunt had just arrived. They all looked older than I thought they would.

I didn't know what to do next. I just stood there in the dark, and for a moment was frightened. What if they looked out and saw me, what in the world would they think? Why is he just standing there? Why doesn't he come inside? What would I say then? I honestly didn't know. I had no ideas.

Face it, I told myself. You aren't used to being around or talking with "normal" human beings. Nobody has a gun and no one is going to shoot at you . . . that's all in the past now. You're home and everything is all right.

I took a deep breath, knocked, opened the screen door, and stepped inside. Their faces turned toward me, and surprise was followed by joy. I moved forward, and all of us stood there, not saying a word, arms around each other, tears in our eyes. We stood like that for what seemed a long time.

It had been quite a trip, but at last it was over.

The book was finished.

The last chapter written.

And, I was home.

This time, to stay.